The Essential Groupworker

of related interest

Practice Teaching – Changing Social Work
Edited by Hilary Lawson
ISBN 1 85302 478 3

Learning and Teaching in Social Work
Edited by Margaret Yelloly and Mary Henkel
ISBN 1 85302 237 3

Taking the Group Seriously
Towards a Post-Foulkesian Group Analytic Theory
Farhad Dalal
ISBN 1 85302 642 5

Handbook of Theory for Practice Teachers in Social Work
Edited by Joyce Lishman
ISBN 1 85302 1 098 2

Competence in Social Work Practice
Edited by Kieran O'Hagan
ISBN 1 85302 332 9

The Group Context
Sheila Thompson
ISBN 1 85302 657 3

The Essential Groupworker

Teaching and Learning Creative Groupwork

Mark Doel and Catherine Sawdon

Jessica Kingsley Publishers
London and Philadelphia

The right of Mark Doel and Catherine Sawdon to be identified as authors of this work has been asserted by them in accordance with the Copyright, Designs and Patents Act 1988.

First published in the United Kingdom in 1999 by

Jessica Kingsley Publishers Ltd,
116 Pentonville Road, London
N1 9JB, England
and
325 Chestnut Street,
Philadelphia PA 19106, USA.

www.jkp.com

Library of Congress Cataloging in Publication Data
A CIP catalog record for this book is available from the Library of Congress

British Library Cataloguing in Publication Data
Doel, Mark
The essential groupworker
1. Social group work 2. Interpersonal relations
I. Title II. Sawdon, Catherine
361.4

ISBN 1 85302 823 1

Printed and Bound in Great Britain by
Athenaeum Press, Gateshead, Tyne and Wear

Contents

Prelude

We have written this book as a celebration of groupwork. It springs from our commitment to a philosophy which values collective responses to problems, troubles, opportunities and discrimination. The book draws on our direct experience of groupwork and from our knowledge that it works. This knowledge has been refined over a number of years by the Groupwork Project to develop a programme of education and training in groupwork with a mainstream social work agency.

Why does the title of this book make reference to the 'essential' groupworker? In the ebb and flow of professional fashions, it might be felt that groupwork is past its time, as outmodish as its cousins, community work, family work and casework. Surely, the collectivist ideal which groupwork embodies has been washed up on the postmodernist beach, stranded by the tide of privatized, atomized experiences in an environment which is no longer capable of supporting lifeforms like groupwork. In these circumstances how can we ever consider groupwork as 'essential'?

Nevertheless, groups continue to be a central feature of human experience. Skilled groupworkers are essential in order to transform an experience which might amount to no more than merely 'working in groups' into something we know as *groupwork*. This book is all about what this 'something' is, and how to learn to do it.

We also use 'essential' in the sense that the book explores the essence of groupwork; that core which makes groupwork meaningful to practitioners in a wide variety of settings and circumstances. The Groupwork Project has been, and continues to be, the testing ground for the development of this essentialist practice model capable of adapting to an enormous variety of contexts.

We hope that the book attests not just to the existence of groupwork (life on the postmodernist beach!), but also to the possibility of enriching existing groups and giving life to entirely new ones, all in the context of mainstream social work and social care. A groupwork service is a hugely important resource for people who use social services, and it has a significant impact on the confidence and professionalism of the agency's workforce, too.

In *The Essential Groupworker* we link groupwork to a central human need for togetherness. We also link it to another need – creativity. Opportunities to express our creativity should feature throughout our lives, not just in the parts we call 'play'. Creativity can so easily be stunted by lack of confidence, failure of imagination, want of opportunity or constraints of culture and role. Groupwork offers members and workers the opportunity to tap into their mutual creativity. We hope this book will contribute to this process.

Finally, it is important to find ways of consolidating learning and practice in groupwork and seeing how it might play a part in the notion of lifelong learning. The development of a 'portfolio with signposts' has been significant in helping learners in the Groupwork Project to capture their groupwork and to make it available to other people. Whereas much professional practice lies buried in crowded memories and dusty case files, the signposted portfolio provides the learner with a lasting way to celebrate their own work and the profession with a means to develop a body of evidence-based groupwork knowledge and practice. Brief extracts from these portfolios are included at the end of each of the chapters in Part 2.

It is difficult to know what directions social work practice will take; however, we do know that people will continue to face deprivation, disadvantage and discrimination, and they will continue to hunger for togetherness and empowerment through collective thought and action. We think it is essential that social workers, social carers and their agencies are able to respond to this need with skilled and creative groupwork. It is our hope that this book will help.

Acknowledgements

We would like to acknowledge the work of all the groupworkers who have worked with us in the Groupwork Project. Their feedback, encouragement and experiences have been an invaluable source of strength and inspiration. Their groupwork has been of enormous benefit to many people.

PART I

Groupwork in Context

CHAPTER ONE

Why Groupwork?

Introduction

Groups are a central feature of human society. They permeate and mediate a large part of our experience – of growing up and being grown up, of work and play. This is reflected in the extraordinary number of terms we use to describe groups: *grouping, gathering, team, forum, association, collective, band, club, meeting, social, bunch, gang, rally, movement, company, outfit, assembly, union, trust*. We have a host of terms to describe groups which have a specific purpose, too, such as *orchestra, symposium, guild, troupe, congregation*. Each term provides its own subtle testimony to the human appetite for social contact in groups, and there is a similarly rich supply of collective nouns to describe groups in the non-human world – *flock, herd, school, flight, pack* – attesting to our fascination with groupings.

Our use of language also reflects the ready distinction we make between an individual, a collection of individuals and a group. We speak of one fish, three fishes and lots of fish, reverting to the singular form when we are talking about more than a set of individuals. One human, four humans, one humanity. We know when one musician becomes two, three or four musicians, and when four musicians become a quartet.

Groups are, therefore, of enormous significance to all of us. We have an innate understanding of how to describe different kinds of groupings and how to differentiate between sets of individuals and something we know is 'a group'. Of course, the boundaries are very fluid. Consider eight people sat around a table, sharing a meal. Early on in the meal one or two persons, perhaps the hosts, lead the conversation; indeed, it is not so much a conversation as a set of interchanges. As the meal progresses a number of conversations break out – three people here, two there, another three here – some are sustained, others peter out. From time to time the conversation engages all eight people together *as a group*. We have all been in such a situation, collectively known as 'a dinner party', 'a pub outing' or whatever, and experienced this fluidity between groupings and group.

A shared meal is rarely orchestrated as such (though the careful pre-party preparations of Malcolm Bradbury's character, Howard Kirk, in *The History Man* make him a consummate, if highly manipulative, groupworker!) It is not difficult to see how the same kinds of process which come to play in these informal, social gatherings are at play in other settings where we are collected together. Certainly, we know whether we have enjoyed the gathering, especially if our role as host makes us feel some responsibility for it; and we know whether it has been 'a group' or just a collection of eight individuals who failed to connect.

There is an 'art of gathering together' (Douglas 1983), along with some 'science' in our understanding of what can help or hinder this process. For example, we know that a round table has the practical effect of allowing each person equal access to sight and sound of each other. We know that there are ways in which we can contribute to the processes of getting to know each other, and we know that the skills which help us to interact successfully on an individual level (careful listening and the like) are just as important round the table. Our attempts to control the environment (or not) have some impact, as well as the quality of the meal and the comfort of the chairs, but we also know that the particular chemistry of this group of people is hard to predict and is likely to be full of surprises, some delightful and some not so. When we are conscious of the processes occurring around the dining table and attempt to understand the art and science of gathering together in order to influence it, we are 'doing groupwork'.

Why this book?

This book is about doing groupwork, and takes its first premise as the universality of groups. In other words, a 'good' groupworker is as interested to learn from experiences around a dinner table as from any other gathering of people. Although our focus is the gathering of people in the course of professional practice, we will set this in the broader context of what happens when people come together in groups at home and at play, as well as at work. This will help to remind us that the enormous spread of groupwork in professional practice – from street to clinic to home to Nissan hut – is just as broad as the collectivities we mentioned earlier. Read through the references at the end of this book and follow some of them up in the text, and you will quickly acquire a sense of the astonishing breadth and potential of groupwork – much wider, in many ways, than one-to-one work seems to allow. What unites 'streetwork with Hong Kong gangs', 'art therapy with abused children' and 'focus groups for research work' is what also connects the dinner party, the pub outing, the quartet and the seminar. They are all examples of doing groupwork, sometimes successfully and sometimes not so. Taken together, they exemplify the astounding diversity of groupwork.

There are plenty of books about doing groupwork (again, turn to the references). This one does not seek to summarize, replicate or better those excellent groupwork books already written. In writing this particular book, we have taken a somewhat different starting point – the teaching and learning of groupwork. This perspective derives from our own experience of learning about groupwork by doing it, and then learning more about it by teaching it. The action research project which we have developed and refined over ten years with a medium-sized social work agency has, itself, generated many successful groups and 'discovered' and helped sustain similar numbers of existing groups. (We refer to this project as the Groupwork Project and describe it in more detail in Chapter 2.)

This book is designed to help groupworkers learn more about their art and craft by developing a generic model of groupwork practice and illustrating what this means in practice. The book also provides resources for people teaching others about groupwork.

The attraction of groupwork

We wrote this book because we like doing groupwork. It is probably safe to assume that one of the reasons you are reading this book is that you do, too – or that you would like to do groupwork. What are the attractions of groupwork? We have already put our finger on one, and that is the central position it holds in our lives both inside and outside of work. Groupwork is a potentially integrating experience because it connects the universal experience of being human, as a member of a family, a friendship group, a team, a citizen. It satisfies a need and desire for the company of others.

In addition to the 'humanness' of groups, another central theme of this book is one which also lies at the heart of groupwork: power. For many reasons and in many different ways, groups address issues of power head on. They are powerful in themselves; the power can be used for better or worse, it can be shared or withheld, but its potential and its presence are undeniable. Groups can provide a more effective environment to experience empowerment because they can be used to replicate or simulate the larger society; in many respects they are microcosms of the wider society, but more amenable to change, at both a personal and a group level. The theme of power, oppression and empowerment runs throughout this book, with a particular focus in Chapter 3.

Allied to the issue of power is the potential for greater equality in groups which attracts many to groupwork. At a very basic level, the mathematics of a group is inescapable; the groupworker is outnumbered by the other group members. Note the use of the word 'other' in the last sentence, because the groupworker is also a group member, just as the host at the meal we described earlier is also a member of the dinner party. The equivocation social workers face when deciding what to call the people they work with on an individual basis (clients, service users, customers, etc.) is not faced in groups; these people are unequivocally 'members', with that sense of being equal and of belonging. In fact, any uncertainty about nomenclature is reserved for the workers – groupworkers, group leaders or group facilitators? (More on this in Chapter 11.)

That others can provide help, support, solutions and strategies in ways which complement rather than threaten the professional role is only possible when practitioners reframe their notion of what it is to be 'expert'; in groups, the professional groupworker is expert at groupwork and the group members are experts in their own lives. This does not diminish professional expertise, it recasts it. In some cases, such as the family group conference in its most radical manifestation, this support and solution can be provided even without the presence of professionals.

Another of groupwork's strong attractions is variety. Groupwork provides a professional experience which is stretching and challenging and often *different* from much of the rest of the work. This applies as much to those who work in groupcare as it does to those in more individualized settings. It is this sense of variety, and dare we say fun, which contributes to one image of groupwork as somehow subsidiary rather than complementary to the main work – almost a 'hobby'. We all know that anything we do at work which we actually enjoy cannot really be called work! Perhaps this is why such a lot of groupwork seems to happen under, rather than round, the table; for some, this increases its attraction.

One of the definitions of a group might be that its members have a sense of *belonging*. Helping to create a place and a space where people can begin to feel that they belong, that they have membership, is one of the strongest attractions of groupwork. People who may never before have felt a sense of community can discover it through membership of a group. This is quite a gift.

A sense of belonging also generates a sense of 'not belonging'. Some groups achieve their identity and purpose by defining themselves in contrast to the mainstream. Others are grouped, willingly or not, according to certain characteristics; this is part of the stereotyping process, which we explore in more detail during the course of this book. A powerfully destructive example of this tendency to group people together was reported in the newspapers in 1998, when 58 guests were evicted from a holiday camp in north Wales 'simply because they were deaf'.

> A Royal National Institute for the Deaf (RNID) spokeswoman said: 'We are not disputing that two deaf people caused damage or that there was a disturbance. But the 58 [deaf] guests were made up of groups from across the country … So why were we all thrown out?'
>
> In a statement, the company said … 'whilst it is true that the group of 58 people all made separate bookings, it was clear during their stay that they constituted *one large group* who had planned to meet at the Centre'. (*Guardian* 19 September 1998, our italics)

In the course of this book we will continue to revisit the paradox that anti-oppressive groupwork requires both the recognition of difference defined by social 'groups' (race, gender, age, class, sexuality, disability, etc.) and the commonalities within social groups, whilst combating the destructive effects of stereotyping and generalizations. So, we recognize that the people with hearing impairments in the holiday camp would face a general level of discrimination (vividly demonstrated by the response of the camp management) whilst having individual needs and personal characteristics (for example, that a few deaf people become violent when drunk, just as a few hearing people do).

In describing the attractions of groupwork we should not minimize the challenges. Some people feel uncomfortable in groups, either as members or workers. They feel on display and, in the more severe phobic circumstances, this can induce a kind of paralysis in which the person is unable to think or act because of their extreme self-consciousness. The group is a semi-public arena and when things go wrong they are seen to go wrong. Even if there is a tight band of confidentiality around the group itself, the visibility of the group to itself is challenging. Groups have a tendency to hold large mirrors up to themselves, and this requires everybody to take a look. Moreover, the sense of belonging which we have described as one of the attractions of groupwork can just as easily degenerate into feelings of *not* belonging; these are difficult to manage in the wider society but they are intensified in the smallness of a group.

If we consider groups from an economic point of view they are a relatively high-risk investment. They require much time for preparation and yet are prone to factors, many of them unpredictable, which can prevent a successful outcome. As we will see from the chapters which follow, there are many fences at which a group can falter. However, preparation time for a group which does not run is not necessarily wasted time, for the individuals involved can learn a lot from the experience (this includes prospective members who may have been contacted individually), as can the agency. The reasons why a planned group fails to run are significant and might tell a story which can help the agency provide a better service in future, though not every agency and manager takes this enlightened view. We have to be careful to ensure that groupwork is not subject to a separate system of accounting, more arduous than those used to account for other resources and approaches. How much time is 'wasted' in one-to-one interventions, perhaps because of the lack of preparation? The semi-public nature of groupwork makes it more amenable to audit and this is a strength; however, the same standards need to be applied across the board.

Groupwork and social work

> At a time when so much of social work energy appears to be directed towards private practice, third party payments, (etc.), it is with some pride that I see groupwork providing professional leadership in dealing with the social issues and problems which were the reasons most of us entered the profession. (Shulman 1988: 16)

Shulman's words, written in another time and another place, have their echo here and now. They anticipated many changes which currently lead social workers to wonder how they might deal with the social issues and problems which motivated them to enter the profession. It has become the orthodoxy that the welfare state is part of the problem rather than the solution, and collectivist approaches to people's difficulties have been undermined at many levels. In the United States the flight into clinical practice funded by insurance claims has even led to a special project aimed at re-engaging social work students with public, statutory practice (Grossman and Perry 1996). This tendency is less pronounced in the United Kingdom, but moves towards voluntary, private and combined provision of social care present a challenge to social work's definition of itself, largely because the profession in the UK has grown up with such a close identification with public sector social services.

Other changes, such as the purchasing–provider split, the blurring of boundaries with other professionals and the increasing reliance on procedure-led practice, have all brought into question what 'social work' is. There is a concern that social workers are not so much professionals as gatekeeping technicians or case managers. All of these changes are of crucial significance to social workers who wish to practise groupwork, because they reflect the context in which groupwork can either flourish or wither. In addition to the themes already raised, the Groupwork Project exposed the significance of *context* on the group's success, and this is reflected in our emphasis on context in this book.

Changes in social work and social work education are so numerous it is a struggle to catalogue them all. In addition to those mentioned, the reorganization of services away from locality-based work to specialisms is also significant for groupworkers. For example, Bodinham and Weinstein (1991: 29) note the decline in agency support for the Allsorts women's group, with groupwork no longer a departmental priority, and a reorganization seeing specialisms replace patch-based initiatives. Although these changed priorities alter the focus and context of groupwork, they do not necessarily alter the relevance of groupwork; for example, groups in specialist settings can replace groups in localities.

Before we consider the impact of these transformations on groupwork, it is important to remind ourselves that although political orthodoxies and organizational structures have changed, people's problems have not. People still live in poverty, continue to feel powerless, are abused, abuse, experience discrimination, become carers, break the law, live in substandard housing, feel depressed or suicidal and make decisions about whether to live in residential care. Despite all the turbulent shifts in the explanations for these problems and society's responses to them, the problems themselves change little. It is important to savour this fact, because we can become so overwhelmed with 'internal' changes – agencies restructuring, governments changing policies, professional tasks and roles being redefined – that we mistake them for 'external' ones. Most people who come to the attention of social workers, voluntarily or otherwise, are not directly concerned with these kinds of change.

One response to the political, organizational and professional transformations which we have described is to defy them, emphasizing the observation already made that people's problems are unchanged, and that the 'classic' groupwork response is as relevant to meeting these needs as it always has been; a return to 'real groupwork' (Ward 1998). This approach asserts the commitment to the collectivist ideal and attempts to resist the challenges to this ideal.

Another response is to embrace the changes and to 'modernize' groupwork. Interestingly, this approach has been most vigorously adopted in a profession which, after a long association, is disengaging from social work. The probation service has long been a friend to groupwork but Senior (1993) notes a transition from expressive goals to instrumental ones when he charts the evolution of groupwork in the probation context. Groups which in former times would have met voluntarily for mutual support are now more likely to target specific offending behaviours as part of a court order made as an alternative to custody. The cuddly 'Monday Group' has become the hard-nosed 'Crimestop Programme'. It is not just the purpose of the probation group which has become increasingly prescribed, but the process, content and structure of the new groups is preordained by ready-bought, off-the-shelf 'kits' which tell group leaders when to do what (Chapter 7).

In this book we propose a framework which is capable of housing a variety of different approaches to groupwork. We have been able to put this approach to the test and to refine it through the Groupwork Project, which we will be considering in more detail in the next chapter. We use a framework derived from systems theory to incorporate the best of 'classic' groupwork, together with the significant developments in the profession's analysis of power and oppression, and an increasing understanding of the components of competent groupwork practice. This is a complex process and, throughout it all, our purpose is to accentuate the creative potential of groupwork practice.

Groupwork's presence

When we survey the state of social work practice, where is groupwork? What presence does it have? In short, how much groupwork is there? The evidence from the literature is mixed. 'Where has all the groupwork gone?' asks Ward (1998: 149), noting that groupwork used to have a clear place in the social work firmament – casework, family work, *groupwork*, community work – when social work had a confident continuum of methods. However, this concern has a history, with Tropp (1978) asking much the same question, 'Whatever happened to groupwork?' twenty years earlier. Trevithick (1995: 16) writes of 'considerable concern that groupwork is being practised less than it once was within social work'. On the other hand, Brown and Caddick (1993: 2) claim that 'the use of groups in the probation service – particularly in direct work with offenders – is now probably more extensive and more varied than it has ever been', a view supported by Senior (1993). Certainly, there are examples of groupwork (or work in groups) being the primary way in which probation clients are supervised (Henchman and Walton 1993), though this is also contrasted with a retreat from groupwork in youth justice, where it is tainted by a perception that it represents expansionist welfare intervention (Drakeford 1994: 241).

The best guess is that groupwork's presence is patchy. Whereas an offender might be more likely to be offered groupwork than a one-to-one service, an Asian deaf woman is very unlikely to have the opportunity of groupwork (Kohli 1993). Preston-Shoot's (1988: 147) description of groupwork as 'largely a fringe activity' remains true for many users of health and social services. The most accurate, but less satisfying, answer to questions about the extent of groupwork is that we do not know. Indeed, the evidence from the Groupwork Project suggests that the existence of many groups is unknown even to the host organization. Breton (1991: 42), too, writes of a group for homeless women in a drop-in centre which 'did not exist' because of the absence of communication between the social worker leading the group and the staff at the centre.

Even if we had a clear idea of the *amount* of groups in existence, this would not tell us about the *kind* of groupwork which is being practised; for example, the increase in groups in the probation service might be to exert greater control and restraint on probationers, which would be groupwork of a very different character from former times (Caddick 1991: 198).

Experiences from the Groupwork Project

The Groupwork Project has led us to a number of conclusions, though we acknowledge that they are tentative, so we must be careful about making any generalizations beyond the agency in question. The first conclusion is that it is not straightforward to gather evidence about who is doing groupwork and how they are doing it. If a member of staff was interested in a group for women with eating disorders, would there be any way of finding out whether such a group was running now or had existed in the past? In the Project agency, informal networks would unearth some information, but even from our vantage point at the crux of the Groupwork Project it was difficult to know who was doing groupwork, how and where. This agency is probably typical in not collecting this kind of information in the systematic fashion which would allow it to be aggregated and accessed.

The thirty or so groups which came under the spotlight of the Groupwork Project yielded detailed information about the quality of groupwork being undertaken in those groups, but all is in darkness beyond this exposed area. It seems reasonable to assume that this reflects the situation in many, perhaps most, social work agencies. It is difficult to know how representative the Project-inspired groups are of the kind and character of other unreported groups; nevertheless, these groups have much to tell us about the factors which sustain groupwork of good quality and the impact of groupwork on people's lives. It is these factors which have helped to shape this book and to feel confident that creative groupwork practice is possible and desirable in modern social work agencies.

Contrary to the orthodoxy that groupwork no longer happens, the experience of the Groupwork Project is that there are groups waiting to be 'uncovered'. There is something potentially subversive about groupwork, perhaps illustrated by the woman in a group for refugees who recalled a 'knitting group' she had been a member of in her homeland. 'This was in fact a political group, but when the police checked up on them, their needles would be innocently clicking away as they switched their discussion to knitting patterns and wool colours' (Tribe and Shackman 1989: 162). There is a way in which some groups in social work agencies operate on what we might call the 'innocent knitting needles' policy! Groupwork is associated with forms of non-traditional work and perhaps there is an inherent covertness to many groups which encourages it to avoid the mainstream.

In an information desert, it is inevitable that there are more groups happening than the agency knows about. Moreover, the lack of information gives a message, intended or otherwise, that the agency is not looking, with a temptation to 'go it alone', perhaps on the principle that it is easier to ask forgiveness than for permission. However, there are a number of reasons why this is not a good idea. The first and most obvious is the difficulty in resourcing a 'home-grown' group. Those who have tried this approach and had the courage to write about it are frank about the difficulties it caused (O'Connor 1992: 84). Another consequence of undercover groupwork is the lost opportunities for learning, both in terms of individual practitioners improving their skills and the agency's potential to understand how its services might be diversified and improved. Groupwork is capable of revealing discrepancies between the quality and quantity of services which people are receiving from individual workers (Badham et al. 1989: 34) and compensating for other poor practices which are not immediately amenable to change. For example, Mullender (1988) describes the establishment of a group to develop a sense of black identity for black children in white foster homes, and a parallel group for white foster parents to challenge white racist views.

The commentators who ask 'where has all the groupwork gone?' are often surveying the landscape of qualified social work practice. However, a tentative conclusion from the experience of the Groupwork Project is that groupwork might increasingly be practised by people who are not social workers. Many of the groups associated with the Project, or uncovered by it, were run by staff who were not styled social workers; a few of these workers had contact with service users more commonly in groups than singly. These staff have relatively little power and are not definers in the agency or the social work literature; they do not send articles to journals about their practice (though they have begun to write about their groupwork through the portfolio devised by the Groupwork Project – Chapter 2). This experience may or may not be typical of other agencies in the UK but it is borne out in some of the available literature. For example, the only stress and anxiety groups known to be running in Oxfordshire when Weisen (1991) conducted her survey were run entirely by non-social workers: one was led by two psychology graduates in a community centre, another by a psychology graduate and a clinical psychologist in the same centre, a third by an occupational therapist in a health centre, a fourth by a community psychiatric nurse in another community centre, and a fifth by a health visitor in another health centre. It may, therefore, be less of 'where has all the groupwork gone?' and more of 'why have all the social workers gone?'

If there is a retreat from groupwork in mainstream social work practice, is this because the roles of groupworker and statutory social worker are seen as incompatible? Examples both from the groupwork literature and from the Project do not support this view. For example, Bodinham and Weinstein (1991: 27) describe a groupworker who used her statutory powers to commit to mental hospital a woman who was a member of the group where she was a groupworker; as a group leader she later went to the hospital to take the woman away for the group weekend and this was seen as acceptable practice. In the Project we have seen a number of successful groups run by social workers with statutory powers in both child care and mental health fields; and the statutory powers of probation officers are seen as central to the effective use of authority in offender groups. Nevertheless, it remains possible that there is a common *perception* that groupwork is appropriate only for non-statutory work.

When we consider the relationship of groupwork to social work the agency context is critical. Staff in social services and health care agencies are not independent clinicians. They are usually employed to work in teams (which, we need to remind ourselves, are groups), so that their work is sanctioned by immediate colleagues, by line managers and by agency policies and procedures. Groupwork may or may not be recognized as a legitimate context for practice. The Groupwork Project highlighted the agency as a critical factor in creating a climate for groupwork – favourable, hostile or indifferent – and the support of middle management in particular can be crucial (Jones *et al.* 1991: 228). The learner groupworkers in the Project were required to have the backing of their line managers (and, by implication, their teams); as the significance of this support became apparent, the programme required line managers to attend the initial consultations with paired participants, serving both symbolic and practical purposes (see Chapter 2). All groupworkers need to ask themselves who in the agency has the power to promote and constrain groupwork (Preston-Shoot 1992: 26). Where can groupworkers find support for their practice? We explore the context of groupwork in greater detail in the next chapter.

One final observation from the Project is that the growth in self-help groups noted in the European groupwork literature (Habermann 1990; 1993), has either not had its parallels in the UK, or has not come to the notice of the particular services of the agency. There was very little networking with, or knowledge of, informal groups in the community and no indication that part of the role of social work staff might be to service or liaise with existing community groups.

In conclusion, there is a conundrum. Has groupwork all but disappeared (Ward 1998)? Is it flourishing but in a different incarnation (Senior 1993)? Or is it now largely hidden because the main protagonists are relatively less powerful and visible in their agencies and less written about in the journals (such as staff in daycare, outreach projects and prequalified staff in field settings)? Our experience via the Groupwork Project in one mainstream, middle-sized, statutory social work agency supports the third view. However, like a prism, it all depends from which side you view it, so that there is a sense in which all three propositions present a facet of the truth.

Although this book's main focus is groupwork in the context of social work and social care, let us not underestimate its universal significance. For example, running a world-class airline company might seem as far removed from social work as we can imagine, but the following paragraph from a book written by the boss of Continental Airlines could be taken straight from a text on groupwork:

> The (previous) chief executive sat at the head of a long table. His closest cronies sat by his side, and down at the other end of the table sat the people who had most to fear for their jobs. At the first managers' meeting we had after I took over, I sat down the middle of the table ... if you want a collegial atmosphere, you have to do something to make it collegial.

> Mixing up the seating is one easy, tiny thing to do ... Everybody had to think about where they were going to sit rather than just sit where they expected to sit. And they got the message: ... things are different. (Bethune 1998: 34)

This chief executive helped turn around a failing $6 billion company by employing techniques familiar to any groupworker. Clearly, groupworkers' skills are marketable well beyond the confines of social work practice because groupwork is an essential part of human activity, be it social work or airline work. The only difference is the level of pay.

Groups, groupings and groupwork

Earlier in the chapter we looked at the 'art and science of gathering' by using the analogy of a group of people sharing a meal. We were able to distinguish people gathered *in* a group and people acting *as* a group. The skill of helping the transition from one to another is a reasonably concise definition of what groupwork is.

Although there might be a place for 'work-in-groups' (Ward 1996: 108) this book is concerned more with the active and creative use of group processes rather than the mere convenience of having a number of individuals gather together. However, there is no standard group. Groupwork can take place over the course of several years and it can consist of a single session, as in critical incident debriefing (Parkinson 1993). The continuum activity which introduces Chapter 4 demonstrates the enormous range of possibilities for any particular group's profile. One of the aims of this book is to help to answer the obvious question – what makes these all groups?

Although there is no standard group, Brown (1990) suggests that much of the social groupwork literature has a 'fieldwork' group as its template, meeting once a week and created from scratch. The notion of 'groupings', an idea that people are already in collectivities, is useful to understand what Brown calls the mosaic of residential and day centre life. Brown and Clough (1989) have developed the following typology to describe the range of groups and groupings.

- *The 'whole community'*: the sense of identity with the totality of the centre will differ from setting to setting.

- *Living together 'groups'*: for example, mealtime groups, bedroom groups.

- *Informal friendships/affinity groups:* people choosing to associate with each other, perhaps on the basis of a shared interest.

- *Groups to discuss group living issues:* such as house meetings of staff and residents to discuss matters of shared concern.

- *Organized groups:* such as behaviour change, activities, reminiscence groups – similar to social groupwork groups in fieldwork settings.

- *Organized groupings:* people come together for an activity such as educational classes, but there is little attention to interaction and group processes.

- *Staff groups and groupings:* formal groups such as staff meetings, smaller task groups, and subgroupings of staff who share interests or characteristics (gender, race, etc.).

- *Groups and groupings whose membership crosses the boundary of the Centre:* groups which contain 'insiders' and 'outsiders'; drop-in groupings.

Ironically, the very diversity and prevalence of group experience in residential and day centre settings might inhibit the development of more formal group structures. Calls for residents' forums might be dismissed because of a feeling that *there is always the chance to air your views, so why do we need a group?* Indeed, the need for a group might be seen as admitting failure in the general channels of communication (Booth 1985).

The paradox is that, whatever the setting, most of us experience groups much of the time, but our experience of groupwork is much more limited. We can understand the meaning of Rhule's (1988: 44) statement that some group members 'had never attended a group before'; in fact, it is their experience of *groupwork* which is new.

Why use groupwork?

> I myself feel better when I am helping someone else ... usually a person whose loss is more recent than my own, although not always. (Part of a group member's evaluation of a family bereavement group, quoted in Hopmeyer and Werk 1993: 114)

We have already begun to rehearse the attractions of groupwork and the reasons for using groupwork are well documented (see Otway 1993: 212). Nevertheless, it will be useful to summarize these, and we begin with one of the most significant; the value of reciprocity, both the giving and the receiving of help. For example, 40 per cent of the respondents in Hopmeyer and Werk's (1993) survey felt that they had received and given equally (55% felt that they received more than they contributed to the group, and only 5% that they had received less than they had contributed). This contrasts with one-to-one interventions which are more likely to cast the service user as a mere recipient.

Linked to reciprocity is the 'all in the same boat' phenomenon and the feeling of strength in numbers. Groupworkers place themselves in a numerical minority in a group and this is frequently empowering for group members, especially when they begin to discover the companionship of experiences held in common. This gives credibility to the group members and facilitates challenges to the groupworker where this is appropriate.

The group can provide an effective medium for change and development, 'a laboratory for learning' (Shulman 1988: 6). It can become a microcosm of the larger world, yet provide a safer environment to rehearse new feelings and behaviours. The group can provide remedial help, and groupwork processes can accelerate 'natural' forces, in the way that 'involvement in reminiscence groups appeared to help new residents in their transition and incorporation' (Gibson 1992: 36).

Crucially, groupwork can highlight those aspects of a person's life which are *not* problematic. For example, a group for teenage cancer patients emphasized the fact that they are not always ill, but they *are* always teenagers – with the interests common to teenagers (Martin and O'Neill 1992: 63). A group which helps participants discover and celebrate their strengths is an exceptionally empowering experience. A place where, as well as sharing pain, people can have fun.

The philosophy of groupwork is based on a belief in the power of the collective solution. 'Collective action generates power' (Mullender and Ward 1991). It is a place where individuals can find their voices, individually or together, learn together and challenge together.

There are two particular issues to consider before concluding this section. The first is whether expediency is a valid reason to consider groupwork. There is no lack of examples of groups as 'the management of numbers', such as Allum's (1990: 135) frank response to a mass disclosure of abuse by one perpetrator of 15 children, using groups as a matter of convenience. However, it is likely that if expediency is the sole justification, then the experience will be one of 'work in groups' rather than groupwork.

The second issue is the value of groupwork to the practitioner. Groupwork is an excellent opportunity to continue to develop professional skills, especially where co-working means that practice is observed and feedback is an integral part of the debriefing (see Chapter 11). Also, groupwork can be a safer environment for the workers as well as the other members; as an example, Erooga, Clark and Bentley (1990: 174) point to the value of groupwork for the professional worker in cases of child sexual abuse, to prevent the collusion which can take place when being supportive on a one-to-one basis can be taken as active agreement (such as head-nodding meaning 'yes, go on, I follow' interpreted as 'yes, that's right, I agree'). Moreover, the emotional stresses of this kind of work can be shared through co-working in groups.

Why not groupwork?

In general, the question 'why not groupwork?' relates to the appropriateness of an individual to join a group rather than the appropriateness of groupwork itself. A review of the literature reveals that all areas of social work practice are amenable to a groupwork service, even those concerned with the most private and troubled of circumstances, such as bereavement, suicide or sexual abuse. However, there are many reasons why some individuals will not benefit from groupwork, usually because their differences are so great. Sometimes these differences do not exclude them from groupwork in general, but this group in particular. At other times, their own phobic or destructive responses to group settings prevent them enjoying the benefits of groupwork.

We should not minimize the fact that practitioners' responses to groupwork are also a factor which limits it. Some settings, such as group care, seem tailored for groupwork, so it seems reasonable to ask why it seems to happen so infrequently. There is evidence to suggest that there is widespread anxiety among staff about being in and working in large groups (Ward 1993). The power of large groups is undeniable and staff may not have had the experience of being part of a successful large group themselves, or the training to facilitate such a group.

In general, it is fair to assume that there are more people who could benefit from a groupwork service than there are groups available to meet the potential demand. There is also a view that groupwork would be a 'hammer to crack a nut' in much current social work and social care practice; so that proceduralized assessments do not justify the resources of groupwork. This is a judgement which agencies and practitioners must make, but there are examples (especially in the probation service) where groupwork has become the routine. 'Why not groupwork?' deserves an answer on its own merits, not 'because we never have'; just as 'Why groupwork?' also requires a considered answer, not 'because we always do'.

Groups for whom?

The bibliography on pages 266–275 reveals the vast range of groups and groupwork. Groups for people in all kinds of situation, groups for service users and groups for staff, groups with many kinds of purpose and groupworkers with aims so varied they even include those who neutralize existing groups (degrouping), as in the work with gangs in Hong Kong (Lo 1992: 61).

Even when it has been established that there are the skills and resources for groupwork, 'Groups for whom?' is not a straightforward question. Consider a situation where there has been sexual abuse against children. How does the groupworker decide whether to work with a group of the children who have been sexually abused, a group with children abused solely within the family, a group of siblings of these children, a group of perpetrators, a group of mothers of children who have been sexually abused ... or a number of other possibilities? (Dobbin and Evans 1994). It is always important to consider the context in which any group might be framed and to understand the needs of the people who seem to be on the sidelines as well as those who are centre stage. For example, a pilot study of groupwork with siblings with special needs showed the intensity of the feelings of guilt, resentment and ignorance the participants had in connection with their siblings (Ferraro and Tucker 1993).

The variety of groupwork reflects the range of contexts in which naturally existing groups occur. Hours spent together in groups plaiting hair provides quality time for black women to teach and learn from each other and to discuss issues they face together: 'groupwork is part of many Black women's culture. The interaction they have, however, is not called or viewed as groupwork' (Francis-Spence 1994: 113). The family is an existing group which might provide the nucleus for groupwork, such as Finlayson's (1993) moving account of groupwork with a family group of four siblings who had suffered innumerable losses, including the death of their mother.

We have already made reference to the processes which lead us to make sense of the world by grouping seemingly random or diverse elements within it. This process has been evident from the dawn of human history, when the frightening randomness of the stars was tamed by grouping them and imposing the patterns of recognizable humans and animals. It is important, too, to remember that groupings are not infallible and that they may not be welcomed by those so grouped. Some people find themselves members of a group to which they never requested membership, for example as a parent of a child with a learning disability. 'It felt like I had caught the wrong train and got off at the wrong station', writes Gobat (1993: 228).

Ironically, those persons who are most vulnerable and most in need are often those who are the most difficult to engage in groupwork (Home and Darveau-Fournier 1990: 238). Groupworkers must consider very carefully how to attract 'hard-to-reach' populations, and how to balance encouragement to join a group with the rights of individuals to decline, a dilemma we address in more detail in Chapter 5. The rewards for membership need to be tangible, and for some prospective members they need to be evident and immediate; indeed, there are some rare instances of group members receiving payment to attend groups (for example, a parent education group reported by Mischley *et al.* 1985).

'Who is groupwork for?' also raises the question of the composition of a group. A greater emphasis on equal opportunities and anti-discriminatory practices is reflected in the development of women-only groupwork, though there is less conclusive evidence when we consider black-only groups (Caddick 1991; Mistry and Brown 1997). We revisit the issue of sameness and difference and group composition in more detail in Chapter 4.

Groupwork and policy making

Social work's response to the attack on welfare and collectivism has not been robust. Where much of the practice of social work is individualized, so is its impact; social work's temperament, tradition and training has, ironically, long been 'privatized' and practitioners and agencies have not been versed in presenting the wider case to the community.

Although groupwork can be similarly 'privatized', and is subject to the same traditions, temperament and training just described, the groupwork philosophy carries a greater potential for wider connections to be made. The very existence of the group is an acknowledgement of other realities and other systems which have a semi-public nature. Groupwork is capable of providing a forum to link private troubles with public policy and a platform to influence a wider system.

An example of this is a report of a group for young mothers published by the Children's Society. At a time when teenage mothers were being blamed for the breakdown in family values, the report 'gives a positive account of the achievements of the young mothers and calls for social policy changes which would help to alleviate some of the difficulties they face and provide opportunities for a better future' (Norman 1994: 234). The young mothers felt empowered by their involvement in compiling the report together with the group leaders. In the field of youth justice, Drakeford (1994) makes a case for groupwork with the parents of young people in trouble as a way of offering courts an alternative to using their powers under the 1991 Criminal Justice Act to bind over the parents of young people who offend.

The experience of groups can also influence organizational and professional policies. For example, policy was changed in relation to siblings' access to hospital wards and the intensive care unit when their brother or sister was very ill or dying. The policy change resulted from the experience of groups for bereaved children in which social workers had encouraged parents not to 'protect' their surviving children but to include them in the grieving process (Harmey and Price 1992: 27). As a result, the organization developed an understanding that the needs of children must be catered for as well as adults when developing bereavement services. The relationship between the group and its setting is even more critical when they are conducted by outsiders who 'import' all sorts of activities which are largely unconnected with the life of the unit or residence itself (Lewis 1992: 56). The groupworker's task is to connect with the staff and the setting, so that the group is not seen as an oasis, but something which can be integrated into other aspects of group living and owned by the full complement of staff and residents.

As well as groupwork's impact on policy making, it is important to consider the way policy can facilitate groupwork. Mullender (1988) calls for policies which enhance the work of groups such as the 'Ebony' groups for black children in white foster homes.

Theoretical perspectives – the essential groupworker

> Two thirds of psychologists and half of the social workers based their groupwork on a particular theory. The majority of psychologists based their groupwork on a behaviour or cognitive approach. Approximately half of the social workers based their groupwork on systems theory or used an eclectic approach. (Schonfeld and Morrissey (1992: 46) on groups for people with learning disabilities)

Theory has an uneasy place in social work practice and the priority for most busy practitioners is one of *doing*. Memories of the need 'to integrate theory and practice' are rekindled in those who supervise students, and experimentation with new practices is more likely to encourage a rethink about what makes it 'tick', a process which often involves a consideration of theory. If this hypothesis is correct, it is likely that theory will play a less explicit part for those running groups as a regular part of their work, whilst those embarking on a new groupwork project might be more interested in underpinning theory. There are, of course, many different kinds of theory and theories for practice are the ones most likely to prove the most readily applicable (Payne 1991). If groupworkers are to make use of theory, it has to be accessible, and organize knowledge and experience in ways which can be translated into practice. Participants in the Groupwork Project responded to theories which helped to make sense of their experiences in groups and which guided their practice.

Even if theory is not articulated, it is always present as a kind of 'theorizing'. There is a sense in which all our actions are governed by personal theories about why things are as they are, why people are motivated to do what they do, who has power and how they use it, what works and what doesn't. These explanations, hypotheses and beliefs guide our actions and might be considered 'personal theories' (Doel and Shardlow 1998: 23–31). They are based on our experiences, mediated by our beliefs; the more open we are to challenge, the more we will search out new information, perhaps based on formal research studies. However, if we act on these personal theories without reflecting on them, we are unaware of their impact and unable to test them out.

When considering theory and groupwork, then, it is important to start with your own personal theories. What current beliefs do you hold in respect of groups and how do they help you to understand what happens in them? How do you explain the behaviour of people in groups (such as in your team) and what purposes do you suppose groups to have? Whatever you read in this book or others will be mediated through your current beliefs. It is likely that these informal theories will influence what you will do in groups more than formal theory, so it is important that you articulate them.

In an overview of theories for practice in social work practice, Payne (1998: 125–9) considers three different views: individualist-reformist; reflexive-therapeutic and socialist-collectivist. The first focuses on individual problems and help for individuals to adjust to society. The second is concerned more with helping people to achieve personal growth and express or cope with emotions through the development and use of relationships. The third focuses on the effects of structural inequality and a dialogue with clients to raise consciousness about the way their problems arise from this inequality and oppression. Payne (1998) names specific practice methods as examples of one or other of the three general categories; for example, cognitive behavioural methods as an example in the first category; counselling methods in the second; and feminist practice in the third. These categories, proposed in relation to theories for general social work, are just as relevant to groupwork. The approaches used in groupwork and their theoretical underpinnings span the same range.

Groupwork is complex because the term is used not just in relation to a context for practice but also as a method of practice. So, in addition to the possibility of using social work practice methods in a group context (counselling groups, feminist groups, etc.) groupwork is, itself, a practice method. There are groupwork elements, therefore, which are common to counselling groupwork and feminist groupwork – as well as the differences which define them as 'counselling' or 'feminist', etc.

One of the aims of the Groupwork Project which has inspired this book has been to develop a generic model of groupwork. In other words, it has sought to take the essential elements of groupwork and develop a model of practice which is adaptable to the many variants of groupwork practice. An example of a 'generic element' is the development of the concept of group theme, which provides a conceptual tool for analysis and a practical tool for application and helps the group to move towards a sense of commonality. From our experience of the Groupwork Project, it is applicable across groupwork methods and settings (see Chapter 10 for a more detailed discussion).

Models of groupwork which emphasize 'phases' and 'stages' imply a sense of chronology which participants in the Groupwork Project found less easy to identify in the reality of a group session than on the pages of a book. For this reason, we have tested a model with the dual purpose of helping groupworkers to understand groups at a conceptual level and to practise groupwork at a concrete level; principles of practice tested in a variety of groupwork approaches. As might be expected from a practice model which is eclectic and essentialist, the theoretical underpinnings are various. The organizing principles, however, are derived from systems theory. For example, when we begin to analyze obstacles to group functioning from the point of view of a number of interdependent systems, it is possible to see that a concern 'here' might in fact be an expression of difficulties 'there', in other parts of the system. It is also possible to understand how the best response is not necessarily at the system level where the problem is evident; a gushing hose pipe is more effectively halted by turning off the water supply than trying to plug the end of the hose. It is important, therefore, not to overlook the wider systems which have an impact on the group. An example from the Groupwork Project was the effect on the dynamics in a group for foster carers where there were close family ties between various members (sisters-in-law, etc.) which were not known to the group leaders until later in the group. (See

Chapter 10 for a full discussion of systems theory and the groupwork model.)

Postlude

Finally, a comment on the place of metaphor in groupwork theory and practice. A metaphor can help to illuminate groupwork practice by allowing group members to consider processes in a parallel world, but safer than the one which is too close to home. A metaphor can also help our understanding of model-building in groupwork; for example, we began this first chapter by using the distinction between four musicians and a quartet to illustrate the difference between a set of individuals and a group. This is not yet quite a metaphor, but as you progress through the book, you will read about tuning in, the development of themes, the group's tempo, and co-workers in harmony. This chimes with a sense of groupwork as orchestration and groupworkers as conductors (Whitaker 1985). The musical metaphor is apt, since music and groupwork are both generic concepts which encompass an enormous variety of styles. We hope this book will help you to differentiate 'music' from 'noise' and encourage you to make your own kind of music, and maybe experiment with some other kinds, too. We hope it will encourage creative groupworkers who know when to follow the score and when to improvise.

CHAPTER TWO

Education and Training
for Groupwork

In Chapter 1 we explored the difficulty of judging the range of groupwork practice in contemporary social work. There is a parallel problem when gauging the prevalence of education and training for groupwork, whether at prequalifying, qualifying or postqualifying levels. Groupwork does not figure in the 'national curriculum' for social work in the UK (CCETSW 1995), nor does any other practice methodology. Whereas schools of social work in the USA require students to have basic knowledge and skills in leading groups, the situation is patchier in the UK (Reid 1988: 124). The groupwork literature allows us glimpses of this scene, but no clear picture of its reach (Doel and Sawdon 1995; Kerslake 1990; Lumley and Marchant 1989). However, if we reframe 'education and training for groupwork' as 'learning groups', whether in an educational setting or as training groups, we can see the extraordinary importance of an understanding of groups – their planning, their composition and their dynamics. Much of the experience of professional education and vocational training is in groups, and it is likely that much of their success or failure lies in the success or failure of the groupwork. So, even when the education and training is not about 'Groupwork', it is about groupwork.

Groupwork is not an esoteric practice method. It is an understanding of groups and an ability to work with and in them and, as such, it is an integral part of a professional's experience and competence. The significance of an education and training in groupwork is not, therefore, confined to a specialist methodology. This kind of training nurtures confidence and abilities which transfer to many different contexts and to situations which we often fail to conceptualize as groups, such as meetings. In the previous chapter we introduced the Groupwork Project, designed to promote groupwork in a mainstream social services department; although the focus was a training programme for groupwork with service users, many learners reported their experiences of generalizing their learning to other aspects of their work, such as meetings, staff groups and case reviews. The reflective nature of the groupwork programme encouraged this transfer of learning, which leads us to the view that the essentialist model which has evolved out of the Project is both a training and an *education* in groupwork.

The context for teaching and learning about groupwork

The context in which groupwork is taught and learnt has considerable significance. College-based education for groupwork has all the advantages and disadvantages of learning which is focused on practice but located in an educational setting. There is plenty of opportunity for reflection and simulated rehearsal but none for direct practice. The student group itself can be used as an exemplar of group processes, but there are limitations and dangers to this approach. One possible solution to this difficulty is to link the learning in college with direct practice experience, such as Kerslake's (1990) account of a groupwork option on a social work qualifying course combined with a practice element. Courses which combine college-based and agency-based learning and practice are valuable, but complex and time consuming to arrange. Moreover, it is difficult to take account of the impact of the setting and agency context on the group.

Training programmes held within agencies can be tailored for particular staff. They have the potential to bring immediate and direct practice into the training workshop and they can take account of a common factor (the agency) which shapes the participants' practice. The training programme itself can be shaped to the agency. There are also disadvantages in agency-based training. Organizational issues such as the uncertainty over a recent, current or impending reorganization can loom over the programme; other preoccupations such as staff changes and closure of residential units are magnified when all the participants are employees of a single agency. The close 'fit' between the content of the programme and the participants' job might become uncomfortably tight. Learners emerging with increased assertiveness from the programme, critical of some aspects of current agency practice, will be welcomed by an enlightened agency genuinely concerned to provide a quality service, but not all can be described in this way as 'learning organizations' (Senge 1990).

Groupwork is unlikely to have a high profile in the agency. Both in the training for groupwork and the groupwork itself, workers are likely to be called to other duties first. The experience of a staff member 'sent on a course at short notice' and therefore missing the second session of a group in which she had agreed to lead members in a reminiscence session, is not unusual (Lewis 1992: 54). It may be necessary to establish the value of a group before it becomes properly resourced: 'gradually ... this work is being recognized as an important and integral part of the task of the Probation Service and attempts are being made to resource it adequately' (Cowburn 1990: 165, on male sex offenders' groups). This movement from avant-garde to mainstream also describes the evolution of the training programme within the Groupwork Project.

A model for education and training in groupwork

Five cohorts of learners (66 learners in all) have participated in the Groupwork Project and it is the evaluation of their experiences which has shaped the training model. This evaluation has been complex and has involved a wide range of factors, including the structure and content of the training programme and the systems and mechanisms for assessing the groupwork skills of the learners. Well over 200 people have been served by groups directly spawned by the Project (these number 27, but many learners have continued to run further groups). The quality of the groups, in terms of the impact on the lives of the group members and their associates, has been accessible through the evaluations gathered by learners and via portfolios of groupwork practice.

The following seven principles have been developed and refined in the light of these experiences and we explore each in more detail in the rest of this chapter. As we go to press with this book, a sixth cohort of learners is adding its experience to our understanding of this model for education and training in groupwork.

- *Parallel*: a training model which parallels the development of the learners' own groups.

- *Compatible*: a training model which is congruent with the model of groupwork practice, in terms of the value base and the methods used, and a training group compatible with learners' project groups.

- *Essentialist*: a training model based around a generic model of groupwork practice applicable by people working in very diverse settings with similarly diverse educational backgrounds and groupwork orientations.

- *Contextualised – agency resource*: a training model designed to foster a pool of groupwork knowledge and experience in the agency, heightening the profile of groupwork.

- *Accountable*: a training model in which lines of accountability are visible and explicit to take account of the various 'stakeholders'.

- *Assessable*: a training model which uses a common assessment tool, accessible to all learners and enabling them to 'capture' their practice accurately and in ways which benefit their learning and encourages completion of the programme.

- *Contextualised – professional development*: a training model which dovetails into a greater scheme of professional development and supports an expression of lifelong learning.

Parallel

We have already begun to describe the shape of the Groupwork Project and its rationale in this chapter. The programme is designed to shadow the running of a group by the learner. Given the immense spread of groups being run by the learners, the precise format of the training programme has to be a compromise. Some learners are already involved in running groups (though not necessarily involved in groupwork), whilst others are starting from scratch. Although the majority of the groups which have been supported by the programme fall into Brown's (1992: 7) 'Individual Change/Support' category, there have nevertheless been examples of all types of group. Inevitably, the training programme cannot run in exact parallel with every learner's group.

There are many parallels between the training project and the group projects. The preference for learners to join the training programme as pairs, usually agreeing to co-work their proposed group, has parallels in groupwork practice, where small subgrouped pairs can provide the strength and companionship needed to engage in the larger group. For example, in Regan and Young's (1990) group for children of divorced and separated parents, the sibling pairs provide a buffer between the parental divorce and themselves. The parallels continue with the consultation interview between the course leaders and each pair of co-workers, which mirrors the offer of groupwork to individuals which we explore in more detail in Chapter 5. The consultation is an opportunity for all concerned to learn more about the programme and to help the co-workers to formalize their plans for the group project, in the way that the individual offer of groupwork to prospective members is a chance for them to find out more about the group and to have an input into the plans.

The first consultation is also an occasion to involve others who might be significant to the project's success. These 'associates' are usually the learners' line managers. Experience indicates that the support of the co-workers' team and supervisor is important to success, so they are invited to participate in the process. Their presence confirms their interest in their supervisee's development, and enables them to understand the extent of the commitment necessary for the group project to be successful. There is no expectation that they will offer supervision in groupwork (though this is a bonus where these skills are apparent), but that they will help to manage the learners' work environment. Many line managers will be aware of the time needed for planning, leading and evaluating the group, but not all appreciate the further time needed to assimilate the learning from the programme and to gather evidence of groupwork ability.

Learners are asked to plan the start of their group soon after the first set of workshops, which allows time for them to firm these plans in the period between the first consultation interview and the first workshop. There are indications that an ability to plan the group project in sequence with the training programme is a factor in its ultimate success, though an alternative explanation could be that if the learners have the ability to steer their group alongside the training programme, this in itself indicates good planning skills. Moreover, a few learners have launched a successful group even after the programme finished (in one case almost a year later).

The collective sense of starting out together is a powerful factor in helping the learners become a training group. Even though groups proceed at their own different pace, with a few ending by the time the second set of workshops is held, a common starting place has a lasting effect. Because of the varying lengths of learners' group projects, the very final day of the training programme is held five months after the last workshop. This provides a stage on which to celebrate not just the groups which learners have been running, but also to congratulate them on completing the course and, in many cases, successfully completing a portfolio. This process mirrors the ending rituals of groups described later in Chapter 13. Indeed, the parallels are very close; not long after two of the groupworkers expressed their embarrassment at the misspelt names on the certificates given to members at the closing ceremony of their foster carers' group, we trainers had a similar experience when we mislaid the certificate for one of the learners.

It is necessary to signal caution about being over-explicit about the parallels between the training group and the learners' own group projects. Learners can easily feel self-consciously 'groupworked' and the course leaders are already seen as powerful people without augmenting this through expert analyses of group processes within the training group. Shifting the focus 'from binocular to microscope' is powerful and should be used sparingly.

Compatible

In addition to the parallel running of course and group, it is important to achieve congruency between the learners' experience of the training programme and the experience which they create for their own groups. Clearly, a training programme advocating empowering, participative groupwork must be empowering and participative (Szmagalski 1989: 245).

The methods used in the training group mirrored methods which the learner groupworkers would use in their own groups. A striking example of this was the use of sculpting. Asking learners to recreate their groups in the workshop proved illuminating and gave the training group a good feel for them. This technique was used to review the way learners had marked the last sessions of their groups. In turn, each pair of co-leaders was asked to mark out the territory in the training room to reproduce their own group spaces, repositioning chairs, tables, flipcharts, etc. to reflect the usual 'shape' of their own group. The co-workers then picked fellow learners to represent each group member and sit them down in the group. In almost all cases, the co-workers said that group members usually sat in the same place from session to session, and in all the example groups the basic shape which was reproduced was an oval or flattened horseshoe, with the co-leaders sat either side of a flipchart at the opening of the horseshoe. This illustrated the power of modelling, because these sculpts faithfully replicated the 'shape' of the training group sessions.

Once we were all seated, the co-workers were invited to move from individual to individual describing them, evaluating their contribution to the group, and physically manoeuvring the learner in a pose which was characteristic of the person they were representing. The first 'round' had been very powerful, but there was an unspoken sense that individuals might have been chosen because of some perceived similarity between themselves and the group member they represented (and this was frequently unflattering). So, in the next and subsequent rounds, people would opt for a group member before his or her character had been described. This was an interesting example of the training group taking care of itself by finding a safe way to continue with a challenging activity.

The most powerful sculpt was the final one. We were introduced to each of the members of the Wednesday Group for people who were socially isolated and in varying degrees of becoming confused. The painfulness of their individual circumstances and the abusiveness of many of their families was strongly felt. So, too, was the power of the able-bodied co-leaders standing over us, coupled with the difficulty they faced in helping a collection of individuals to become a group. In particular, learners experienced the poignancy of the sudden and unannounced departure of individuals from the group, off to 'The Sycamores' nursing home, for example. No celebrations, cakes or certificates for these group members, unlike the pictures painted of other learners' group endings. Sculpting proved to be a powerful method of recreating learners' groups in the workshop and it was a method which was compatible with the methods used by the learners in their own groups, too. This is just one example of the congruency between the input of the training groups and the output of the learners' groups.

Essentialist

To what extent can one particular training model serve learners from such a variety of settings working with such diverse groups? Can a model of groupwork practice based largely on learning theory and systems theory satisfy learner groupworkers who might have other kinds of theoretical orientation (for example, psychodynamic theories)? To meet this objective, it would be necessary to distil and present the elements which are the *essence* of groupwork. The design of the training model would be tested to capacity by learners with different levels of experience and educational attainment from almost every section of the agency, working with an enormous variety of groups and with a range of orientations to groupwork.

The authors were by no means certain that it would be possible to develop such an essentialist model of groupwork practice, as well as an associated training model to act as a vehicle for that practice, capable of supporting such a broad constituency. Experience of Tuckman's (1965) famous model of 'developmental sequences in small groups', summed up in the mnemonic 'Forming, Norming, Storming, Performing, Adjourning' was not encouraging. Although it is a well-established generic concept, these developmental sequences were not especially helpful when generalized across different types of group. Phases in groups might best be considered as specific to different kinds of group, such as the clear phases in work with child sexual abuse perpetrators detected by Erooga et al. (1990: 185–7): guilt and false motivation; awareness and resistance; awareness and internalization; maintenance/relapse prevention. These phases might be more helpful to co-workers training to lead this kind of group than a generic model of group development. It seems important, then, to tread carefully when considering the possibility of discovering what might be essential elements of groupwork.

Ultimately, the model which came to underpin the training model and the groupwork model was based on systems theory, and this helped to provide the 'essentialist' model which proved durable across settings and styles. Over the course of the rest of the book we explore the elements of this model which has provided a framework or template capable of supporting a rich diversity of groupwork. Whatever the profile of a group, for instance as 'plotted' on the continuum chart on pages 73–74, learners have consistently reported the relevance of both the training model and the practice model in supporting their groupwork learning and practice.

There are no shortage of indicators by which to test the model's general relevance. The most obvious is the number and diversity of groups run by learners, with four out of five (79%) learners who completed the training programme running groups to successful completion. This is indicative rather than conclusive, since we do not know on what factors the success of the groups depended. However, further evidence arises from the learners' own testimony, explicit in written and verbal feedback taken regularly during the programmes, and implicit in the fact that, for example, six pairs of groupworkers listen attentively to each others' presentations, even though the groups are of very different complexion and serving different user groups. In fact, learners reported that the opportunity to train alongside colleagues from across the agency was unusual and was one of the most successful aspects of the programme. Of the learners, 56 per cent were based in field and community settings, 24 per cent in daycare and day centres and 17 per cent in residential care. The populations served by the learners' groups were as follows.

- *Groups for adults* (mixed gender eligibility): 8 (29%)
  - Day centre users with mental health problems (5)
  - People with enduring mental health problems
  - Parents group, where children at risk
  - New foster carers and adopters to manage behaviour problems with under-8s
- *Girls-only and women-only groups*: 6 (22%)
  - 'Girls just wanna have fun' 'not-therapy' group
  - Women with eating disorders
  - Women with learning difficulties

- Women who have been sexually abused
- Women with enduring mental health problems
- Women developing self-esteem
- *Children and young people groups*: 5 (19%)
  - Children who have been bullied at school
  - Young people in residential care group
  - Teenage boys who have been sexually abused
  - Young people who are homeless and seeking accommodation (2)
- *Groups for elders*: 4 (15%)
  - Older people with mental health problems or dementia (3)
  - Reminiscence group
- *Staff development/training groups*: 4 (15%)
  - Staff development group (children's residential)
  - Senior residential social workers support group
  - 'Quality circle' group for staff in mental health residential unit
  - New support workers, with assessment component

The diversity of learners' groupwork experience and qualification status is also testimony to the essentialist nature of the Project. There are few, though notable, examples in the literature of groups run by unqualified social work and social care staff (Bernard *et al.* 1988); by contrast, the Groupwork Project attracted twice as many prequalified staff as qualified, with 82 per cent running groups to a successful conclusion. Though they are the least likely group of staff to write about their successes in the journals, 53 per cent of the unqualified staff who completed a group 'told their stories' in a portfolio for assessment.

So, the training model helps learners learn about groupwork and practise groupwork in a variety of situations. Using an art metaphor, the model provides a palette of colours and some instruction in how they might be used. Each of the colours seems to be an essential aspect of leading and participating in a successful group, but the mix of 'crimson reds', 'cobalt blues' and 'yellow ochres' varies considerably so that an immensely rich variety of pictures is possible, all created from the same palette.

The groups in the Project were located in the same agency, which could be seen as a limitation on claims to an essentialist model. It was interesting, therefore, to take the model out to probation services, where one factor which had been absent previously was ever-present in probation groupwork

– the element of compulsion. This did not undermine the model overall, but it did mean that one facet (the 'Prussian blue' on the palette, if you like) coloured all of these groups. Moreover, the heavy reliance on manuals gave many of the groups in the probation service a 'painting by numbers' feel, which restricted the degree of experimentation suggested by the palette metaphor.

The diversity of practice models in groupwork is matched by a similar diversity in training models (Kerslake 1990: 65). In this eclectic environment it is important, therefore, to be able to articulate what basic expectations of practice we have of people who claim that they 'do groupwork'. In essence the rest of this book aims to do exactly that, so that by the conclusion of Chapter 13 we hope the reader will have an understanding of these groupwork essentials, of what these 'reds', 'yellows' and 'blues' are and how they might be used.

Contextualized – agency resource

We began to explore groupwork in the context of the agency in Chapter 1. These contextual issues were especially prevalent in the Project because all of the groupworkers were located in the same agency. This increases the potential for groupwork to be seen as an agency resource as the numbers of groups and the 'amount' of groupwork reaches a critical mass.

For groupwork to become an agency resource rather than a bolt-on interest pursued by some of the staff, there needs to be an explicit strategy in which groupwork knowledge is used systematically. At one level this knowledge is as straightforward as an accessible database which keeps track of groups in the agency; at another it is the way the accumulated experience of groupwork in an agency is consolidated. The latter requires a strategy which goes beyond the scope of groupwork to the broader notion of practice knowledge and the development of a learning culture (Senge 1990). An agency with 'the knowledge' might prevent the need for the following response from one learner who, when asked 'What do you think will help your group to be successful?' replied 'Being assertive enough to clear obstacles along the way'.

One indicator of the extent to which an agency perceives groupwork as a resource is the availability of consultation. The consultation interviews between the groupwork learners and the course tutors (the authors) was rated by learners as important to the overall success of the groups. It was an occasion to put the teaching into context. This is important where the groups under the umbrella of the programme are at different stages, some yet to begin, some nearing conclusion. In their groupwork with children who had been sexually abused, Lebacq and Shah (1989) and Dixon and Phillips (1994: 92) stress the value of consultancy. The former identify the need to set up consultancy arrangements before the general terms of reference for the group are agreed and with a frequency of at least once a fortnight (the group was weekly). With hindsight they also advised that groups which aim to address the needs of black sexually abused children recruit a black consultant, and that group leaders of different races should consider whether to have individual as well as shared sessions with a black consultant. In the trade-off between quality and efficiency, this level of consultation is not always practicable; the experience from the training project indicates that consultations which are reliable (i.e. ones which are planned well in advance, not interrupted, nor cancelled) compensate to a degree for relative infrequency.

The Groupwork Project is far from reaching the point of 'critical mass' at which groupwork becomes self-sustaining, a major mode of delivery throughout the agency. However, there is a developing network, in which past learners meet potential learners before the latter make a decision to apply for the training course, and current learners are put in touch with others who have already run similar groups. The transmission of learning also takes place via the availability of past portfolios of groupwork practice as exemplars, and past learners acting as mentors for current ones. Without doubt, the groups are an important resource to the agency, but it is less certain what value they hold for the agency at large; set aside other work in the agency, their profile remains low. The findings of a survey to discover the extent to which learners continue to run groups and practise groupwork after their involvement in the Project will help shed light on this question.

Accountable

The issue of accountability in groupwork is often neglected. In the many different kinds of group described and evaluated in the pages of the UK journal *Groupwork* there is rare reference to accountability. If the group members are already service users of the agency, the accountability usually continues through their allocated worker; if they are not known to the agency prior to the group then there may not be even be a discussion of accountability. The implicit model of accountability reinforces the conventional view of groupwork as tangential to the mainstream.

Manor (1989) identifies three types of accountability: parallel, dual and multiple. In dual and multiple accountability, there is more direct access to the group from the line mangers and sometimes other agencies. The loss in confidentiality with so many others involved is compensated by the greater sense of involvement, so that groupwork is more integrated into the life and understanding of the agency and sister agencies. It is likely that dual and multiple accountability are rare.

The implicit model of accountability has many consequences. The obvious one is the cumbersome lines of accountability, with some group members being the 'cases' of one of the group leaders and others having workers not in the group. The groupworkers themselves can find themselves 'double-accounted' if they have both line manager and consultancy arrangements. In all of this, the lines of accountability tend to parallel the traditional, hierarchical model, and there is rarely a sense of accountability for the group as a whole.

The training model in the Project ensures that lines of accountability are visible and that team managers are integrally involved in the planning of the group and make an explicit statement of commitment to the group. This openness is especially important because of the assessment component of the model, in which learners' groupwork practice is exposed in a portfolio. However, the model takes a view of accountability which is broader than line management. Learners are asked to consider who are the associates who have a stake in the group; accountable groupwork takes proper account of these stakeholders, especially when evaluating the group's progress (see Chapter 12).

Assessable

There is a tradition of supervision in British social work agencies, but not one of appraisal or assessment. However, developments such as NVQ (National Vocational Qualifications) and the Post-Qualifying Award in social work are producing a keener awareness of issues of competence and assessment of practice ability in the workplace. A practitioner running a group would not ordinarily expect their practice as a groupworker to be formally assessed, though good groupwork practice would include the proper review and evaluation of the group and an examination of the workers' part in its progress. However, this is unlikely to require the systematic collection of evidence to illustrate their ability and their learning at each stage of the group's development. Standard evaluations of groupwork are unlikely to require the use of a wide range of methods to assess the competence of the groupworkers. For example, a trawl of the groups described in articles in the journal *Groupwork* reveals that few, if any, group leaders used video *on themselves* to capture their skills in groupwork, still less to make this video material available to an independent assessor.

The groups run by the participants in the training programme had a number of purposes. Their primary purpose was to meet a recognized need, where groupwork was acknowledged as the best way to provide the service. However, one of the consequences of planning and running a group is the learning which the workers derive from the experience and, for the leaders of these particular groups, the quality of their learning and practice was subject to independent assessment.

Learning from an experience is not automatic. If the learning is to have an impact on subsequent practice, it needs to be 'named' – made explicit and available for reflection and retrieval. Taking a mathematical analogy, if we are told that 'nine plus nine equals eighteen', we can answer the question, 'what is nine plus nine?' If we wish to answer this question a day, a week or a month later we must *know* that 'nine plus nine equals eighteen' in order to give a correct answer. And if we are to answer attendant questions, such as 'what is eighteen minus nine?' we must know *how* and *why* 'nine plus nine equals eighteen'. There are parallels with the learning of professional practice, in which groupwork experiences need description, reflection and evaluation in order for the experience to guide future practice.

There is some evidence that the process of gathering evidence using various methods and from a variety of sources, with the aim of collecting it into a portfolio of materials, enhances the participants' *practice* (Doel and Shardlow 1989). The term 'portfolio' is often used loosely and interpreted as meaning many different things, so it is important to clarify how the portfolio developed for the Groupwork Project is constituted. The notion of the portfolio is an attempt to accommodate what is essentially a three-dimensional experience (interactions in groups and around them) into a two-dimensional format. The format used for the Project portfolio has evolved out of the experiences of many users, starting with the 'frontier portfolios' which tended to be formless and unwieldy (Doel and Shardlow 1995). The 'signposted' portfolio developed for the Groupwork Project aims to balance the blank sheet approach with the tick-box competency model, the former often felt to be providing too little guidance, the latter too much. The signposted portfolio consists of a number of sections which follow the pattern of the training programme, which in turn follows the progress of groups. Each section has a sequence of pages headed by prompts; those on the even-numbered pages beg descriptive answers and those on the facing, odd-numbered sheets trigger evaluative reflections based on the descriptive evidence. The discipline of separating observation from commentary is, in itself, beneficial to groupwork skills, and this pattern is maintained throughout the portfolio.

In order to increase the number of windows on the learner's practice, a broad range of assessment tools is encouraged, including a video, a commentary on the video and a report of direct observation (as far as possible by a skilled groupworker, though this is sometimes the co-worker). The groupworker is prompted to consider issues of power and oppression throughout the portfolio, as well as consolidating these into a specific section on anti-oppressive groupwork. The aim is not to rely solely on the learner's ability to write about their groupwork practice, but to acknowledge verbal skills as well as literary ones, so each learner has a *viva* as an opportunity to provide additional evidence.

The feedback from those who have used the signposted portfolios has been universally positive, despite the hard work. Indeed, in a number of cases candidates have expressed uncertainty about whether they would have completed the assessed part of the programme without the portfolio structure. Clearly, the form of the assessment can support or hinder the completion of the assessment and consolidate or fragment the learning.

LIKELIHOOD OF COMPLETING A PORTFOLIO

Twenty-eight learners completed a portfolio of their groupwork practice (that is 46% of the learners who completed the programme). Training is a valuable resource and to know which prospective learners are most likely to complete successfully would be valuable knowledge. As a small step towards this, we considered how accurate learners were in their self-assessments. We surveyed one cohort of learners to measure the reliability of their judgements of how likely they thought they were to complete a portfolio. (To complete a portfolio the learner has, by definition, to finish the programme; we felt that asking people whether they thought it likely they would complete the programme would be a dispiriting question to ask at the start and unlikely to elicit honest answers. On the other hand, the portfolio was seen as a potentially difficult addition, and optional for prequalified participants.)

How realistic are people in their assessment of how likely they are to complete a portfolio? The 'confidence rating' of learners was monitored at two points during the programme. They were asked 'At this point, how do you rate your chances of completing a portfolio by the autumn?' and asked to choose from percentages rising in tens from 0 per cent (totally certain not to complete) to 100 per cent (totally certain to complete). The first reading (Column 1) was taken at the close of the first two-day workshop in February, and the second (Column 2) at the close of the second two-day workshop in April. Column 3 in Table 2.1 is the actual outcome in the autumn.

Table 2.1 Self-assessments of the likelihood of completing the assessed component ('signposted' portfolio) of a training course in groupwork					
Name	*1*	*2*	*3*	*result*	
Doreen ✕	100%	90%	YES	(passed)	
Mary	100%	90%	YES	(passed)	
Simone ✕	80%	60%	YES	(passed)	
Mavis	(absent)	80%	YES	(referred)	
Louise ✕	40%	70%	YES	(passed)	
Peter	30%	40%	YES	(passed)	
Molly ✕	50%	50%	YES	(passed)	
Sally	80%	90%	NO	–	
Suzanne ✕	70%	50%	NO	–	
Greta	70%	50%	NO	–	
Wanda	50%	90%	NO	–	
*Ken	90%	(absent)	NO	–	
*Genny	50%	(absent)	NO	–	

* did not complete the programme (all names have been changed).
Note: ✕ indicates co-workers. Percentage (%) figures represent self-assessment of the degree of certainty of completion: Column 1: First reading (Feb); 2: Second reading (Apr); 3: Submission (Sept), with result.

This is a very small sample and it is difficult to draw any firm conclusions, other than the fact that there seems to be no pattern to the accuracy of people's self-assessment! The depths of some participants' under-estimation of themselves is matched only by the height of others' over-estimation. The lowest self-assessment came from the only man in the training group to complete the course (Ken dropped out) – Peter's low 30 per cent rose to only 40 per cent, and yet he completed. Wanda's 50 per cent rose to 90 per cent, but she didn't. Doreen and Mary's original certainty (100%) was vindicated, Ken's (90%) and Sally's (80%) wasn't. Two people became more confident of completing (and did), whilst three people became less confident of completing (but did).

Taking 50 per cent as the divide between less and more likely, of those who eventually completed a portfolio there was a greater proportion who rated themselves as *less* likely to complete at the first self-assessment than those who rated themselves as more likely to complete! Even by the time of the second reading, two of the seven completers still rated their chances of completion as 50:50 or less, and two eventual non-completers had raised their self-assessment to 90 per cent likely to complete.

One fact which may be significant is a pairing arrangement. All seven who completed the assessment component had partners in the programme who were also co-workers in their groups. Half of the six who did not complete were without a partner in the training group and there was only one partnership where one person completed and the other did not.

Contextualized: professional development

Finally, it is important to develop a model for training and education in groupwork which is consistent with broader aims for professional development. Learners have come to the Groupwork Project at various points in their professional development, some qualified and some not, some with considerable experience of social work and social care, some with little. The programme has offered all learners the opportunity to develop their groupwork abilities and to practise these in a group forum. In addition, learners have been able to demonstrate their groupwork competence via the 'signposted' portfolio which we described earlier. Despite the hard work and exposure involved in compiling a portfolio, 42 per cent of all the learners who began the programme submitted one, and this percentage rises to 58 per cent of all those learners who successfully completed a group. For the qualified learners a successful portfolio represented 40 'credits' towards the Post-Qualifying Award and a clear pathway in terms of their career development. There was no expectation that prequalified staff would complete a portfolio, yet just over half of those who completed a group also submitted a portfolio. Frequently it was the prequalified learners who derived the most personal value and pleasure from their work on the portfolio and the agency 'standard pass'-level certificate which they received. For many, the groupwork portfolio was a significant first step towards recognition of their abilities and the first time they had exposed what they did in their work to a formal, independent assessment. At least one learner used it as part of a subsequent successful application to a Diploma in Social Work qualifying programme.

A significant aspect of the Project has been the empowering effect of groupwork on the learners themselves. This effect was often underlined and reinforced by the process of completing a portfolio of their groupwork practice. For example, at the offer of groupwork training with Carol and Brenda, it was their line manager who did much of the talking and it was evident that it was his idea that they should run a group. Nevertheless, they persevered and, as the training programme progressed alongside their own group, they became increasingly excited by their achievements and more assertive with their supervisor and the team. Indeed, the scale of their groupwork success proved so threatening to their peers and line manager that plans for further groups were scuppered. This kind of negative response from colleagues has been noted by Gibson (1992: 36), where some of the staff involved in reminiscence groups 'were subjected to peer criticism, either implicit or sometimes explicit where reminiscence was seen as 'skiving', a soft option and a neglect of real work'. These kinds of experience, even when negative, have been valuable for the Project as a whole in understanding the significance of the associates who might have a stakehold in the group's success or failure.

Although we describe the model as 'training', the effects are indeed educational. The sense of achievement at a personal as well as a professional level was widespread in the consultation interviews, summed up by one learner who described the Groupwork Project as the best thing that had ever happened to her (exactly mirroring comments made to the learners by members of their own groups). This blossoming was most notable amongst the learners without formal qualifications. It encourages a belief that it is possible to create a reality out of the of lifelong learning. In the trends towards managerialism, a generic model of groupwork can help to re-establish a sense of professionalism, which in turn can benefit agency morale.

CHAPTER THREE

Power and Oppression in Groupwork

Exclusion, inclusion and empowerment

> It is not those differences between us that are separating us, it is rather our refusal to recognize those differences. (Lorde 1994: 115)

Groupwork challenges the often unspoken 'norm' of individual work. For this reason it can be seen as avant-garde and adventurous. One of the authors remembers vividly being required to make a case for groupwork to an entire divisional office of a social services department, in a way that no-one had ever been required to justify casework. Ten years later, Mistry (1989) describes the same resistance from colleagues and a similar 'shock value' for a proposed women's group in a probation service. Perhaps there is an intuitive sense of groupwork's potential for anti-oppressiveness.

Social workers have long worked with people who are excluded in one way or another from social power and influence. In some cases this can be an especially isolating condition, such as people with Aids who 'may come to see themselves as toxic, stigmatized outcasts' (Getzel and Mahoney 1989: 99). Groupwork can provide an environment in which the individual members have an experience of inclusion, with others 'in the same boat'. Nevertheless, we should not assume that coming together as a group of 'men with Aids', 'women with eating disorders', 'children who have been bereaved', etc. is necessarily supportive. The pain of losing friends and lovers to Aids can be reinforced by the potential amplification effect of a group, the exposure to even more pain and loss. One member 'just couldn't stand being constantly reminded of AIDS' and took a leave of absence from the group (Getzel and Mahoney 1989: 103). So it is important to consider how a group experience is going to be supportive and inclusive rather than amplifying any existing sense of exclusion and how to balance this with a sense of respect for diversity and individual difference.

Themes of inclusion and exclusion will always be present in groups. To make them explicit they may need to be introduced as topics in the group itself. An example of this was the use of a game in which all but one member huddles together in a scrum. This game was used in a group for emotionally disturbed children to generate an immediate sense of inclusion and exclusion, in order to explore how it feels (Clarke and Aimable 1990: 43).

In the great majority of instances the people who participate in social work groups do so not because they need treatment or therapy but because they feel they lack *power*. As we have noted, people who come into contact with social work are often at the margins of society, whether on a temporary or semi-permanent basis, and the very purpose of the group might be the situation or behaviour which puts them in a position of relative powerlessness. The effect of gathering together with other people who find themselves in similar situations can be liberating, but this effect is not automatic and we have all experienced groups which replicate the abusive power relationships in the wider society. Certainly, experiments in social psychology which demonstrated the potentially coercive effects of groups have become folklore, and many practitioners seem wary of 'the power of the group'.

Issues of power are, therefore, central to groupwork. Empowerment, in the sense of an increasing feeling of self-worth and a growing ability to feel and use power in constructive ways, should be an integral part of the members' experience of the group. Learning about power develops out of the use of the group itself as a smaller and safer stage to explore, reflect, rehearse and redefine the larger one outside. As a groupworker you have a very real part to play because the way you acknowledge, use and share your power in the group will be noticed. Who you are and what you stand for also reflect your place in the wider society (as a woman, as an Asian man, etc.) Additionally, learning to believe in and accept personal power and responsibility can be an important experience for all members of the group.

Unfortunately there is a tendency to see the exercise of power by group leaders as automatically 'a bad thing'. This reflects social workers' general ambivalence to the exercise of power through statutory responsibilities and the twin roles of care and control. In fact, it is the group leaders' denial of their own power and their inability to use it appropriately which poses the greatest threat to a group. Models of self-directed groupwork such as Mullender and Ward's (1989, 1991) are sometimes mistakenly interpreted as requiring groupworkers to be 'power-free', an impossible state to achieve, even if it were desirable. There are many circumstances when groups will look to the workers to use their power to help secure resources from outside, or to manage conflicts within. Sometimes it is right to exercise this power and sometimes not, but it is never right to deny it.

Different manifestations of oppression

> The notion of whiteness as 'race' is almost never implicated ... Whiteness is unnamed, suppressed, beyond the realm of race. 'Exnomination' permits whites to entertain the notion that race lives 'over there' on the other side of the tracks. (Williams 1997: 5)

Groups are microcosms of the wider society, capable of amplifying and reinforcing oppression as well as challenging it. The power of groups can be used to reproduce stereotypes from the social world outside the group; the very 'whiteness' of a group, for instance, can serve to strengthen an individual's perspective of white as 'normal', to the extent that race and racism are not considered. Implicit assumptions about the dominant culture as white, male and employed will be reflected in the group dynamic and this is the most subtle form of oppression, because it is complicit and unrecognized. This notion of institutionalized oppression gained broader recognition following the Stephen Lawrence Inquiry and the examination of a police service.

Groupworkers must avoid being complicit with institutionalized oppression and help the group to challenge the assumptions which bring this level of oppression into the group itself. They also need to be conscious of the different sources of power and the consequences for members and for themselves. The position of authority of the groupworker cannot be denied, nor the fact that they often have control of resources which are important to the group. Group members might hold particular expertise or knowledge, or exercise power by virtue of their personal charisma or physical strength. There are three processes to be noted in this respect; the assumption of power, the need for access to power and the ascription of power to others.

In addition to the failure to name oppression, there are many reasons why the desire to create a group which is anti-oppressive does not always give birth to the reality. Oppression, prejudice and stereotyping are complex issues and we cannot assume that people who are marginalized because of one attribute fall into automatic alliance with people who are marginalized in other ways. The British Deaf Association's wish to ban deaf lesbian and gay people (Taylor 1996: 117) and the racism in a mixed-race women's group (Butler 1994: 173–4) are examples of the powerful ways in which oppression can be internalized. Describing the power of groupwork for black women in British society, Francis-Spence (1994: 116) writes, 'The stress of being denied the opportunity to achieve your potential can lead directly to an absorption of the hostility and of the racist values on which it is grounded'. This kind of internalized oppression is common and might emerge as a theme, so that group members are able to gain strength through their mutual awareness of this dynamic.

The realization that oppression has many dimensions can be powerfully demonstrated in group contexts, as manifested by 'J', herself disabled, and a member of a women's group:

> I spoke of the doubts which arise about my feelings of equality among non-disabled women. Well the answer is yes, I do feel equal, because I have learned from the women's group that the lives of many non-disabled women are paralysed by various forms of blatant and subtle discrimination and oppression. It's a paralysis that prevents them from developing or discovering their talents or achieving their full potential, in much the same way that some disabled people are prevented. ('J' in Wintram *et al.* 1994: 131)

'Telling your story' and having it listened to is an empowering process in it-self. For many individuals this might be the first time they have had this op-portunity, not just to tell their story but also to listen to others in a similar vein. This is a reciprocal bargain which the group makes with itself, and it is one which benefits all. Feelings of empowerment might sometimes be ampli-fied by the intimacy and privacy of the group, at other times it might be the knowledge that the private stories will inform the bigger picture; for instance, the stories of five adults with learning difficulties and their collective views on the notion of 'adulthood' lay at the heart of a research project conducted by Walmsley (1990). The participants helped to set the agenda for the re-search and to verify and influence its findings.

Group members may have internalized feelings of discrimination to the extent that they find it difficult to see themselves in an alternative light. The experience of encouraging older people in residential care settings to express their views and aspirations can be dispiriting for the groupworkers, as they run up against the internalized view of some older people as passive and compliant, feeling that entering residential care is a sign of failure.

Stereotyping is another potentially oppressive process in groupwork. As-sumptions are made about what certain groups of people like doing best – that groupwork with older people means reminiscence work, for example. Lewis (1992: 57) notes the success of a group for older people in groupcare which looked at environmental issues, with practical changes to a 'greener' lifestyle in the establishment. Moreover, methods associated with one social group can frequently be put to good effect with others, in the way that oral history work, associated with work with older people, was used in a project with young people (Drower 1991).

It is important to avoid a hierarchy of oppressions in groups, but this can be difficult to achieve. In a group where all members are deaf (which might even be called the 'Deaf Group') other factors can easily be overshadowed. A group for deaf Asian women provided an especially supportive setting, because 'in white deaf groups, deafness was the only issue' (Kohli 1993: 242).

The oppression experienced in the wider community by individuals in the group is often brought home when the group goes 'out' and is in direct contact with others. A groupworker makes the following observation in her groupwork portfolio:

> When we were doing our outside activities, such as visiting W. College and the White Rose Centre, we did not tell people who we were – just that we were a group of women. We didn't think it necessary or fair to the group members [to say more because] there is a lot of stigma attached to mental illness. We believe it is their right to make the decision about what they say and who they say it to, regarding their mental health, and not our decision.

The extent to which these kinds of decision are made by the group members or the group leaders or the whole group together, and the extent to which the assumptions and stereotypes of the larger society are challenged or accepted, are central to the group members' experience of the group as emancipating.

Composition of groups

In Chapter 4 we examine various factors to take into consideration when planning groups. One of these is concerned with diversity and sameness in the composition of the group and this relates to both leadership and membership of the group.

The visible differences in a group relate to attributes such as race, gender and age. Sometimes the group might be limited to one common attribute, such as a single sex group, whilst in others the value of mixed groups is recognized. Hard information is difficult to come by, but a survey of groups in the probation service found that 7 per cent of groups were women only, 43 per cent men only, and 45 per cent were mixed (Caddick 1991: 209). The same survey found that less than 1 per cent were black members only (just 3 out of 1463 groups), 39 per cent were white members only and 61 per cent were mixed race. In the Groupwork Project, 22 per cent of groups were women only (some others were all-female, but not by design) and 4 per cent (just one group) boys only.

As human beings we tend to gather with people who have characteristics and points of view similar to our own. We are drawn to others who will confirm our world view and difference can be experienced as challenging, even threatening. Groupworkers need to acknowledge their own 'comfort zone' when considering difference and sameness; this is especially important when considering membership of the group. Acknowledgement of our potential to oppress is a key responsibility for us all. In one training group the black and white co-leaders, exploring issues of group composition, found themselves drawn to those they perceived as sharing their values rather than taking into account the implications of leaving the group with only one male group member. Such dilemmas require openness, honesty and self-awareness, and co-working can redress bias in ways which are liberating.

The group processes might have a differential impact on people with different attributes in ways which are not necessarily predictable. For example, in a mixed-race group in South Africa working on an oral history project, the black participants felt energized whilst the white ones exhibited a 'white man's guilt' phenomenon. 'One of the major flaws in the programme was that insufficient time had been set aside for the possible need to resolve this response' (Drower 1991: 126). A group for black and white children (girls and boys) who had been sexually abused was led by two female workers, one black and one white. The decision to bring children of different races and genders together was deliberate, enabling them to experience each others' cultures and to witness the two co-workers taking equal responsibility for the care of the group (Lebacq and Shah 1989). In another example of a mixed group setting, Norman (1994: 224) describes male workers as providing 'a positive role model for both the children (working with them in a playroom) and their mothers (as co-facilitators in the group) by demonstrating that men can and should be involved in all aspects of child rearing'.

On the other hand, there are equally compelling arguments for not having mixed groups. Discussing mixed-gender groups in the probation service, Mistry (1989) saw women's needs being submerged, often because they were outnumbered by male members, but also because of their own socialization into considering the needs of the men in the group before their own. In these circumstances, the case for a women's group is strong. Mistry goes on to claim that it is difficult to have structured packages of groupwork in the probation service which are of equal relevance to men and to women, and a women's group does not have to start from a male-oriented norm. She also came to believe that black women in the group might benefit, too, from an all-black women's group.

In addition to thoughts about how the composition of the membership will relate to oppression in the group, it is also crucial to consider yourselves as group leaders (Mistry and Brown 1997). How do your attributes conform to or contrast with the membership? What differences and similarities are there between you and any co-workers in the group? In parallel to our discussion of the composition of the membership, there are similar advantages and disadvantages to sameness and difference between co-workers, with groups likely to reflect social attitudes and expectations, for example by 'behaving as though the white co-worker (in a mixed-race leadership) is the senior partner' (Mistry and Brown 1991: 114). In a group for non-white refugees the white, non-refugee women leaders were a valuable resource for members to access their new world, but this positive aspect needs to be weighed against the possible negative effects of their distance from the women's experiences (Tribe and Shackman 1989: 162). Some differences are evident, others are not; for example, a lesbian groupworker must make a deliberate choice about whether or when she will disclose her sexuality. Groupworkers need to feel that the group is safe no less than group members.

The composition of a group is also affected by the access which people have to it, in terms of the knowledge that they have available and their ability to make use of it. This is not simply a question of 'how like me are the other members of the group?' (in term of race, gender, ability, sexuality, etc.) but how equal the opportunities are to join the group. A group for motoring offenders recognized that offenders in rural areas had difficulties in attending a town-based group, so the groupworkers used volunteer drivers, travel warrants and bus fares to try to overcome the transport problems and the urban bias of their group (Hutchins 1991: 224). During group sessions it is necessary to ensure that activities are open to all, or at least balanced so there is observance of different gifts and different limitations. The action techniques used in groups have much potential to redistribute power and develop intimacy (Chapter 7):

> Through reminiscence, the conventional, often power-laden relationships between carer and cared for are blurred, sometimes reversed and an all too rare opportunity afforded for older people to exercise their right to be taken seriously. (Gibson 1992: 30)

Intimacy and authority in groups

Ideally, perhaps, leaders might have personal experiences with cancer. Going through such experiences as surgery, radiation and chemotherapy, or having a loved one experience them, undeniably gives a greater insight into the unique situations in which cancer patients find themselves. (Daste 1989: 66)

A central dilemma for all groupworkers is how different or similar their lives are compared with the group members. The author of the above quotation, Daste, is now leader of the group he had experienced as a member, and his words go to the very heart of the 'street cred' dilemma which can cause groupworkers to feel insecure in their role. They can expect group members to notice and sometimes to challenge their differentness. 'What experiences have you had that can help you understand our lives?' was the question asked by one of the members of a group for Asian women with terminally ill children (Muir and Notta 1993: 131).

A women's group can expect to be led or facilitated by women, but a mother's group might not necessarily be led by women who are also mothers. The female workers in a women's group share a sisterhood with the group members but may have very different lifestyles and opportunities from them. Even if attributes such as gender and race are similar, the issue which brings the members together (such as eating disorders) often separates worker and member. We might expect there to be a contrast in the relationship between members and workers of a group for people with Aids where the leaders also have Aids, and a group where they do not (Getzel and Mahoney 1989). However, what can come as a surprise to members-turned-leaders is that even when they have had similar experiences and attributes to members, their role as groupworker *is* separate from the group.

This separateness can feel an uncomfortable contradiction for groupworkers aiming to provide an experience of togetherness in the group, and it is easy to be tempted to deny it. However, it reflects a general tension in groups between the forces of intimacy and authority; that is, the forces which bring people together and emphasize their 'groupness' and those which separate them and reinforce their individuality (Shulman 1984). The most notable of these differences arises from the position of the groupworker as 'central person' in a group, the one who knows all the members and who has more often than not initiated the group (Heap 1979). This position carries authority, often augmented by the groupworker's professional role, and their perceived knowledge and skill base. In certain settings, such as residential and day care, the groupworker might already hold power over daily lives and, as a consequence, they must be particularly vigilant when they assume the role of central person (Brown 1990: 251).

Groupworkers do not empower groups by denying or abandoning their position as central person; they use it to enable group members and the group as a whole to become central person. One of the ways in which groupworkers can ensure that they do not abuse their authority is to seek feedback from group members, to listen to it carefully and to act on it. Listening is not the same activity as 'interpreting' and the particular theoretical orientation of the groupworker has a considerable bearing on his or her ability to listen unhindered. For example, in a psychotherapeutic group in Northern Ireland, the group leader found himself condemned by members for routinely doing little more than delivering yet another interpretation. He considers two interpretations of the members' hostility towards him; first that they perceived him as 'a depriving and authoritative parent', and second as 'a deep displacement onto me of anger which was really directed at the member who was perceived to distinguish himself by his dress – the wearing of a poppy – as a representative of a hated political authority and rival group' (Benson 1992: 9). The groupworker's own needs, in this case to express power via 'professional' interpretation, prevent him from listening to what group members are *actually* saying and to consider the possibility that leadership style can be oppressive.

Groupworkers divest some of their power by working in a situation where they are outnumbered. In the group the workers often leave the familiarity of their own office for neutral territory, and share their role (as helper, challenger, informer, clarifier, etc.) with many others. 'Whenever Flora speaks, the other members pay attention to her and take serious what she says. If I were to say the same thing, they wouldn't consider it as valuable' (Reid 1988: 125). In some models of groupwork, members are, indeed, 'central persons' from the very beginning (Mullender and Ward 1991), but this is not always possible and there needs to be flexibility about how the groupworker can best achieve this (see Chapter 11 for more discussion concerning leadership and co-working). The question of authority and intimacy is as central to the group as it is to all human relationships and it is best addressed directly. There will be many circumstances when group leaders begin the group as the central person, and a few where it is appropriate that they remain in this situation:

> The clinicians are in charge of the programme and not the participants … the purpose of the groups is not empowerment or for these perpetrators to feel better about themselves. (Crown and Gates (1997: 58–9), in respect of a group for juvenile sex offenders)

So, there are times when authority is exercised firmly by the group leaders as control. Crucially, though, amidst this deliberately authoritarian leadership style, the group has to be a place where the young perpetrators feel they *belong,* so that they can cope with the increasing realization that they have caused tremendous hurt and damage. In order to encourage this sense of belonging, the groupworkers must use their authority to nurture intimacy in the group. The notions of authority and intimacy are inextricably entwined.

Naming the group

In addition to the general patterns of interaction in the group, there are other quite specific activities which can be introduced into the group which help to develop a sense of empowerment. In Chapter 6 we will consider the negotiation of a group agreement in the first or early sessions; the agreement itself, and the way in which the group achieves it, should demonstrate respect for diversity and a commitment to anti-discrimination.

A very concrete way of helping the group to gain a sense of increasing control and responsibility for itself is to help it to find itself a name. How the group acquires its name is significant and symbolic. If you are currently working with a group, consider its name and how this was decided. In the early stages of planning, groupworkers frequently adopt a 'working title' for convenience because the full description of the group is unwieldy. The Group for People Experiencing Difficulties Caring for Older People Living at Home With Them becomes the Carers Group. Often this name sticks, and an opportunity for group members to become involved in a process which helps to accelerate the group's sense of identity is lost. Opening up the decision on what to name the group conveys a number of positive messages about ownership of the group, as well as providing a relatively neutral topic to test the group's ground rules concerning decision making. For example, if there are several strongly supported options for the name, how is the final decision taken? Perhaps in recognition of many agendas, sexually abused boys named their group the Power Group (Dixon and Phillips 1994: 84). One of the groups in the Project was called What Matters? by the workers, but the members decided to change the name to It Does Matter. In some ways symbolic, in other ways very real, the naming of the group by the members provided an early opportunity to work together and exercise power.

Taboos

A taboo is a topic or theme which is considered to so offend or contravene established conventions that it has become 'unspeakable'. Taboos are specific to the particular society, family and cultural group; in some societies homosexuality is taboo; in some families questioning the authority of the father is taboo; in some cultures suicide is especially taboo (O'Connor 1992). The euphemistic name, the Tuesday Group, might shield a taboo topic, the Tuesday Group for Survivors of Sexual Abuse.

Groups are often formed for the specific purpose of confronting a taboo. Whether it is sexual abuse, alcohol addiction, childlessness, or eating disorders, the group's focus is likely to be taboo in general, social terms. Taboos have a way of breaking through the silence barrier (witness Basil Fawlty's failed attempts not to mention the war in front of his German hotel guests), but it is better if this is managed rather than allowed to fall to chance. The group leaders need to articulate the taboo words, perhaps as early as their opening statement of purpose (see Chapter 6); it might be the first time that group members have heard the words spoken in a public forum and naming the taboo starts to break its power.

During the life of the group other taboo topics might emerge, subjects which the group is avoiding or which lie behind the explicit taboo. Fear of failure; fear of becoming emotionally close to someone; anger at injustice; guilt for real happenings, shame for imagined ones. These might develop into group *themes* and have a powerful and beneficial effect on the group's ability to move from a collection of relatively powerless 'I's to a increasingly powerful, collective 'We' (Chapter 10). Taboos are, therefore, central to issues of power and oppression in the group, and they are key to unlocking the group so that it is not experienced as perpetuating the taboo, but as emancipating the group members.

Learning about power and oppression in groups

In the remainder of this chapter we will hear from learner groupworkers telling their own stories of groupwork. Each of these stories provides opportunities for learning about power and oppression in groups. (Names have been changed.)

Gemma and Phil's story: the group as somewhere to be heard

Phil and Gemma are prequalified workers in a residential home for children. They have struggled with their idea for a group, finding the loose boundaries of residential care an unexpected hindrance, not to mention practical difficulties such as the fact that they are rarely on duty together. They have found Brown and Clough's (1989) notion of groupings useful and have decided to build on the 'Chat Times' which have been a sporadic feature in the home. They come to the consultation interview at the training centre even though Phil is on annual leave. The flipchart sheet from the previous two consultations over the past five months is displayed to remind us of where we were and where we hoped to be.

Gemma and Phil are feeling good about developments. They say that there is now a *consistency* that has been missing before and when asked how this shows itself they tell how the Chat Times now happen regularly each Saturday morning (at the request of the young people they have been moved from Thursday evenings which is when they used to happen, if they happened). 'It's very basic, but we [the staff group] are *listening.*' In the first two sentences they introduced two themes which recur throughout the consultation — consistency and listening. A culture is developing that whoever is there, the grouping moves into a group, and there is a consistent thread because either Phil or Gemma always participates. Phil describes how he tunes himself into the young people as early as the night before and how the 'flow' of Saturday morning determines how and when Chat Time begins. Sometimes Chat Time happens round the dining table, sometimes out in the porch; it has a fluidity which is very different from 'formed groups'.

What makes it groupwork? Gemma says that it is moving from the I to the We (see Chapter 7). For example, the previous Saturday the Chat Time moved from lots of individual 'I want a pet' statements, with various different animals in mind, to '*We* want a *unit* pet'. This finally manifested itself into a tank of fish, with a desire for each person to call their own fish by its own name. What a wonderful metaphor for the unit itself, with the individual young people acknowledging their separate but together lives in the same tank. Phil had noticed a similar process when initiating this Chat Time with the theme of holidays, which had begun with wild ideas from individuals and developed through discussion into a more achievable group project. A clear movement from individual preferences to a group negotiated outcome.

Chat Time was beginning to be part of a cycle which included the unit staff meeting each Monday. Issues, questions and requests from Saturday Chat Time were now being brought to the Monday staff meeting and, to complete the circle, from the staff meeting to Chat Time.

When asked how they know the group is working, Gemma and Phil point to attendance and the fact that the young people are able to talk about living together and to talk about it together. The young people are attending when they could as easily walk away or stay in bed. The safe boundary around Chat Time makes this a group rather than a discussion over breakfast or a moan around the telly, and it helps the young people to face riskier items (such as a conflict over taking cigarettes without asking). 'They feel they are being listened to … it's so simple and yet you have to go through all that complexity to get there,' muses Phil.

There are clear indicators that the children are feeling empowered by this experience, even if this is not a word they would use to describe it. Despite its informal and hang-loose name, their Chat Time group provides a safe space to have a direct impact on the way the unit is run and to negotiate through conflict and resolve difficulties. Whatever the reluctance of the workers to accept their own 'positional power' or set clear boundaries, the young people nevertheless ascribed them with power; Phil and Gemma learnt that the key is not about 'giving' power to the young people, rather it is about 'letting go' of some their power and control. They rediscovered the really elegant principle that the crucial part of communication is listening.

Jenny and Linda's story: the group as somewhere to be 'normal'

Jenny and Linda are prequalified workers coming towards the end of their eighth session of the Feeling Good About Myself Group for seven women with mental health problems. They arrive at the session bubbling over and, like Phil before her, Jenny comes to the consultation even though she is on annual leave. Their groupwork mentor, a previous participant of the training programme, had prompted them to consider how they were managing the group's ending and they had exclaimed that 'it's going so well we forgot about endings!' (Chapter 13). They have learned a lot from the successful *closure* of individual sessions, where they used an action technique called 'Woolly ending', in which a brightly coloured network is 'knitted' by group members throwing a ball of wool to another person, keeping hold of their end and saying something positive about the person they throw to (see Chapter 7 for more on action techniques). After the final ending of the group, the members have decided to meet each other, and have said what a shame it is that Jenny and Linda can't join them. Jenny puts it succinctly when she says that 'the group is ending but not the *association*'. It is a precise word for it.

We tutors are familiar with their group via a sculpt which Jenny and Linda conducted during the last workshop, in which they enlisted the help of members of the training group to represent a typical moment in their own practice group, reproducing positions and body language. Lesley, who had sat back from the group in the early sessions, is now much more part of it, though still 'a bit different'. Linda thinks she is dominated by her mother and it has taken some time for her to begin to be her own person in the group.

Though not qualified, Jenny and Linda each want to complete a portfolio of their groupwork learning and practice. They like the fact that the 'signposted' portfolio asks very specific questions to guide the candidate through each section, but the pages on power and oppression just say 'Notes' and they are both stuck. Linda repeats several times, 'I just see "Notes" and a blank page underneath and I just don't know what to write'. Her husband's support has also been enlisted, on many occasions by the sound of it, to read what she has written, but he says he can't help with power and oppression! Indeed, several learners mention partners and family in ways which clearly indicate the significance of this kind of support to completing a piece of work such as a portfolio. Jenny and Linda are asked to visualize the page with what they think their answers would have been if there had been questions. For an instant they are puzzled, but in their mind's eye they begin to sketch a response and to replace the intimidating blank sheet with some text. They remember how they offered the group to potential members (Chapter 5) and, at an individual level, how they responded to Lesley's difference, helping her into the group. They reflect on their own relationship as co-workers and their 'equal but different' approach (Chapter 11). Prompted, they also consider the relative powerlessness which people with mental health problems experience and this triggers a strong memory of the women very much enjoying the session when they had their treatment at the beautician's shop, when they didn't feel treated like clients ... 'in the group they don't feel treated like clients'. The women had also commented on the way Jenny and Linda had joined in, everyone having a makeover (including their mentor, who was observing/participating in this session).

> Jenny (*with some pride*): I've had a training in beauty therapy!
>
> Linda (*with equal pride*): I never wear any make-up at all!

As trainers we learn, too, that the language of anti-oppression does not always go out of its way to shake hands with the uninitiated and that we must find ways to make it accessible. The Feeling Good About Myself Group is undoubtedly an empowering experience for these women, because an ability to participate in society's games seems to be the first necessary step to becoming critical of them. The obvious critique – that learning to apply make-up is an oppressive view of womanhood – is perhaps only attractive to those who are in a position to choose. Jenny and Linda are on a journey, too, and at this point they are experiencing the excitement of helping people who are marginalized to come 'on board'. It is a very significant step if you are not yet on board, and perhaps it is an essential first step before it becomes safe or possible to take a critical view of what 'on board' means and to consider moving elsewhere.

Joanne's story: the group as a place to share the pain

Joanne and Sean are both qualified social workers. They are paired for the training programme, but they have been planning separate groups since they work in separate fields of practice (Joanne in mental health and Sean in children and families). Neither has been able to launch their group yet.

Joanne's planned group is for women who have been bereaved through the loss of a partner. As a result of one of the workshops Joanne decided to enlist a co-worker and together they have been publicizing the group, largely via a brief referral form sent to doctors in local health practices. After several weeks they have still only received one referral, and this does not meet the criteria (the woman has unresolved grief about parents, not partner). Joanne knows from the articles she has read in the *Groupwork* journals on display at the workshops that the experience of others working with people who are bereaved suggests that some flexibility is important but, as usual, it is difficult to know just how elastic the criteria can be (O'Connor 1992).

Publicity is an important factor in recruitment to a group and the respective power of groupworkers and referrer undoubtedly has an impact on the response (Chapter 5). Joanne is interested in the experience of two previous learners, whose group for women with eating disorders was stalled for almost a year because of lack of referred members; now, several groups later, they have waiting lists for the next. The key factor was personal contact with the referrers and attractive posters in direct view of potential members. Success now breeds success and word of mouth publicity is sufficient.

The timescale has moved back four months to an October start, finishing just before Christmas. This has proved a useful opportunity to rethink the pattern of sessions, with a decision to offer a recall session in early January because 'Christmas is a very difficult time'. Joanne has suffered the same kind of bereavement as her prospective group members, so her situation will be very close to theirs. This will add credibility to her position as groupworker, but also requires care with the boundary between intimacy and authority discussed earlier in this chapter. Her own story will offer a significant connection to the other women in the group, but she should not be surprised to be experienced as different by the other women in the group. They will undoubtedly ascribe power to her because of her professional expertise.

Joan and Louise's story: the group as a place to have fun

Joan and Louise are qualified social workers in a specialist child care team. They both have previous experience of groupwork and want to complete portfolios of their groupwork practice to work towards the Post-Qualifying

Award in social work. They are joined by Christina, a student on placement in their team, to lead a group for eight 13- to 15-year-old girls whose families are in contact with social services. The Girls Just Wanna Have Fun group is in the sixth of eight weekly sessions, though the group has decided to have a ninth session (an 'omega' session – see Chapter 13) to evaluate the group and to have a meal together. Attendance has been very good, with seven or eight girls each session.

The group's genesis can best be summed up by Joan's comment in the first consultation four months earlier that 'the minute you say "do you want to do something without the boys?" they say "Yes!".' Fun sessions such as body painting, jewellery making and braiding have been entwined with activities like a sex education game and a drugs quiz. When describing how they see the group, Joan and Louise describe it as participative, safe, supportive and fun, 'a group where the girls aren't social worked'. This same sentiment is echoed by one of the group members, Chloe, who was ambivalent about coming to the group and has wide experience of psychologists, psychiatrists, social workers and groupwork. At the offer of groupwork Chloe said, 'I'd like a group as long as it's not therapy'.

Unlike groups which are defined by the problems and difficulties in the members' lives, Girls Just Wanna Have Fun offers a period of time when its members can forget about those problems and put themselves back in touch with what it is like to enjoy yourself when you are a 14-year-old girl. The problems are not denied, and sometimes they surface in the discussions in the group, but they are set in the context of the existence of another side to their lives. If we can reframe anti-oppressive practice as emancipatory practice, Girls Just Wanna Have Fun provides a measure of release for its members, when they discover their strengths and their connectedness.

Clare and Marina's story: the group as somewhere to develop social skills

Clare is a social care manager in a multidisciplinary team and Marina is a mental health support worker in the same team and neither has a social work qualification. They have completed two sessions of the Tuesday Group with people with mental health problems, which is planned to run for ten sessions over ten weeks. Clare in particular was keen to work with a mixed-gender group (three women and four men ranging in age from 59 to 32) and six out of the seven members have attended for both of the first two sessions.

The group's focus is to develop social skills and the first session had been an introductory one, with the second focused on body language and the way we interpret it. The next one is planned around the theme of assertiveness.

Clare and Marina are pleased with the way the group has started and they feel that it is participative, but they relate this in a low-key fashion and find it hard to say what part they think they have played in generating this participation. Indeed, if you were to 'turn the sound down' and listen only to their body language you would think the group had bombed badly. After some gentle exploration, Clare mentions her fears about the group and when these are teased out they relate to a worry that the group members will find her wanting and incompetent. Marina feels the same kind of performance anxiety.

One of the consequences of this anxiety is a tendency to feel responsible for filling the group's time, resulting in a lot of pressure to prepare and deliver 'material'. This represents holding on to control and power and responsibility and, paradoxically, reinforces the 'positional power' of the co-workers. Being handed some control over the content of the group session whilst responsibility for the process remains with the workers provides a first opportunity for many disadvantaged individuals to get in touch with their own power. We discuss how to encourage group members to start working for the group, building on the participative atmosphere, rather than it feeling like Clare and Marina have to do it all. A piece of homework is suggested, whereby each group member (including Clare and Marina) agrees to watch the same half-hour of soap opera and look for examples of passive, aggressive and assertive behaviour. The first part of the following group session could be a discussion of each other's observations, thus sharing the responsibility for the work of the group and freeing the groupworkers to focus more on the group processes and less on delivering complex material on theories of assertiveness. It is an example of the need for Clare and Marina to feel comfortable and confident about their own authority as group leaders so that they can transform themselves from managers of information to facilitators of group processes.

They are also experiencing some difficulties as co-workers. Marina's style is to have everything cut and dried and planned well in advance, whereas Clare's is last minute and spontaneous. Marina is dependable and less flexible and Clare is flexible and less dependable, but they are not yet in a place where they can see these qualities as complementary. Less fear about their roles as group *leaders* and more engagement with the processes in the group is likely to help the problem of performance anxiety and the difficulties in their co-working arrangements.

We are also reminded of our power as tutors by the anxiety which Marina and Clare experience in relation to the consultation interview. Where tutors see an opportunity to enable learning and an honest review of what has worked well and what has not, learners can perceive an inspection by power-ful assessors looking for faults. It is helpful for groupworkers to reflect that, however powerless they feel, group members are likely to see them in the same powerful light as we were seen by Marina and Clare.

In the coming chapters we present the elements of a practice model through the lens of teaching and learning groupwork. It is a model which we describe as 'essentialist' because of its wide applicability in many different circumstances. We hope it integrates and demonstrates anti-oppressive groupwork, by considering issues of power and oppression at all levels and stages, from group composition at the planning stage through to the dynamics of individual sessions, in which common groupwork themes such as 'silence' are considered from a perspective of power.

PART 2

Groupwork in Action

CHAPTER FOUR

The Planning Phase

About 'Continuum'

There are many factors which it is necessary to consider when beginning to plan for a group. In this activity we look at 12 different but related 'lines', each of which comprises a continuum, joining opposites. The activity is designed to help you identify these various factors, and to consider each of them not as 'A or B', but as a continuum of possibilities. When you read the text in the chapter itself, it will become apparent that there are many other dimensions to each of the 12 lines. Taken together the lines help you to consider the overall 'shape' of the group.

Purpose

This chapter demonstrates one of the many paradoxes in groupwork; the need both to plan carefully and yet to be able to set all those plans to one side. In general, successful groups do not 'happen', they are planned. However, *who* does the planning and *when* they do it are issues which are crucial to anti-oppressive groupwork.

Making plans is not the same as putting them into effect. In other words, the groupworkers can plan in careful detail how the group members will be central to making plans in the group. Groupworkers need to feel comfortable with this paradox, in order to steer a course between abandonment of responsibility for any planning and adherence to a rigid format. A well-planned event looks and feels spontaneous and effortless; only the well-organized groupworker knows just how much planning supports the spontaneity!

Method

- Consider each of the 12 continuum lines in turn. What do you understand each factor to mean? How does it relate to the group you are planning?
- Make notes about where along each continuum you think the proposed group might lie and why. You can photocopy pages 73–74 and put a 'X' on each line in the appropriate place.
- Consider who should make decisions in respect of each factor and when they should be made. For example, by you and your co-worker or by potential group members or by the whole group together? Before contact with individuals, at the offer of groupwork to individuals, or during the initial sessions of the group itself?

Variations

Consider the impact on the group of moving your 'X's in different directions along each line.

Notes for the groupworker

> The skill is in knowing what *not* to plan in advance because it is better left to be discussed with the potential group members. (Mullender and Ward 1989: 8)

> The decision to run a group is often fallen into, rather than being consciously chosen. (Muir and Notta 1993: 122)

All groups need planning, even if the plan conforms to Mullender and Ward's (1989) notion of 'open planning', with a strong emphasis on knowing what to leave until the group itself meets. There is a difference between planning and taking decisions in advance; and the paradox of good planning is that much of it does not need to be put into effect, yet the process of planning can help free groupworkers to be more creative rather than less.

Continuum

People lines

1 Adapted   **History**   Created 1

←—————————————————————————→

(members already know each other and may be part of a ready-formed group or team)   (members do not know each other and are brought together for the group)

2 Open   **Joining and leaving**   Closed 2

←—————————————————————————→

(members can join and leave at any time)   (members must join and leave at specified times)

3 Difference   **Mix**   Sameness 3

←—————————————————————————→

(group members have very different attributes)   (group members have very similar attributes)

4 Self-help   **Leadership**   Practitioner-led 4

←—————————————————————————→

(no involvement by professionals)   (planned, run and ended by professional leaders)

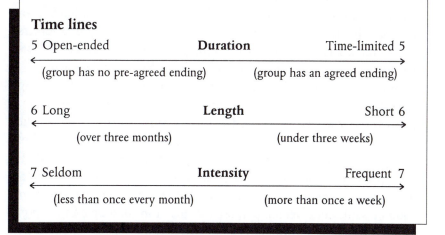

Time lines

5 Open-ended   **Duration**   Time-limited 5

←—————————————————————————→

(group has no pre-agreed ending)   (group has an agreed ending)

6 Long   **Length**   Short 6

←—————————————————————————→

(over three months)   (under three weeks)

7 Seldom   **Intensity**   Frequent 7

←—————————————————————————→

(less than once every month)   (more than once a week)

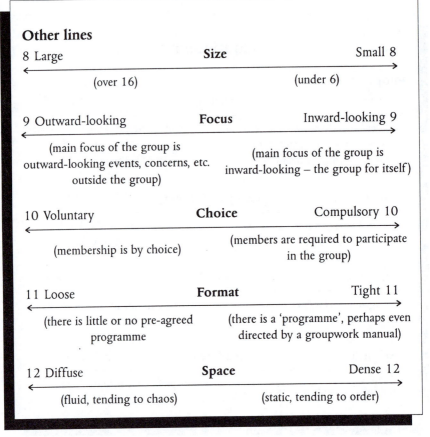

Other lines

8 Large   **Size**   Small 8

◄─────────────────────────────────────►

(over 16)   (under 6)

9 Outward-looking   **Focus**   Inward-looking 9

◄─────────────────────────────────────►

(main focus of the group is   (main focus of the group is
outward-looking events, concerns, etc.   inward-looking – the group for itself)
outside the group)

10 Voluntary   **Choice**   Compulsory 10

◄─────────────────────────────────────►

(membership is by choice)   (members are required to participate
in the group)

11 Loose   **Format**   Tight 11

◄─────────────────────────────────────►

(there is little or no pre-agreed   (there is a 'programme', perhaps even
programme   directed by a groupwork manual)

12 Diffuse   **Space**   Dense 12

◄─────────────────────────────────────►

(fluid, tending to chaos)   (static, tending to order)

Noticing and researching the need

To be successful a group must meet an identified need. The decision to plan for a group should not, therefore, be driven by the need for the groupworkers to run a group! The notion of 'a need' is complex and deserves more analysis than we can give it here. For example, descriptions of people 'by category' – people who abuse alcohol, children with a disability, tenants with housing difficulties – are not the same as descriptions of common need. Even a commonly expressed need – 'we all need to grieve the loss of a parent' – can belie many different purposes, as the question 'why do you need to …' asked of each potential group member will reveal. The differences which can lie behind apparently commonly-held needs do not necessarily mean that different groups are required – no two people's needs are identical, but there should be sufficient common purpose that they can contribute to the proposed group and benefit from it.

Researching the need means finding out whether the work you will be undertaking to plan and run a group is justified. Often your knowledge comes from direct experience of the needs in question, perhaps over many years. It might be that you have thought about the possibility of a group for a long time and that something has happened more recently to release your energies. Sometimes there are formal research findings relevant to your interest, and this can add to your understanding of the potential different kinds of need. For example, 'mothers whose daughters have been sexually abused' is a category that you might consider for a potential group, with likely common feelings of anger, shame and responsibility. On the other hand, consider how the following research knowledge would influence your views as a potential groupworker with this group:

> The mothers fell into three groups: (a) those who denied the incest and took no action (9%); (b) those who rejected their daughters and protected their mates (35%); and (c) those who proceeded to protect their daughters and reject their mates (56%). (Walker, Bonner and Kaufman 1988: 157, quoted in Masson and Erooga 1990: 147).

Groups sometimes have their genesis in an awareness of a shortfall in existing services. For example, a group for children whose brother or sister had died was established because the follow-up service offered by social workers was, in practice, undertaken with the parents of the dead child and 'over time we became aware of the deficiency of this service, and feedback from parents confirmed this' (Harmey and Price 1992: 21). Robertson (1990) canvassed community-based professionals working with 'at-risk' families to focus her groupwork on issues which emerged as common for parents, and found that sleepless children came high on everyone's list. A number of the learners in the Groupwork Project circulated questionnaires to team members to canvass opinion about unmet needs which groupwork might satisfy. Whether systematic or informal, it is necessary to research the need for a proposed group; this process will help confirm or refute the need for the group, bring others on board, and will certainly have an influence on your plans.

Resources

Even if there is an undeniable need for groupwork there are not always the resources to meet it. We will look at the practical arrangements for planning a group later in this chapter, but first of all we look at the fundamental question of resources. It is responsible practice to ensure that any proposed group will not founder through lack of resources. Of course, it is your hope that the group will *become* a resource, but it will need an 'investment' in order to achieve this.

One of the largest resources is your time. If you are new to groupwork it is important that you do not underestimate the size of the commitment. A general rule of thumb is an hour's preparation and an hour's debriefing, evaluation and recording for every hour of groupwork contact, but this is probably a minimum and depends on the kind of group you are planning. If you are collecting evidence of your groupwork abilities, perhaps for an assessed portfolio, you will need further time. In addition to your time, and that of your co-worker, it is also important to consider who else might be 'implicated' and be expected to give time to the group, however indirectly. The support of colleagues, supervisors and other professionals might be a crucial resource in promoting and sustaining a group either directly with group members or indirectly by releasing you from some of your existing commitments in order to put energies into the groupwork.

You need to determine what other kinds of resource are most significant to the success of the proposed group and where these are to be found. This might entail very creative thinking – looking outside the usual channels for sources of funding, for example. An art therapy group secured funding from adult education and a local charity (Otway 1993: 213); parents of learning disabled adolescents contributed £1 per session towards their own group (Gobat 1993: 222). A women's group in the probation service started with a £50 donation from a local solicitor and finally secured £400 from the Prince of Wales Trust for a three-day residential trip to a Butlin's holiday camp. After two years, the agency committed funds for the group, an affirmation of this way of working with women offenders (Mistry 1989: 151).

What other kinds of resource might be necessary for the group to function? Will some potential group members be excluded if there is no creche? How will group members travel to the group? Transportation by female taxi drivers to a group for sexually abused girls was a major factor in the group's success, and certainly ensured good attendance (Peake and Otway 1990). It was also a model of protective adult care, but it came with a price – £1500 (approximately £5 per girl per session). There are many ways in which individuals can be excluded from groups because of lack of forethought. One group lost an Asian member because she spoke very little English (Gobat 1993), but in another group some of the Punjabi- and Urdu-speaking women translated for the Hindi and Bengali speakers (Muir and Notta 1993). On this occasion the necessary resources were found within the group itself, but the potential need for translators should always be considered beforehand. Groupworkers will still sometimes decide to proceed with a group 'in their own time', even in the absence of resources. However, O'Connor (1992: 76) discovered the risk involved in this strategy when a need was unearthed without adequate resources to meet it. Going it alone carries risks and prevents the agency from learning about its own services.

Demonstrating anti-oppressive planning

When planning the group, it is important to consider how these processes are demonstrating anti-oppressive practice. In particular, this means a consideration of how structural inequalities such as racism and sexism have been addressed; for example, are the posters advertising the forthcoming group on display in the local health centre written only in English, thus excluding the Punjabi-speaking local community? The main focus of the group may be bereavement by suicide, but how are the needs of individuals who have other major pressing concerns, such as poverty, to be addressed – through the group or outside it? (O'Connor 1992).

We have already described how the planning itself should be kept 'under control' so that group members do not feel painted into a corner when they arrive at the first session. Needless to say, it is also crucial to check your assumptions, for there are many tenets of practice wisdom which contradict each other. For every advocate of male-female co-leadership in sexual abuse work, there are those who are equally adamant that such groups should at all lengths exclude male workers. On the one hand, so the argument goes, it is an opportunity for positive male role models and challenges to stereotypes about the uncontrollable nature of male sexuality, (Masson and Erooga 1990: 149); and on the other hand, it is said to inhibit the group since 'relationships with men are at the core of their pain' (Peake and Otway 1990: 121). Moreover, the implicit assumption in both these positions that all perpetrators are male could feel excluding to someone who was abused by a woman (rarer though this is).

Avoid 'placard planning' – in other words, planning dictated by slogan and presupposition. The only assumption you should allow yourself is that nothing should be automatically ruled out or in until it has been thoroughly aired. This is especially important in order to develop a mutual understanding with your co-worker (Chapter 11).

Group design – the likely 'shape'

> Children or adults sitting in a circle, talking about life experiences, sharing feelings, and problem solving. The worker, perceived as a calm, benign, parent figure, guides and directs members through

> interpretations, the offering of insight and sage advice. (Reid 1988:
> 132)

We need to check our assumptions not just about what happens during a group but about what the overall design of the group is likely to look like. Eight sessions of one and a half hours over eight weeks for eight members is often used as an implicit template for groupwork, but it needs to be challenged and the continuum exercise will have demonstrated the rich permutations of possibilities for a group. The shape of the group should be cut not from a blueprint but from the agreed purpose and needs which it is designed to meet. The 12 lines of the continuum are explored in detail below; they demonstrate the infinite variety of possible 'shapes' for groupwork.

Lines 1–4: People lines

The first four lines focus specifically on the people involved; whether the group members have previous knowledge of each other or other kinds of relationship outside the group, how they join and leave the group, their differences and similarities, and the nature of the group leadership.

LINE 1 *HISTORY*: ADAPTED GROUPS AND CREATED GROUPS

One of the most significant considerations is whether the group or its members have 'a history'. Do prospective members know each other already? In small communities this is almost inevitable, as in one of the Groupwork Project groups in a small West Yorkshire town where it transpired that a number of the women were related to each other. Is this an existing residential grouping becoming a group, a gang transforming into a group, some of the users at a day centre community selecting into a group? Each individual brings 'baggage' into the group, but if individuals in the group have a mutual history, some of the baggage will be shared and this will make the dynamics of the group all the more complex. When the group is finding out about itself in the first session it is important that every opportunity is given for individuals to be open about their knowledge of each other. Where the group is adapted from existing groupings, such as teams or residents, the boundary between 'out there' and 'in here' should be marked clearly and explicitly (see Taylor, Miles and Eastgate 1988).

LINE 2 *JOINING AND LEAVING*: OPEN GROUPS AND CLOSED GROUPS

To what extent will the membership be open to change during the life of the group? There are a number of reasons why a group might be open in terms of its changing membership. Some of these reasons concern events outside the group, such as the rapid turnover of a larger system in which members are joining and leaving at unpredictable times, and others are specific to the group, such as the need to respond to crisis quickly, continuing intermittent help, or the group members' different rates of progress (Henry 1988: 217). An open group, then, allows a rapid response to potential members who might need the help of the group immediately (Allum 1990; Otway and Peake 1994).

At the heart of the open and closed issue is the notion of *belonging*. One way of defining a group could be that its members have a sense of belonging. Often there is an assumption that a sense of belonging can only be achieved through a closed group and that open membership is disruptive. However, there are examples of very open and open-ended groups which nevertheless generate a great sense of commitment and belonging. The Allsorts women's group ran for eight years and had an attendance which fluctuated between 11 and 24, with about 35 coming at one time or another, yet one woman was greeted back to the group after an absence of two and a half years (Bodinham and Weinstein 1991: 25). There are ways of preserving 'group memory' through written records, photographs, flipchart sheets and the like which stimulate the sense of a continuing entity transcending changes in its membership (Mullender and Ward 1989: 13). Moreover, the situation is complex because although the group itself might be open it might operate within a closed system, such as a group for people in residential care where membership is confined to the larger resident group, though residents can participate as and when they wish (Clarke and Aimable 1990: 41).

One of the difficulties of new members joining a group can be the fact that they are not 'up to speed' so their presence slows the pace. In their work with child sexual abuse perpetrators, Erooga *et al.* (1990: 182) found that having a group that was open at some stages to allow new members to feed into it, and closed at others, inhibited the general progress. They devised a 'level one' six session group, which acted as a feeder group for entrants who were brought up to speed in order to join the main 'level two' groups.

Of course, there are situations where the necessary level of trust, intimacy and disclosure suggests a closed group. Potential participants might be invited to a preliminary, 'zero' session before deciding whether to commit to the group which subsequently closes its membership (see Chapter 6).

LINE 3 *MIX*: DIFFERENCE AND SAMENESS IN GROUPS

The following four brief scenarios raise the same question for the groupworkers involved; that is, how much difference and how much sameness does a group need to work well?

- A group is being formed for older adults related to adjustment in a new setting, within a nursing home facility. Would the best composition include all residents or those who have been there for differing periods of time?

- A group of severely 'clinically depressed' clients has been identified. Would you form a group consisting solely of these people, or would you form a more general group related to 'grieving' and including others who have adapted more successfully?

- A group at a day centre for older people to deal with issues of ageing is composed entirely of gay and lesbian members (although that was not a guiding principle in forming the group). Would you include a new member who is heterosexual who has expressed an interest in dealing with the same kinds of issues?

- An agency providing services for Alzheimer's victims and their families puts together a support group. Should both children and spouses of Alzheimer's victims be included in the same group? (taken from Rice and Goodman 1992: 67–74)

These dilemmas reflect the choices which group leaders and members face when considering the composition of the group. There are no definitive answers, but it is important to think about the choices which you face with regard to the group you are planning and be explicit about why you think sameness (homogeneity) or difference (heterogeneity) is appropriate. Revisiting the main purposes of the group will help to fix the decision, but whether the group achieves the best balance is a matter of luck and serendipity as well as careful planning.

Sometimes a group might deliberately include members who, outside the group, are in opposition. For example, the Dialogue Groups described by Garrett (1995) contained both prisoners and prison officers. Despite early resistance from prison officers to the idea and presence of Dialogue Groups with prisoners, the group facilitators later 'discovered that some officers even chose to come in on their days off simply in order to take part in the group' (Garrett 1995: 59). Other groups might deliberately select members who share at least some of the characteristics which are considered to be central: Peake and Otway (1990: 122) decided on the key factors when considering recruits to a group for girls who had been sexually abused, and they were careful to ensure that at least two girls shared each factor (ethnicity; abuser had been prosecuted; abuser had not been prosecuted, etc.), so that none felt isolated in the group.

An implicit assumption that 'difference' is code for people from minority groups is often shared both by 'majority' and 'minority'. This assumption should be challenged all round. For example, 'J' describes how as a disabled woman it had not even occurred to her to join a non-disabled group or activity, such as the women's group, and she 'was quite shocked by the admittance of self-inflicted segregation (even though it was not consciously done)' (Wintram et al. 1994: 131). 'J's disability was therefore secondary to her membership of the women's group. Sometimes it is worth encouraging potential members who are different from the others to take the risk of membership. The only father amongst a group of seven mothers was also the only black person in the group for parents of learning disabled adolescents; despite the experience in other (all-female) groups that mothers had believed that fathers do not feel, or act, in the same way towards their disabled child, 'this particular father gained the respect of these mothers and destroyed some of their assumptions' (Gobat 1993: 223).

What exactly are we are considering when we ask the question how different or alike group members should be? 'Sameness' and 'difference' are often present in the one group, depending on how these characteristics are defined. For instance, if you were designing a group for people with cancer would it be more important to consider the location of the cancer, the duration of the cancer, the prognosis for the cancer, the family circumstances of the individual, the attributes of the person with cancer (in terms of race, gender, age, etc) or … what? Even if we can agree which factors are important, can we decide whether they should be characterized by homogeneity or heterogeneity? In their survey of a variety of groups for people who have suffered bereavements, Hopmeyer and Werk (1993: 113) found that the majority of respondents to their questionnaire 'indicated a desire for groups which were homogeneous to problem but heterogeneous in terms of relationship to the person who died and to length of time since bereavement'. In other words, considerable strength was derived from being with people who faced the same kind of problem (a family member who has committed suicide), and less concern that fellow group members share particular attributes (age, race, gender, etc). In another study Harmey and Price (1992: 23) discovered in their groupwork with bereaved children that it is not necessary for children to share similar causes of sibling death in order to develop a shared understanding of each other's situations and feelings. However, it is necessary to avoid having a group in which there is only one child who is the sole surviving child in his or her family.

Evaluating what group participants have found helpful and unhelpful in terms of difference and sameness is one way of developing collective knowledge of which differences matter and which do not.

LINE 4 *LEADERSHIP*: SELF-HELP GROUPS AND PRACTITIONER-LED GROUPS

Nothing seems to polarize the world of groupwork quite so strongly as the question of the location of leadership. Nevertheless, it is important to bring an open mind to this question and to consider what kind of leadership suits the nature of the group. Is it the natural, spontaneous processes which occur in groups of peers, or an acceleration of these processes under the direction of professionals, or a place somewhere in between?

Self-help groups are groups of people who have joined together because they have a common problem or purpose; they hope to offer support to each other and, often, to do something about the mutual problem. Usually they are not led or directed by professionals. The best-known self-help group is Alcoholics Anonymous, with the first such group in the US in 1935 spawning many others, both in terms of number and genre. By their very nature, it is difficult to know how common self-help groups are, but a study in Denmark suggested that about 1 per cent of the Danish population were participating actively in them (Habermann 1993: 22). The growth of the Internet perhaps extends our concept of self-help groups to those where contact is electronic rather than personal, contrary to Matzat's (1989: 249) definition of a self-help group as specifically one where people have face-to-face contact – otherwise he describes them as self-help *organizations*. In Scandinavia, self-help groups are 'developing almost the character of a movement' (Habermann 1990: 221) but there is an ambivalent response amongst professionals. If there is an 'explosion' in self-help groups does this contrast with a decline in professionally led groups? In Chapter 1 we tentatively suggested that this decline was not necessarily an accurate assessment.

There are undoubted benefits to self-help groups, not least the empathy of people who are living with the same problem, and the destigmatizing effect of a group of people all of whom are in the same boat, undiluted when the group has no professional helper. In an Alcoholics Anonymous group, alcoholism is no longer a minority. Matzat (1993) reminds us that the skills and attributes of professional groupworkers come principally from their humanity; that is, most groupwork skills and techniques are merely natural helping behaviours used more systematically and with greater sophistication. Indeed, 'lay' group participants may be more inclined to focus on the strengths of group members than those particular professionals who have been trained to seek out and highlight the pathological.

Nevertheless, the practitioner has a valuable role to play with self-help groups. Whether as initiator, facilitator or consultant, the practitioner can advocate the idea of collective self-help amongst existing service users, provide support from outside (for resources, etc.), and network by referring people to self-help groups. Self-help groups often need some level of professional assistance to help them survive. For example, a 'move-on' group for women who had been attending a probation group was launched with the help of a student social worker. The group did not survive and required agency help to become reestablished (Mistry 1989: 156).

Values can differ between practitioner-led groups and self-help groups. Although members of self-help groups might feel more direct empathy towards each others' situations, they can also be more judgemental and make more demands of one another and can take their own experience as the 'defining experience'.

Professionally led groups can move towards self-led status, so that any particular group is not static on this 'line'. In this section we have focused on self-help to redress some of the balance where the focus in much of the book is on groups with practitioner leadership or facilitation (see Chapters 3 and 11 for further exploration of notions of leadership). This reflects the reality that, by and large, groupworkers are creating a service rather than responding to one requested by users.

Lines 5–7: Time lines

Time is an extraordinarily significant factor in groupwork and the word encompasses at least three complex dimensions, which we explore below along Lines 5, 6 and 7 of the continuum.

LINE 5 *DURATION*: OPEN-ENDED GROUPS AND TIME-LIMITED GROUPS

Time limits are particularly useful if the group wishes to galvanize for action and seeks a specific outcome. The predetermined ending of the group provides a focus for activity and a safety net for workers and members alike, in the knowledge that their commitment to the group has a boundary. A time limit defends against drift, and is likely to help a group end on a 'high' before energy and purpose start to peter out. Flexibility is important if the group requires some additional time to meet its purposes, but the ending should not be postponed merely because it is experienced as 'difficult' (Chapter 13).

There can also be compelling reasons to have a group which does not have a time limit, especially where membership is open so that the group can be replenished as existing members drop out over time. A group which serves as a resource to a wider population, and which becomes known within the community from which it draws membership, survives on its merits as a group rather than because of the needs of its specific members. So, whereas the time-limited group focuses primarily on the individuals in the group, the open-ended one develops a life of its own.

The single line of this continuum does not tell the full story. The group itself can be open ended, with members contracting to participate in a set number of sessions, as illustrated by a women's offending group in which offenders agreed a limit to their participation, with no newcomers to the group for five weeks, in order to allow stability (Jones *et al*. 1991: 218). In agencies where a 'menu' of groups is offered an individual can have a two-step group experience; for example, when prospective group members continue to deny a problem, they might be offered an opportunity in an open-ended group to explore whether they do have a problem, and if they come to acknowledge this the next stage is a group programme which helps them to achieve the changes they desire. Membership of the second (time-limited) group is made possible only by participation in the first (open-ended) one (Behroozi 1992: 38).

Finally, groupworkers have demands on their own time which need to be respected. It might be that the group runs with an agreed time limit (thus limiting the demands on the workers) or not at all.

LINE 6 *LENGTH*: EXTENDED GROUPS AND BRIEF GROUPS

> In week twenty, the boys quite unexpectedly talked directly about their abusive experiences ... there was a reluctance to continue talking about the abuse in subsequent meetings, but the boys' relationships with each other and with the workers were much less guarded. (Dixon and Phillips 1994: 85–6).

So, did it take 20 weeks because it took 20 weeks? If the group had been limited to 12 sessions would it have happened earlier, before the end came? If the session had not begun as it did with the mask-making as an activity would it never have happened at all?

When you come to consider the optimum length for the group you could be forgiven for thinking that it is easier to answer 'how long is a piece of string?' Different people have notoriously different senses of time; in the group described above, the group leaders were preparing for what they saw as a long group of 40 weeks only to find after four weeks that one of the boys expressed disappointment that it had to end soon.

Plans for groups of a certain length may prove unrealistic. In their groups for mothers of children who had been sexually abused, Dobbin and Evans (1994: 118) discovered that 'it quickly became clear that [weekly for six months] was too short a time and the second group met weekly for almost a year'. Judging the appropriate length of string becomes easier with experience, though every groupworker must be prepared for groups of very differing characteristics.

Some groups are exceptionally brief, others run over a period of years. A group of four residents of an old people's home met over two consecutive days; the first morning three of the women went shopping with the staff member and the next day all four cooked themselves a fine meal. The processes described in this 'group for independence' do not follow the conventional idea of groupwork, but it is clear that some very effective groupwork was accomplished; 'during the five hours we spent together that day all the ailments previously mentioned seemed to disappear or were forgotten … we are now discussing the possibility of further meetings on a weekly basis' (Bernard *et al.* 1988: 119.) At the other end of the spectrum are groups which endure many years, usually with some turnover in the membership, but with a sense of continuity often provided by venue, purpose or name.

In addition to the length of the group's life, it is also necessary to consider how long each individual session will be and whether this will conform to a regular pattern. We return to the notion of sessional patterns in Chapter 7.

LINE 7 *INTENSITY:* GROUPS MEETING SELDOM OR FREQUENTLY

The time dimension in groupwork is significant, but it is difficult to know to what extent the shape of a proposed group is taken for granted, and whether options are considered in connection with the frequency of the group meetings. In a survey of groupwork in probation settings, the once-a-week session was near-universal, but there were some clear distinctions between the group's focus and its duration:

> Offending behaviour, alcohol education, motoring offenders, temporary release, induction, drugs/addiction and control of anger and temper groups tend to include ten or fewer sessions; women's groups and sex offenders' groups generally involve many more sessions; life and social skills groups fall somewhere between these two poles and activity programmes and residents' meetings tend, not surprisingly, to be provided on a rolling, open-ended basis. (Caddick 1991: 207)

Schonfeld and Morrissey's (1992) survey of groups in Ireland for adults with a learning difficulty also confirms the dominance of the once-a-week shape, with only 2 out of 35 groups not running weekly.

All three of the timelines are interconnected. A group which meets frequently (more than once a week) is likely to be short and time-limited, too. Often this short, fat shape is called a course or module, and is prevalent in probation and prison settings: five-day prison 'culture groups' (Towl 1990); anger management groups, (Towl and Dexter 1994); intensive three- or four-day modules for offenders, (Mackintosh 1991). Frequency might change with the group's progress, as with a group of older people with learning disabilities which started on a weekly basis, but moved to fortnightly (Atkinson 1993: 202). Similarly, an intensive ten-day course for male sex offenders evolved from a relatively diluted group experience, initially running once a week over a period of time (Cowburn 1990). Groups might vary, then, from the intensity of a one-off weekend to once a week over the course of four years such as long-term support groups for people with chronic schizophrenia (Cwikel and Oron 1991).

The continuum lines are multidimensional; for example, in addition to the frequency of the group meetings, it is possible to consider whether group members might have different intensities of involvement in the group. A groupwork method called 'open grief groups' has a complex pattern of membership, with some members new and others about to leave, some attending 'twice a week, others only once a week, and still others only once every fortnight' (Davidsen-Nielsen and Leick, 1989: 188). Examples such as these help us think creatively about all the possibilities.

As with all the lines in continuum, the questions 'Who decides?' and 'When?' are central. Who decides the frequency? The leaders of a Who Cares? group had assumed it would meet monthly, but when its young members came together they wanted it weekly. The compromise, fortnightly, suited no-one. Discussing frequency in the individual offer of service (see Chapter 5) would have pinpointed these different expectations earlier and it might have been possible to consider adding to the co-leadership so that group members' wishes could have been met without an increase in time commitments for individual workers (Mullender and Ward 1989: 17).

Lines 8–12: Other lines
LINE 8 *SIZE*: LARGE GROUPS AND SMALL GROUPS

The size of a group should be determined by its purpose and the desired mood. Conventional wisdom suggests that the smaller the group the more intimate the experience, and the larger it is the greater the diversity and the re-sources. However, size is not just mathematical but also experiential, so that a group of 16 will seem large if it is the whole of the staff team and users, but small if it is part of a conference of 200 people. Size is also personal to each groupworker, and the prospect of groups of over 16 or so persons intimidates some. Ward (1993: 66) suggests that for many people the definition of large group is 'a group just larger than I can cope with'.

Much of the groupwork literature tends to assume a group size of about 6 to 12, but there are many advantages to groupwork with larger groups, bearing in mind that the size of the team of groupworkers might need to increase with a larger membership. In these larger groups, Mullender and Ward (1989: 15) describe the role of 'spotter', where a groupworker sits amongst the membership and listens out for those with ideas, but who are more inclined to whisper to their neighbour. A larger group also allows for the possibility of 'clustering'. Writing about Dialogue Groups in a prison setting, Garrett (1995: 56) states that 'the group needs to be large enough for sub-cultures to be able to reveal themselves and for individuals to notice themselves identified and aligned with others'. This does not happen with groups smaller than 12, and the preferred size for these groups is 15–30.

It is useful to record your own experiences of the effect of group size, especially since even the smallest differences can have a noticeable impact. For example, the group leaders of a group for emotionally disturbed boys found that a session when there were only three present 'lacked energy and was disconcertingly orderly' whilst a session with six or more boys 'generated more interaction than we could reasonably cope with' (Clarke and Aimable 1990: 41). In other cases the same group framework might be flexible enough to accommodate very different numbers such as a group for bereaved children which was adapted for use with a class of 25 ten-year-olds bereaved by the sudden death of a classmate (Harmey and Price 1992).

When determining group size, the unit might not be the individual, but the family, as in a multifamily group where 'it was found that four to five families is the ideal size for a group' (McKay et al. 1997: 97). In practice this could mean anything from 10 to 22 individual members.

The size of the group ultimately depends on the very obvious factor of who turns up, so it makes sense to start with a group which errs on the large size, since you will be more likely to lose members than gain them (Dixon and Phillips 1994: 82). It pays to have a plan for the group which is not dependent on a specific number; for example, if you are planning to break into smaller subgroups at some point in the session make sure you can break into combinations of two's, three's and four's. Once again, flexibility is crucial in the planning phase and beyond.

LINE 9 *FOCUS*: OUTWARD-LOOKING GROUPS AND INWARD-LOOKING GROUPS

> It seemed important to help the women to look outwards, to explore what they could do outside the group and in their own lives. This was not to say that the members would not be allowed space in the sessions to talk about the crises in their lives, but the workers wanted to avoid the traditional social worker/client relationship where the women could end up feeling that they were little more than the sum total of their problems. (Allsorts women's group, in Bodinham and Weinstein 1991: 24)

The focus of the group will have an impact on other lines in the continuum. Most groups are likely to have both extrinsic and intrinsic aspects, in other words the focus will move between what-is-happening-in-the-group and what-is-happening-outside-the-group. These will influence the kinds of activities the group engages in, the optimum size and the timelines. The self-directed groupwork in Mullender and Ward's model (1989, 1991) is avowedly extrinsic, designed to achieve external change. A group for refugee women was almost entirely inward looking, providing a sanctuary of safety and comfort in which women could talk about their experiences and traumas if they wished (Tribe and Shackman 1989).

Even groups which are primarily inward looking, such as therapy groups, will make some links with the group's external reality (perhaps drawing on experiences from outside the group, or developing 'homework' tasks for participants to complete). Groups which have a high degree of outward-looking focus, such as campaigning groups, will not be exclusively so, for example using group processes to develop collective goals and strategies. Otway and Peake (1994: 160) describe how a group for women whose children had been sexually abused was able to offer telephone contact to a woman who had concerns that full membership of the group would bring her into contact with the 'authorities' and a detrimental effect on her standing in the community. This is an interesting example of an essentially inward-looking group including a person on the outside in its sense of membership.

LINE 10 *CHOICE*: VOLUNTARY AND COMPULSORY MEMBERSHIP

It might seem that there are only two opposite poles on this line; the decision to join a group is either voluntary or not. However, this picture does not do justice to the various subtleties of the line between voluntary and compulsory. There are many ways in which members of some 'voluntary' groups would prefer not to be eligible for membership, and other 'compulsory' groups which are a welcome relief from the alternative on offer. All decisions are, then, constrained to a certain degree.

Probationers might agree to the making of an order with a condition to attend a group, but the alternative of custody puts the choice in context and alerts the groupworkers to possible difficulties in motivation (Henchman and Walton 1993). Some groupworkers feel that coercion to join a group is inadmissible because it is so contrary to the spirit of groupwork (Canton, Mack and Smith 1992). This problem is, of course, no different from individual work with service users and the link between the degree of compulsion and the depth of motivation is far from straightforward.

The link between compulsion and probation groups is not exclusive and there are other circumstances where choice is constrained. For example, critical incident debriefing (CID) in groups has been shown to be such an effective response to people involved in severe traumas such as major accidents and disasters that there is a case for making it obligatory (Parkinson 1993). Certainly, it is less stigmatizing if CID is seen as a procedure which is routinely followed, rather than something which is viewed as a sign of weakness and inability to cope.

It is possible to consider a mixed membership of voluntary and compulsory participants (Jones *et al.* 1991: 22). In any group it is important to allow time early in the first session for members to give an honest account of how they came to arrive in the group (see Chapter 6).

LINE 11 *FORMAT*: LOOSE GROUPS AND TIGHT GROUPS

The lines in Continuum become 'poles apart' when groupworkers take an ideological stance at one end or other of the line. This is especially evident when we look at the format; the differences between structured and unstructured groups crudely sketched around caricatures which push them even further apart; unstructured groups inflict long periods of excruciating silence, whilst structured groups stifle free expression and speed from task to task.

Bensted *et al.* (1994: 39) detect 'a reaction in groupwork generally, and specifically in groupwork with offenders, against the ubiquity of highly structured groupwork packages and predetermined programmes. Some of these may be quite effective, but they have the limitation of fitting the person to the programme rather than vice-versa. We detect a possible revival of interest in responsive, "person-centred" approaches to groupwork with offenders.' Off-the-shelf packages can, indeed, be delivered insensitively, and so can home-grown 'non-plans'. It is a common fallacy to place 'person-centred' and 'structured' groupwork at opposite ends of a continuum.

The paradox is that the format of the group can have a highly structured framework which houses a very flexible, responsive content. For example, two learner groupworkers were expending so much energy preparing material for a social skills group that they forgot how to make the group work for itself. They found themselves preparing barrels of material about assertiveness, neglecting the value of making demands for work from group members. Instead of cramming their own materials into the prepared structure, they could use it to ask members to consider examples of assertive behaviour between one session and another and to bring these examples to the group. The format can, therefore, be highly structured, whilst what goes into the structure can be unpredictable and generated by the group.

As well as the format for the internal structure of each session (the pattern), there are choices about the overall plan (the shape). The group might be relatively *ad hoc* from session to session or it may have a detailed programme; it might be relatively free-standing or form part of a larger, structured programme such as the Newcastle Intensive Probation Programme, in which various modules of groupwork are offered to offenders over a period of time (Mackintosh 1991).

As with all the previous ten lines in the continuum, when it comes to making decisions about the format of the group overall and individual sessions, forget your preconceptions and your prejudices. Consider the group for itself, its needs and its potential, its members and its purposes. Consider where the power lies to make these decisions and how that power can be redistributed. Consider when and how these decisions are best made; is this before the group starts, during the early sessions or later still?

LINE 12 *SPACE*: DIFFUSE GROUPS AND DENSE GROUPS

We have referred to the shape and pattern of a group and now we consider 'space'. The use of space in groups is a rather more abstract construct than the lines we have been describing so far, but space is a curiously significant factor in the feel of a group. The empty chairs where absent members should be sitting, the intimacy of a physical contact warm-up activity, the wholeness of a circle of people, the disruptiveness of members coming in and out of a group room, all illustrate the way in which the feeling for space has an impact on the group. The terms 'dense' and 'diffuse' are used by Clarke and Aimable (1990: 38) to describe the contexts of groupwork with emotionally disturbed boys in residential care, pointing to the different dynamics arising from an open, moving game of football and the static confines of the schoolroom. This notion of denseness and diffusion is helpful in considering the use of space in all groups.

How much emotional and psychological space will the group provide? DeVere and Rhonne (1991: 140) describe the photo-language technique as allowing the *space* for participants to examine their emotional responses to a range of social behaviours and phenomena. Some groups, such as offence-related groups in probation, are very packed and leave little space for things which are not designated in the programme. On the broader plane, it is worth considering what kind of space the group will occupy in the lives of the group members.

Density and diffusion are also related to the use of physical space. You may not have considered anything but a circle of chairs, but there are some purposes which might be better suited to a different use of space. Residential groupings can have a very indeterminate space. Critical incident debriefings, which we described earlier as taking place after major traumas, seat participants around a large table because 'sitting in an open circle could be threatening and feel like a therapy session' Parkinson (1993: 145). One learner in the Groupwork Project had described her group several times in the training workshops, but only when she drew the group on flip-paper did the limits and opportunities imposed by space, the group's own space and the space around it, became apparent. Whether it is emotional space or physical space, its significance should not be underrated.

Practical arrangements

The practical details of groupworking should not be underestimated. Groups require excellent planning skills, available time and careful organization. This is one area where a checklist approach can help:

- place
- timing
- budget.

PLACE

> To be quite honest, had the group required me to travel any further than the local school, I don't think I would ever have made it. ('K's statement in Wintram, *et al.* 1994: 133)

The group's location is critical, in terms of accessibility and the appropriateness of the room or space where the group is held. Where groups are adapted from existing groupings, the location needs to mark out some distinct 'territory' for the group. Sometimes it is appropriate to find a place where group members might congregate naturally, and at other times it is preferable to find a place which is noticeably different. It may be best to link people into their local resources, such as literacy classes, welfare rights and creche facilities. On other occasions privacy and quiet might be the main priorities; in discussing confidentiality in the context of two groups for mothers of sexually abused children, Dobbin and Evans (1994: 118) describe the usefulness of a centre which was open only four days a week, so they could use it on the fifth day when no other people were around. Check to see if the venue is likely to have any symbolic meaning for group members, such as the potential infantilization of a junior school setting.

In terms of physical space, the notion of 'turf' is useful. Whose turf should the group be held on? Discussing professional practice in non-professional settings, Breton (1991) asserts that work with people at the margins of society, like homeless women, needs to be done on their own turf. This is especially important because of the questions of transport and cost. Who will be expected to meet any costs (for travel, creche, outings, refreshments and the like)?

This list of advantages for a particular venue for an art therapy group for women provides a useful general guide:

1. It was local.

2. It was not attached to a social services office, so possibly avoiding the stigma that can accompany a client of social services.

3. There was a separate room for the creche on a different floor.

4. Refreshment facilities and toilets were close by.

5. Materials and equipment could be locked away when not in use by the group.

6. The room was free on the day we had set aside.
   (Otway 1993: 213)

At all times it is right to be flexible about the location of the group. This was demonstrated by a long-standing open group for gay men with Aids which voted to meet on alternate weeks at the home of one of their members who had become too housebound to attend the group in its usual venue (Getzel and Mahoney 1989: 105).

TIMING

The timing of the group might be rather different from other individualized forms of help, for example, meeting outside office hours. A group for bereaved children was held on Saturday mornings since 'the children clearly stated that they did not want to attend the group during school time as this would identify them within the school setting as different' (Harmey and Price 1992: 22).

Co-workers need to be clear and explicit about their own limits. Family and social commitments might preclude weekend or evening groupwork, and it is right to be honest about this at the very beginning of the planning. Moreover, the groupworkers' agency should also have a system for workload relief to compensate for additional out-of-hours work.

Selecting a time and a day convenient for all group members, whether inside or outside normal working hours, can be surprisingly difficult.

BUDGET

In addition to possible costs for group members, it is necessary to consider any additional resources which need to be budgeted for the group, such as materials and equipment (flipcharts, 'props', video hire, etc.), fees for any invited speakers, refreshments and the like. The sums involved are often quite small and it is always worth asking the agency whether there are budgets available for these purposes. Not all groupworkers can expect to have their own budget, though it is clear that this is a major benefit and an indication of the agency's support. A sound budget enabled the Newcastle Intensive Probation Programme 'to provide good quality course materials, effective publicity including a high-quality annual report, and a good standard of accommodation for the groups' (Mackintosh 1991: 265). A small budget can be a valuable aid.

And the rest . . .

Planning needs to address the 'in-betweens' from one session to another. Will there be any contact with group members between meetings and what will happen if a member does not attend a session? Such questions should be discussed either in the offer of groupwork to the individual (Chapter 5) or in the first session (Chapter 6). Similarly, everybody concerned should know if there is any other work which needs to complement the groupwork and what links will be made with this.

Finally, no matter how much planning takes place, there are always occasions when it is necessary to respond to the unplanned. Groupworkers need flair and creativity to make the best of the situation as they find it; they are better prepared if they have planned, even if those plans sometimes need to be abandoned.

Portfolio extract

Our first mistake was not fully addressing Brown's (1992: 35) first stage of planning and preparation: 'the groupworker must be satisfied that a need or problem exists and is shared by a number of people for whom some common aim can be identified.' We assumed that the need was there in sufficient numbers and we concentrated on planning the venue, transport, content, etc.

Consequently, having realised that there were insufficient numbers within our own agency, the time available for referral, assessment, interview and offer was severely curtailed. Not only did that put pressure on us but it affected the process. Ideally the [offers of groupwork] would have been carried out with two workers, the girls would have visited the proposed venue and we would have interviewed and assessed more girls allowing us to be more selective. It would also have allowed us to be more supportive to the girls, some of whom were more apprehensive than others. One girl dropped out prior to the group starting having previously indicated that she would come. Several weeks later her social worker telephoned to ask if she could attend – clearly she was just too nervous to begin with and if we hadn't been running around like headless chickens we could have followed it up.   JA (1998)

CHAPTER FIVE

Offering Groupwork

About 'Tuning in'

This activity is designed to help you attune yourself to the group. It is especially helpful to be 'tuned in' for the first session and it is a technique which is valuable to use before every group session. Tuning in is designed as a short-cut for this process, portraying your efforts in a graphic manner. It resembles the 'graphic equalizer' found on the modern music deck, where the various frequencies of the music are displayed in rising and falling columns to give a picture of the 'shape' of the music in any one instant.

Purpose

The theme of this chapter is attuning to the group, and an offer of groupwork service to prospective individual members is a significant part of tuning in. Groupwork is not, therefore, confined to the time spent in a group, and the essence of good groupwork lies in the way in which you demonstrate your early commitment to the individuals who comprise the group. Part of this process is also anticipating the 'mood' of a prospective group; what are the prevailing emotions and feelings and what is the likely impact of this? This, in turn, helps you to keep the group's activities and processes in tune.

Method

- Consider the set of emotions in the columns in the upper half of the activity. Thinking of a particular individual group member, colour in each column to the extent (height) appropriate, depending on whether you think they will be feeling this emotion strongly, somewhat or not at all. Use a red pen.

- Consider the lower set of 12 columns. Thinking of the same individual, colour in each column in the same way. This time use a green pen.

- There are six unnamed columns (numbered 1–6). Consider six emotions which have not been named, but which you think group members might also be feeling. Colour the columns accordingly (the stronger the emotion, the higher the column): use red for unpleasant emotions and green for pleasant ones.

- What do your completed 'wavebands' tell you about the group member, the group and yourself?

Variations

To what extent do you think the group member you have chosen is typical of other group members? How might this profile differ from individual to individual?

What is the balance of pleasant and unpleasant emotions – which are the higher columns? What proportion of the additional six columns are red/green?

How might newcomers to an existing group feel (in other words, new members about to join an open group), and how might these feelings be different from members who are about to form a group from its beginnings?

So far you have been considering the possible feelings of group members, but you have feelings about the coming session, too. What kind of 'graphic equalizer' do you create?

Some of the other feelings which have been named by groupworkers and learners using the tuning-in activity:

> afraid, bored, cautious, defiant, ready to be disappointed, distrustful, frustrated, isolated, numb, sceptical, suspicious, unsure, wary.

Notes for the groupworker
What is 'an offer of groupwork'?

The notion of an offer of groupwork implies that the group is the creation of the groupworker rather than the groupworker's response to a requested service from others. From our experience, and from a review of the groupwork literature, this appears to be the most common genesis for a group, though there are some rare examples of the latter (Ferraro and Tucker 1993). In general, then, it is the groupworkers who are taking the initiative, whilst basing the planning on their understanding that there is a need for a group. Groups

Tuning in

Consider a group member coming to the first session of the group. What feelings might they be experiencing, and to what extent? Shade each of the columns as appropriate, using red for the first 18 columns and green for the second 12.

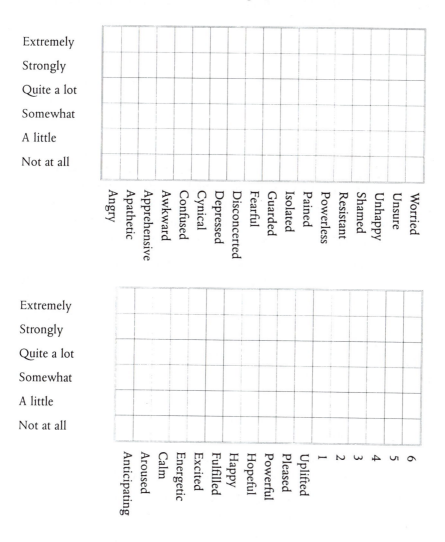

Use the numbered columns in the second set of columns to add six other feelings you think the group members may be experiencing before they come to the first session. Shade them in the same way you have with the other named columns, using red shading for feelings which are generally unpleasant and green for pleasant ones.

are not necessarily created 'from scratch' – they can also emerge out of existing groupings of people, for example in residential and day centre settings.

As we discovered in Chapter 4, potential members should be involved in the planning of the group, and the offer of groupwork is an important first step in this involvement, whether the aim is for self-directed groupwork or a group more heavily directed by the groupworkers.

Recruitment and publicity for the group

> We needed some publicity to attract women who didn't have contact with our referral agencies. We were afraid of frightening women off if we advertised the group as being about challenging personal and institutional racism and so played safe and publicised the group as looking at issues such as hair and skin care, multi-racial books and toys, coping with parents' reactions, experiences of racism towards their children and helping their children find a positive identity. We wanted to illustrate the leaflet showing a white woman with a black child but this proved difficult so we had to join two separate pictures. (Rhule (1988: 43), on publicizing a group for white women with black children.)

Once the groupworkers have formulated their initial plans for a group, it is important that they are put to the test. It is necessary to discover whether the need is real and whether it can be met by attracting sufficient people who are interested in the idea of a group. The groupworker's own knowledge of the kind of people they hope to attract to a group will help them to answer the following questions essential for recruitment to the group.

- How will people find out about the group?
- Are we likely to attract more recruits than we want (in which case we need to restrict numbers) or to have to broadcast fairly widely to attract sufficient numbers?
- Are potential members likely to be more attracted by a group which is already 'programmed' or one which is yet to be finalized?
- What choices do the groupworkers and potential members have in respect of these questions?

One of the key questions to consider in the offer of groupwork to potential members is how they are likely to perceive their needs, and to be open to the possibility of differences in perception. For example, there is some evidence that there is a difference in the preferences of men and women in allotting time in groups to specific issues. In a survey of bereavement groups, in which people were asked to select their preferred topics, men selected items related to problem solving, coping and information gathering, whilst women stated a preference for sharing feelings, rating information on bereavement very low (Hopmeyer and Werk 1993). A group wishing to attract both men and women would need to include topics which covered broad ground.

Potential recruits might be hard to reach for a variety of reasons. Reluctance or forgetfulness by social workers to refer their clients, the isolation of potential members, unwillingness to admit to a socially stigmatizing disorder (such as bulimia), are all very powerful reasons why people in the target group might fail to become members. Moreover, there is also the possibility that, in some circumstances, individuals who wish to attend the group might not be allowed to. This was the situation when a number of the women who wished to join a group for Asian women with terminally ill children were 'refused permission' by their husbands (Muir and Notta 1993: 131).

There are some situations where the group on offer is for those people who have regularly been selected out of other groups, such as group therapy for sex offenders with severe learning difficulties, where the learning difficulties have, themselves, been an automatic rule-out criterion from other sex offending groups (Cormack 1993).

Informal networks play a large part in recruitment to some kinds of group, especially if membership is open so that word of mouth can attract new members once the group is established and seen to be successful. The Allsorts women's group ran for eight years, with recruitment aided by an enthusiastic member who worked part time at the local greengrocer's: 'with every pound of potatoes, as it were, she also sold the group' (Bodinham and Weinstein 1991: 25).

So far, we have considered publicity only in terms of attracting would-be members to a potential group, but publicity is a two-way street. Once established, a group might wish to publicize itself, either to gain new members or to let the wider community know of its activities so that it can gain in influence. A programme of oral history groups in South Africa culminated in an evening presentation at which various aspects of the group's research were presented to the public (Drower 1991). The Kids Like Me group of teenage cancer patients in Ireland went so far as to appear on national television and to make a video of a dramatized account of a teenager with cancer to publicize its cause (Martin and O'Neill 1992: 66). However, not all groups will wish, or be able, to achieve such a high profile.

In an institutional setting it is possible to consider a survey of needs to discover what groupwork might be most welcome and appropriate. Ashe

(1991) conducted such a needs profile questionnaire in a prison setting and found a range of topics requested, such as employment briefing, families group, drugs support and parole information. The success of this approach is evident from the number of prisoners attending the groups (1500 inmates took up voluntary membership of the groups in a year).

The worker in a group for parents with sleepless children attributed some of the group's success to clear advertising of the group as focusing specifically on children's sleep difficulties, and this 'discounted any inappropriate or unsuitable referrals' (Robertson 1990: 251). Having a tight focus does not mean that other themes cannot or will not arise during the course of the group (parents being controlled by children was a strong theme in the parents of sleepless children group), but it ensures that participants share a primary focus in the group.

For groups which are run on a regular, recurring basis, the pattern of recruitment might change. As a group format moves from avant-garde to mainstream, the numbers of people referred or referring themselves might increase (Cowburn 1990: 167 notes this in relation to a programme of courses for male sex offenders, where it was initially difficult to attract referrals from colleagues, but latterly each group was doubly subscribed); on the other hand, the pool of potential group members might begin to dry.

Reluctant and involuntary members

Although this chapter is primarily concerned with the process by which prospective members select themselves in or out of a proposed group, there are circumstances when people do not have this choice. In most probation groups the choice is nominal, in that the alternative to attendance at the group under the terms of a probation order is a custodial sentence. In these circumstances, the purpose of this phase of groupwork is to develop 'remotivating strategies' (Behroozi 1992). In other words, this stage is an opportunity to address the source of members' reluctance about the group and to tempt prospective group members by helping them to see the relevance of the group to their own needs, and the possibility of change via groupwork. These strategies are best employed with each individual *before* the group itself starts.

Perhaps there will be an opportunity for recruits to test the group's usefulness over an agreed number of sessions, or perhaps they are 'stuck' with the group (and the group stuck with them) for the duration. Whatever the case, it is crucial that individuals know where they stand and that the period before the group starts is used to engage compulsory group members.

As we saw in Chapter 4, the gap between voluntary and involuntary group members, whether they are mixed in the same group or not, is often not as great as it might first appear. In many groups, there are members who would prefer not to be in need of the group – prefer not to be children who have been sexually abused, prefer not to be people bereaved by suicide, prefer not to be abusing alcohol. Reluctance and ambivalence may be as common in 'voluntary' group members as 'involuntary' ones, but it may be less overt. If we view teams as groups, we can also see how membership of the team group is voluntary in the sense that each person accepted the offer of employment, but involuntary in the sense that they did not have choice about who their team colleagues would be.

Offering the service to hard-to-reach people requires special thought and skills and it is important that the whole person is invited to participate in the group and not just the 'troubled, or broken or hurt part' (Breton 1989). Sometimes it is better to offer a low-demand group service, such as a drop-in, which can prepare people for other kinds of more intensive group involvement.

Some potential members may be reluctant because competing attractions may win greater favour. The notion of 'opportunity cost' guided the timing of a group for emotionally disturbed boys in residential care, so that participants would not be missing out if they joined the group (Clarke and Aimable 1990: 39). The balance of costs and benefits is always important to keep in mind when recruiting individuals to a group.

Criteria for membership

Whether you judge it likely that the group will be oversubscribed or undersubscribed, it is useful to develop some criteria for membership to the group. This aids co-workers' understanding of each others' ideas about who and what the group is for, and highlights any major differences at an early stage. This process does not mean that decisions have been finalized; planning and preparation does not mean closing options.

However, it is important to challenge a common assumption in groupwork that there needs to be a careful 'membership specification' to give to colleagues who can then refer people on. This is one kind of groupwork, and it may have a place for some kinds of groups in some kinds of setting, but groupworkers should start from the premise that the offer of groupwork is an opportunity for potential members to make a decision.

Some of the criteria are likely to be defined by circumstance. For example, O'Connor (1992: 78) describes how the limited resources outside of the group and the time constraints on the group (ten sessions) helped to define how the criteria were drawn up for a group for people bereaved by suicide. Initially, the criteria required participants to be bereaved by at least eight months (and preferably by one year), the suicide was to be the primary issue for the participants, the applicants were to have at least one good supportive confidante outside the group, and parents who had lost children through suicide were not to be mixed with other categories. However, the reality was that there were insufficient recruits who met these stringent criteria, so they had to be adjusted. In the end, it worked fine to mix 'categories' of suicide and to have people who were at different stages of their grieving, but it was the two group members whose primary problems were other than the suicide who dropped out before the end of the group. Experience will alert groupworkers to which factors are likely to be the crucial ones, but having common purpose is usually important.

If the membership of the group is open, prospective new members need to know whether there are any exit criteria; can members leave as and when, or are there specific circumstances which will trigger their leaving the group. Is it possible to re-enter the group at some later stage?

The significance of the offer of groupwork to individuals

The experience of the Groupwork Project has led the authors to conclude that the way in which the group is offered to individual service users is critical to its success, and yet it cannot be taken for granted that individual offers of groupwork will be made in person. Many of the groupworkers in the Project would have relied on a letter or referral from colleagues, but decided to offer the groupwork in person as a result of the advice from the training programme. The additional time spent in meeting potential group members before the group starts is repaid several times over in terms of the effectiveness of the group itself.

We prefer to avoid the term 'selection', which is often applied to the process of deciding who is and who is not a member of the group (Brown, 1992: 59). The ideology of selection emphasizes the power of the group leader and though we do not underestimate this power, we do not wish to reinforce it. The notion of offering a service to individuals who are prospective members of the group (with a right of veto by both parties), implies the beginnings of a partnership in which there is an exploration of the group. To what extent is there is a fit between the workers' ideas for the group and each potential group member's needs and interests? To what extent can the group itself be adapted to the individual's needs? It is not, therefore, a question of the captain of a soccer team selecting the best players, but a meeting of people, in which one (or two) invite another to discuss the likely conduct and purpose of a game and their interest in playing.

Manor (1988) describes four 'rungs' on a ladder to characterize the offer of groupwork, which he terms 'an interview'. These move between engagement, linking, induction and mediation. It is very valuable to rehearse how you intend to offer the group to potential members.

Let us explore five reasons why the individual offer of groupwork is significant:

1: REHEARSE AND REFINE THE GROUP'S PURPOSES

The need to describe your ideas for the group in words and ways which people interested in joining the group will understand provides a series of rehearsals for the 'opening statement of purpose' which you will make to the whole group towards the beginning of its first session (Chapter 6). Your experience of making individual offers will help to shape the opening statement and introduce the prospective group member to some of the issues which the group itself will face. Describing a group for children who had lived with domestic violence, Mullender (1995: 86) tells how the child and the mother were offered a pregroup interview which 'began to confront the secrecy in advance of the group and also to introduce the kind of questions which would be asked there'.

No matter how well planned and definite your ideas for the group, they will benefit from the need to formulate them in order to present them to potential recruits. Discussion and negotiation with service users will help to refine your suggestions, to develop concrete examples to use as illustrations, and to test the viability of the group. If you listen carefully to your potential membership, they will be the source of valuable ideas to shape the future group. You should take careful note of the degree to which your plans are confirmed, modified or contradicted by the experiences derived from the individual offers of groupwork service. In some circumstances you may wish to consider more formal ways of collecting information, such as a questionnaire to identify any particular concerns (Ferraro and Tucker 1993).

Even when you are starting a group programme with which you are very familiar – perhaps it is the fifth or sixth time that you have run this highly structured and predictable programme – it is a mistake to skip the individual offer of service. Each group is a unique experience, primarily because of the different individuals involved and no matter how predetermined the aims of a group, it should be possible to accommodate a different membership and be open to review and change. A 'winning formula' for a group is one which responds to the particular chemistry of each different set of group members.

2: SET THE TONE AND ENCOURAGE PARTICIPATION

The individual offer is an opportunity to increase motivation for the group by offering potential members tangible benefits and hope. As groupworkers, your enthusiasm for the group is important to show how groupwork can be worthwhile, and the respect you show for each individual's concerns at this early stage will set the tone for the group itself.

First sessions of groups can be anxious occasions as individuals get to know each other. If the group members are also unfamiliar with the groupworkers, this adds to the level of discomfort. It builds confidence if the groupworkers have already had contact with each member; as groupworkers, you will recognize faces and know names, and group members will already have developed some confidence in you from the offer of groupwork, feeling less need to test you out.

The individual contact prepares you for any quirks as they may become apparent during the offer of groupwork, though be prepared to find some people behaving quite differently in the group setting (for example, somebody may have been chatty when the individual offer was made, but is silent in the group).

After individual visits to mothers of children who had been sexually abused, Dobbin and Evans (1994: 119–20) sent letters of confirmation in order to reinforce a sense of clarity and reassurance about the forthcoming group. Indeed, follow-up letters inviting or reminding people of the start of the group can reinforce the mood established at the individual offer.

3: MEET AS INDIVIDUALS

Members enter a group as individuals and they will leave as individuals. It is your hope that they will work together and develop a group spirit, but they may have very different expectations about the nature of the group. An individual offer made in person enables people to express these views in a relatively uninhibited fashion. It is possible to take account of these differences before the group itself begins in a way which is more difficult once the group is in session, because some individuals find it too challenging to express differences openly in the early stages of a group.

Even when the potential group members already know each other (perhaps the proposed group is for people already living together in residential care), it is just as important that they are given space to express their opinions and concerns as individuals. They may too often be seen as part of an existing grouping (the residential group, for example) and it may be important that the proposed group is seen as different from established groupings. The individual offer is a way of emphasizing this difference.

The offer of groupwork is an opportunity for the would-be recruit to become familiar with the groupworkers as individuals, too, and begin to build a sense of trust in them. Contextual issues are important, such as how the person came to the notice of the groupworkers and how the groupwork service relates to any services they already receive. Answers to these and similar questions put the group in its broader context, so that the first session starts from a position of mutual understanding.

4: OFFER PEOPLE A REAL CHOICE

An individual offer of groupwork demonstrates your commitment to the principle of choice. The primary choice is usually one of attendance, but even when this is not an option, there are other issues where a commitment to choice can be similarly demonstrated; in determining the content and process of the group, for example. Most important, the offer of service gives people the chance to change their minds, even if the groupworker feels this is the wrong decision:

> At least one woman who had originally been interested [in joining a group for women with sexually abused children] decided not to join the group in the end: while waiting for it to begin she had moved from belief in her child to a stance of disbelief in order to retain the relationship with her partner – an indication, perhaps, of how isolated and unsupported she felt. (Dobbin and Evans 1994: 119)

'Choice' is relative. In some circumstances people may feel that to refuse groupwork might be detrimental to other aspects of the services they receive. In other cases, there may not be a choice (for example, the alternative to attendance at the group is a custodial sentence). The offer of service provides the opportunity to open up this central issue of choice, in preparation for wider discussion when the group itself meets. Where there has been little or no choice about attendance this will inevitably be a theme when the group meets, and the individual offer begins this process.

There are many reasons why a person might choose not to come to the group. They may not feel sufficiently motivated, they may fear that it will be too challenging, or not challenging enough. Some people might decide not to join a group because they want 'to think less, rather than more, about what had happened' (Dobbin and Evans 1994: 119). Individuals need to know that the group is likely to be both more and less intimate than their experience of one-to-one work. There may be practical obstacles, such as the time the group is being held. It is important that groupworkers make a record of why people have decided not to come, to discover any patterns and learn from them.

In addition to giving potential members a real choice, an offer of groupwork helps to prevent 'professional assessment' obstructing true potential. This phenomenon is carefully documented by Gibson (1992) in a study of various reminiscence groups for older people, some held in residential homes and others in daycare centres. Staff's low opinions of the ability or willingness of residents to participate were almost invariably proved wrong; if the groups had depended on a selection process controlled by the staff only a few 'select' older people would have been chosen to participate and many others would have been denied the opportunity.

Individual recruits also need the chance to change their minds a little later than the offer of groupwork. In Chapter 6, we consider the idea of a 'zero session', when individuals are settling in but have a chance to opt out of a group which thereafter becomes closed. The offer of service cannot always convey the 'feel' of a group, as illustrated by a woman who came to feel that a group for people suffering with schizophrenia would be intrusive only after she had been to a session (Randall and Walker 1988: 64).

5: SCREEN FOR UNSUITABLE GROUP MEMBERS

We have been careful not to talk about selection, but there are occasions when groupworkers consider that the needs of an individual will not be met by the group and, on occasion, that the individual could be seriously detrimental to the potential group. Where the person does not recognize the lack of fit, the leaders have a responsibility to screen by vetoing their attendance. Where possible, other more appropriate services should be suggested. It is safer to discover any mismatch during an individual offer of service than in the first session of the full group.

An example of the appropriate use of screening is described by Mullender (1995: 86), where a number of pregroup interviews were conducted for children who had lived with domestic abuse, in order to exclude 'children who could not verbalise sufficiently, and families where risk or denial was too high'. In another group, child sexual abusers were interviewed twice and, if accepted, had a social and sexual history taken and a contracting meeting with all the agencies involved (Erooga et al. 1990: 179). Dixon and Phillips (1994) describe the significance of the preparatory meetings with boys, their parents and any social worker involved prior to a group for boys who had been sexually abused. This was especially important in one instance where it became evident that the two referred boys (brothers) were still having contact with their abuser, a cousin who kept coming to the house. Apart from the immediate child protection issues involved, the group was intended for boys where abuse had ceased between six and twelve months before. These necessary safeguards strengthen rather than undermine the general principle of choice over selection.

Methods of offering groupwork
WHO TO INVOLVE

In addition to the people who are eligible to come to the group, it can be appropriate to include others in the initial offer. For example, a group for girls who had been abused by the same perpetrator was launched by inviting the parents of the girls to an initial meeting to explain the group and seek their consent for the girls' attendance. In fact, this meeting spawned not just the girls' group, but a group for the mothers, too, with a broader remit which addressed their own personal needs (Allum 1990). Sometimes it is helpful to involve other professionals who are involved with the potential group member, as long as due regard is paid to the power balance in this kind of encounter. If the group is to be co-led it is important not to cut corners and for both co-leaders to meet the potential recruits together.

GROUP OFFERS

The offer might not always be an individual affair. For example, a 'listening survey' was used with a religious community, in which pairs of Sisters interviewed one another about the concerns they had about their lives in the community (Grindley 1994). The responses were collected and categorized and then used as the basis for the design of a workshop. This is a form of offering groupwork in a ready-made community of people who can be canvassed so that their collective response frames the group itself. The Kids Like Me group (see page 99) was launched by an invitation to an open day for teenager cancer patients, their families and friends, and out of that day a committee and a group was formed (Martin and O'Neill 1992). Prospective members of a hospital-based group for people suffering from schizophrenia were given the workers' planning notes 'to involve them in generating ideas for the group' (Randall and Walker. 1988: 62). The four issues which most concerned prospective members were that the group should be closed membership, a strong demand for information about schizophrenia, spontaneous requests for ice-breakers to ease anxieties and an agreement about confidentiality, especially in connection with other staff.

How the group is offered depends on how wide you want to canvass for membership and the opportunities available to put these recruitment plans into action.

'Tuning in'

> Over the next few days as our first Wednesday approached, some resistance was evident. Residents did not want to go through with it; some did not feel 'up to it', and other objections were made. I think people were frightened and anxious about their capabilities; it was safer to do nothing, rather than embark on something new with the possibility of 'failing'. Of course, I was going through the same anxieties. (Lewis 1992: 54)

The ability to anticipate the likely thoughts and feelings of group members prior to the first session is an important factor in the success of the group. This process of 'matching the mood' has been called 'tuning in', something very much like finding the right frequency on a radio. It is your attempt as a groupworker to put yourselves in the shoes of the group participants. Shulman (1984: 22) describes four important factors when tuning in:

1: FOCUS ON FEELINGS RATHER THAN THOUGHTS

Tuning in is more 'affective' than 'intellectual'. To continue with the waveband metaphor, the process is less about finding the radio station by knowing the frequency and following the digital counter and more about twiddling the knob and listening carefully until it sounds 'right'. The process of tuning in is less about understanding what group members are likely to be thinking and more about you actually *experiencing* what they may be feeling.

2: TUNE IN TO YOUR OWN FEELINGS AS WELL AS THOSE OF THE GROUP MEMBERS

How you feel has a big impact on how you act. Tuning in to your own feelings lessens their power to block you; sometimes it will feel right to disclose your feelings in the group, though this must be handled with care. Are your own feelings 'in tune' with those of the group members or are they quite different? If the group is taking place at the end of a long day is this true for group members, too? Have you had similar journeys to arrive at the group venue? All of these arrival issues will affect the group's take off.

3: TUNE IN AT A NUMBER OF LEVELS

At a broad and general level

Adolescent boys in trouble with the law are likely to come to the first session of a group in a different frame of mind than old people who are considering whether to enter residential care. At this broad and general level you are able to use your experience and imagination to consider how people of this age, in these circumstances, etc., are likely to be feeling about the group. Tuning in at this general level helps you consider how a particular social group (as opposed to the group you are working with) defines itself. For example, if one of the group members was deaf you would be aware of their disability, but would you be aware of the fact that 'deaf people have their own language, culture and community, and thus they see themselves not simply as a disabled group, but as a cultural linguistic minority' (Kohli 1993: 235)?

At the level of individuals in the group

Although you have an idea of the likely feelings of 'people in these circumstances' there are important individual differences. If it is the first session for all members of the group, you need to rely on information you gathered in offering the groupwork service individually. In terms of the prospect of residential care, for example, you know that Mrs Khan feels resigned to it, Mr Freeman is very anxious about any changes, and Mrs Short is similarly anxious, but more about change not happening quickly enough. In addition, group members also have varying feelings about the prospect of being in a group. All of these factors give an individual gloss to the general kinds of feelings which you anticipate they may have.

Individuals who enter an existing group are likely to have different kinds of feelings as they anticipate their first session. Uppermost is the sense that they are the only one who is new and how this feeling of being different will be handled.

At the specific phase of the group's life

The tuning in technique is useful at every stage in the group's development. Will the mood of the previous session prevail in the coming one? How will events between this session and the last have influenced these feelings? Has there been any contact with individual group members outside the group? All of these factors, and many more, have a bearing on how well you can tune in to the feelings which group members bring to the session.

4: THE CONCLUSIONS OF YOUR TUNING IN PROCESS MUST BE TENTATIVE

It is paradoxical but, after all the energy which you have put into anticipating the feelings of group members, 'the key to the successful use of the tuning in skill rests in the worker putting all hunches aside when beginning the engagement' (Shulman 1984: 25). Tuning in is designed to sensitize you to *potential* concerns and feelings, not to produce a caricature of group members. It is just as important, therefore, to be able to attune to the *actual* feelings when the group is in session. Returning to the metaphor of the radio wavelength, it is important to know when you are tuned in to the wrong station, and to be able to retune accordingly.

Checking assumptions

> Had the young men considered the effects on their female partners of their being in prison? (Badham *et al.* 1989: 31)

Tuning in alongside a co-worker is a way of checking out assumptions. Paradoxically, a co-leadership which is very attuned to itself may make assumptions in common; for example, heterosexual co-workers might make the assumption that all the members of a group are similarly heterosexual. A discussion about relationships in which leaders and members together presumed heterosexual relationships, as in the example above, would feel very excluding to any gay people in the group. They would not have an expectation that a gay person would necessarily 'come out' (especially in the circumstances of a prison group) but it would be right to expect that the groupworkers' own language would be inclusive, to signal to all group members that other kinds of partnership in the community are possible.

There are commonly held assumptions in all fields of groupwork practice. For example, we might readily assume that people who are bereaved all feel loss, yet 'some are made free by bereavement but dare not admit it' (Rimmer 1993: 135). Checking assumptions does not preclude acting on experience. For instance, if your experience of working with people suffering with schizophrenia tells you that thought disorder and a flat mood could be problematic in a group setting, it is important to act on this knowledge, perhaps by emphasizing physical activity to counter some of the 'slowing down' experienced by people with schizophrenia (Randall and Walker 1988: 65).

In addition to assumptions, it is important to be aware of any bad fantasies you harbour as a groupworker. What if nobody shows up? What if the group gets out of control? What if you're 'found out' as not being skilled enough? What if everybody sits in silence? (Reid 1988: 126). Tuning in, before the individual offer, before the first group session and before subsequent sessions, helps you to check out these assumptions.

First feelings

> As a person enters a new group, he/she scans the situation for signs that indicate to what extent he/she is welcome. There is great sensitivity to non-verbal communications, such as tone of voice, facial expressions, or gestures. (Fatout 1989: 73)

Feelings in themselves are neither good nor bad. Even a feeling that is believed to be bad, such as guilt, must be considered from different perspectives; the aims of one group may be to reduce feelings of guilt, such as carers wanting to spend time away from those they are caring for, whilst another group might have the specific aim of inducing and encouraging feelings of guilt where they are absent, such as a group of juvenile sex offenders denying the pain they have caused others (Crown and Gates 1997).

Feelings are influenced by group norms and it is important to anticipate potential conflicts between the norms of the leaders and those of the members. In the group for juvenile sex offenders, for instance, the leaders have to avoid colluding with the members' attempts to minimize the effects of their abusing.

Finally, the debriefing for groupworkers after the group's session should include time to consider the accuracy of your tuning in and the extent to which it was possible to anticipate the mood of the group as a whole from the experiences of the offers of groupwork to individuals.

Portfolio extract 1

As a result of attending the Skills in Groupwork course, the offer to individuals was done differently to how I normally would have. As we work closely with all these individuals and see them regularly at informal groups, I may have offered this group to them informally at one of the other groups … However, I found that the letter and an individual visit explaining the aims of the group was very successful.

This method I would use in the future. All potential members were very excited at having received an appointment letter from us. This, along with the separate visit … did a lot to stimulate motivation and interest. It also gave them the opportunity to ask questions, put forward suggestions and mention any problems or fears that they had. I also think it was important for both co-workers to do all the visits together as it demonstrated commitment on our part. As this method worked well, I don't think I would change the approach to individuals next time.

One of my concerns in making our offer to the individuals was in getting the balance between, on one hand being encouraging and enthusiastic about the group, and on the other not coercing the individual to join against their will. I am aware that most of the individuals may feel very powerless in their lives and that they may be likely to go along with things that we suggest. However, I think that all attending members genuinely wanted to be there.

JW (1998)

Portfolio extract 2

[Although I think I was accurate in the main], I was not prepared for one group member's anger to be expressed in the form of complete silence – Paul did not speak until the team building work was well underway and so when the anger was expressed verbally it was a shock. I was also not prepared for the amount of knowledge this particular group had about each other from outside. A number of the group members had known each other from prison. This made for a lot of solidarity and a reluctance for some people to go against the dominant thoughts or feelings of another.

LE (1998)

CHAPTER SIX

The First Session and the Group Agreement

About 'Best of intentions'

Good intentions feature strongly in social work generally and groupwork in particular. The dialogue in this activity represents an 'opening statement of purpose' at the beginning of the first session of a group led by Ken and Beverley. Their hearts are in the right place but, sadly, their mouths are not. In a light-hearted way, this activity is designed to highlight the important themes when considering how to state your purposes at the beginning of a group.

Purpose

This chapter focuses on the first session of a group. The elements of a successful first session are examined, as are the core themes of authority and intimacy in groups. We also consider how groups can move to a sense of common purpose, whether this is a formal group contract or a looser form of mutual agreement.

Method

- Read through the transcript of Ken and Beverley's opening statement of purpose.

- Reread each of the eight sections. You will be tempted to make critical comments about Ken and Beverley's performance. Resist! Before criticizing the *how*, consider the *what*. What are their intentions, do you think, at each juncture of their joint opening statement? In the columns to the right of each section make a note of their intentions and any themes arising.

- Finally, try rewriting the opening statement of purpose staying true to the good intentions but communicating them more skilfully.

Variations

The exact nature of the group in the 'best of intentions' activity is deliberately non-specific. Consider the impact of different kinds of group on the way you might rewrite the opening statement (young offenders; people with alcohol problems; tenants in a housing estate, etc.)

Best of intentions

Everybody has been introduced in the new group. Ken and Beverley have planned their opening statement of purpose and are full of the best intentions for the group, but – as you read through what they say – you will find it easy to be critical. So, rather than criticizing what they say, identify the themes and issues which you think they are trying to explore. How would you express them differently? Complete this exercise before reading the notes which follow.

	Intentions	Themes
1 Ken This group is at the interface of service users and our Agency. As such, I hope to be able to facilitate your access to available resources and therefore empower you to use them yourself. In this way, as you'll remember from the one-to-one sessions, the aim is for you to become self-determining and to function autonomously.		
2 Beverley As part of a training course we're doing called Skills in Groupwork, we need to run an actual group so we can practise our skills and gain evidence for our portfolios, so it's only right to share with you that this group has a special interest to Ken and me. We think you'll get an even better service from us because we're so keen to do our best for the group.		

	Intentions	Themes

3 Ken

It's interesting, but when I first had the idea that a group of this kind might be useful, I wasn't exactly certain that there was a real need out there, but coming to see you each individually to make the offer of a group confirmed my gut feelings. I particularly remember Jaswinder telling about his great sense of loss at his particular misfortune and his overwhelming sense of injustice; it convinced me that the group was going to fulfil a much-neglected need. So, I have high hopes of the group, and I know Beverley does, too.

4 Beverley

Yes, although Ken and I have never been in the sort of situation you find yourselves in, we can understand what it feels like and it's not too difficult to put ourselves in your shoes, so we really know how difficult it's been to come here and how courageous everybody has been. Well done!

5 Ken

I thought I'd put people's minds at rest if I gave an illustration of some of the things we'll be doing during the group. For instance, next week I'll be setting up the video, so you can rehearse some of those really tricky situations you've found yourself in, but not known what to do. The research tells us that people feel a lot more confident when they've practised things – and the video is a great opportunity to get direct feedback about how you're doing. I've used it with other groups I've run and they've all enjoyed it. We'll be doing some exercises, some sculpting, and using the flipchart for ecograms. But above all, I want us to have fun and enjoy these group sessions.

	Intentions	Themes

6 Beverley

But, of course, this is your group not Ken's or mine, so we want to know what you'd like to do, as well. We don't see ourselves as the leaders of the group, as such, so we want you to tell us what you want. We think structure is oppressive to the group, so it's all up for grabs and we're really very easy about what goes on. For instance, if the start and finish times of the group aren't convenient with everybody we could renegotiate these to fit in with you all. And we don't want to have too high expectations of the group – there's a limit to what can be achieved, so let's keep our feet on the ground.

7 Ken

Finally, before we move on to finding out more about you – just a few words about ground rules. I don't want to get heavy about things, but the centre doesn't allow smoking, so you will need to confine that kind of activity to outside the building. It's bad manners to interrupt people when they're speaking, and it's a matter of respect to listen carefully to others and – of course – not to gossip about what goes on inside the group. I hope you agree that these seem reasonable things to stick to.

8 Beverley

So, to start the group moving, why don't you break into pairs and share with the person next to you something you like about yourself ... it's OK, don't be shy, we're going to do it, too, aren't we Ken!

Notes for the groupworker

The early stage of the group, when it is beginning to get to know itself, is sometimes referred to as 'contracting in'. The notion of contract has an established place in work with individuals, families and groups (Corden and Preston-Shoot 1981; Shulman 1984; Smith and Corden 1981), though we prefer the term 'agreement' in order to emphasize the element of negotiation and to recognize that there are seldom the legal sanctions which contract implies. So, 'contracting in' is shorthand for the various processes which help the group to form an agreement with itself, both on an individual basis between member and workers, and on a group basis, between the members and the group and the workers and the group. Secondary agreements with family members, colleagues in the agency, or other people with a stake in the group may also be necessary (Preston-Shoot 1989: 40). The notion of contracting in is designed to help the present collection of individuals begin to reach agreement about what their group might be.

There are three components to contracting in:

- the first is the groupworkers' responsibility to set out their own stall and to set the scene via an opening statement of purpose

- the second is to introduce group members to each other and to enable them to share their own vision for the group and to agree the processes which will help the group to work effectively

- the third concerns agreement about goals and outcomes, whether these are held individually or commonly.

Let us explore each of these components in more detail.

Opening statement of purpose

Towards the beginning of the first session of a new group, the leaders should share their vision for the group. Why do they think there is a need for a group? What do they see as the purposes of the group, and how might the group achieve them? The groupworkers are laying out their stall, carefully and honestly. It is an early stage in the process of negotiation around what the group is for, where it wants to go and how it might get there.

This process began with offering groupwork to potential individual members of the group (Chapter 5). This was a rehearsal for the statement to the whole group, helping to refine and shape the statement of purpose; what was said privately is now stated publicly, avoiding any fantasies that different things have been said to different people.

Let us pick up on some of the themes arising from the opening statement of purpose by Ken and Beverley in the best of intentions activity. We will see that these themes are common to all groups at this initial stage.

USE OF LANGUAGE

Groupwork is just one of many different kinds of work setting in which group leaders find themselves. Few people are employed solely as groupworkers, so the group setting is not necessarily a familiar one, and certainly has to be seen in the context of all the other activities which workers undertake. For example, a medical social worker might be making an opening statement of purpose to a new group only minutes after attendance at a hospital ward-round, where a professional language code is all too often seen as a badge of authority and credibility. The transition to the different language code needed for the group setting is not easy.

In his first words (1), Ken hopes to demonstrate the agency's stake in the group. He wants to signal the importance of the links with the agency, especially if there is an intention that the group will develop into a ginger group, with a direct impact on the agency. It is evident that he also intends to show his commitment to the ideals of independence and self-confidence, but expresses this in a way which is likely to confuse, alienate or antagonize his audience. His good intentions come over as jargon because he has not paid attention to language and how best to express these ideas. Even words like 'ground rules' (7) are probably better stated simply as 'rules we can all agree on' or 'guidelines'.

Beverley's language is more direct but she, too, uses some words whose meaning is likely to be obscure to group members – for example, 'portfolios' (2) and 'oppressive structure' (6). It is impossible never to use an occasional word or phrase which will be seen by some or all group members as jargon. What is important is to recognize this by listening to yourself and watching people's responses; when you hear yourself using this kind of term, point to what you have done and use it as an opportunity for everyone to learn from the experience. The learning is not particularly about what the word means, but more about the acceptability of making mistakes and learning from them. You are able to model a process whereby you check out whether people are understanding, and you demonstrate the confidence to apologize if necessary.

WORDS AND ACTIONS AS ONE

Using appropriate language is not simply a question of avoiding jargon. There must also be a congruency between the words and the actions; in other words, the various messages which are being conveyed should be consistent. Although Ken and Beverley use the language of participation, they employ the techniques of a steamroller. Ken 'doesn't want to get heavy about things' (7), then does exactly that. He confirms with himself that 'these seem reasonable things to stick to', but fails to check them out with the group, and therefore fails to put his earlier commitment to 'becoming self-determining' (1) into practice. His language and his behaviour are not compatible, and its effect on group members is very unsettling.

Attempts to ensure that the language is clear and accessible can feel patronizing. Making an assumption that group members have not understood a particular word or concept can be as damaging as an assumption that they do. Avoiding being patronizing on the one extreme and high-handed on the other is not easy. It seems to be a matter of authenticity. Rather like taste, or whether colours 'go' together, authenticity is an elusive almost aesthetic quality – 'we know it when we see it!' Beverley's 'Well done!' (4) is well intentioned, but does it convey authenticity or condescension?

MUTUAL EXPECTATIONS

The opening statement of purpose is an attempt to answer the kinds of question which the groupworkers anticipate the members are asking themselves. One such question concerns the workers' stake in the group: 'why are they interested in running this group?' The members' interest in the group is usually self-evident, the workers' less so.

The offer of groupwork to individuals (Chapter 5) has already provided an opportunity to discuss your interest in the group on a private basis, and the opening statement of purpose allows this to move to a public level. Beverley tackles this head-on in her first pronouncement (2). She is open about other agendas (their involvement in the training programme), and expresses the view that these are valuable because they serve to increase the workers' stake in the group. However, this is a very secondary consideration for group members, who could find it confusing to be exposed to this detailed information so early in the session. They might also feel a pressure for the group to do well, because of the repercussions for the groupworkers if it does not.

Your stake in the group includes your expectation of the group's success. Communicating your confidence that the group can work, and that it is worth investing time and energy, is part of the animation which group members expect from leaders. Indeed, it is one of the functions of leadership to provide this kind of vim and buzz. However, your drive towards a positive approach has to be balanced against two other factors.

- Your relish for the group might be misinterpreted as insensitivity towards its subject matter (bulimia; childlessness; severe and enduring mental health problems, etc.). It is important to distinguish between your hopes for a positive outcome for the group and your awareness of the potential painfulness of the path ahead.

- Your expectations for the group must be realistic. People whose situations have been stuck for many years might sustain only tiny changes, and it is important that they experience these as small successes, not large failures.

Achieving a balance between the enthusiastic cheerleader on the one extreme and the dour sceptic on the other is not easy. The leadership in the best of intentions example veers between the two, with upbeat high hopes in the early part, and a rapid about-turn with Beverley's feet-on-the-ground dose of reality later (6). Groupworkers should aim for balanced, rather than mixed, messages.

WORKING WITH DIFFERENCE

Groups expose and highlight differences. After all, this is one of the reasons for using groupwork and why it can be such a powerful method. There are many dimensions of difference in groups (Chapter 3); at this stage, in the opening statement of purpose, the most potent is the one between group members and group leaders.

In most cases the groupworkers know every individual member of the group, whereas the members frequently know no-one but the workers. The groupworkers might be privy to intimate details about individual members, which can encourage group members to fantasize that the leaders know more about other members than is the case. All in all, the workers are in a powerful position, often made the more so by the members' fantasies.

The workers attend the group for different reasons than the members (in most cases, the groupworkers are not sex offenders, not carers, not alcohol or substance abusers, not suffering dementia, etc.) This 'apartness' is a factor which everyone must face, but the manner and timing are not straightforward. It is evident that Beverley feels her difference from the members acutely, and her anxiety to confront it leads her to raise the matter very early in the opening statement (4) and in a manner which tries to minimize it. Her reluctance to accept leadership responsibilities is an attempt to minimize the worker–member differences, but her discomfort is evident (6). She returns to this theme in an implicit way when she seeks to reassure the group that she and Ken 'are going to do it [an activity], too' (8). This discomfort is common in groups but often unacknowledged. It is related to power differentials; in this case, the group members' direct experience of the group's focus (for instance, eating disorders) provides them with a knowledge and a credibility which the leaders lack. The leaders know that a group member's claim that 'you don't really know what it's like' is powerfully true. This credibility gap is potentially strong and deep, but often one which groupworkers are not prepared to face squarely, and the abdication of leadership is an attempt to 'trade', with the language of equality as a smokescreen for these differences.

There are also differences *between* co-workers. There may be differences in attribute (gender, ethnicity, age, etc.), as well as in individual style and personality and, of course, their perceived powerfulness. Group members observe these differences and the way in which the group leadership handles them. The choice of personal pronoun is an early indication of how each co-worker views their position, *vis-à-vis* the group and the other co-worker. The transcript of the opening statement of purpose in the Best of Intentions example allows us to indulge in some textual analysis; Ken and Beverley each use the personal pronoun ('I' or 'we') 17 times, but the proportion of singular to plural forms is very significant:

	I		**We**	
Ken:	14	Beverley:	16
Beverley:	1	Ken:	3

So Ken's use of 'I' ('when I first had the idea ...') stands in sharp contrast to Beverley's 'we' ('we think you will get an even better service ...') Do you have any hypothesis about why this might be?

When is it right to use 'I' and when 'we'? Reread the best of intentions transcript and consider each of the 34 times the personal pronoun is used, deciding when you would you keep it as it stands and when you would change it. How do you make your decision as to which is appropriate?

A similar textual analysis can be employed to discover how group leaders move between 'you', the group members, and 'we', members and workers together.

HANDLING YOUR OWN FEELINGS

A failure by groupworkers to recognize or deal with their own feelings can obstruct the group's progress. In the example, Ken and Beverley fail to observe the most important aspect – a welcome. Even if they have already welcomed people as they came into the group, a collective and public welcome at the beginning of the opening statement is crucial. The *tone* of the opening statement is likely to have a greater impact than the specific content, and the tone must be welcoming. In the Groupwork Project, learners participated in videoing a rehearsal of opening statements of purpose and were regularly surprised at the details which they had missed 'live', but which they noticed when watching the video subsequently.

Both Ken and Beverley seem anxious about their authority and credibility with the group, as indicated by the tendency to use jargon and the efforts to deal with their own differences from group members. They have not resolved their ambivalence about the notion of leadership, which shows itself as an unhelpful mixture of heavy-handedness and abandonment. The mistakes which the co-workers make in this opening statement of purpose suggest that they have not considered the issues and themes which lie behind their statements, and have not tuned in to their feelings about the group and their own position in leading it. Sadly, this opening statement of purpose is not a parody, but a real illustration of what can happen if co-workers do not consider the core themes carefully.

Group agreement about processes

If we liken the first session of a group to a card game, the opening statement of purpose has been an opportunity for the groupworkers to show their hand. They have also begun to demonstrate what kind of card game they hope it will be; not a game of poker in which cards are held firmly and competitively against chests, but one which encourages everybody to show their hand as they feel able. The next step is to find ways for group members to begin to show *their* cards, in terms of their hopes and fears for the group. There are various ways of doing this and the action techniques in Chapter 7 provide many ideas for the first step of introducing group members to each other. Craig (1988: 52) makes literal use of the card game metaphor, asking each person to write their answers to the question 'what am I doing here?' onto cards, dealing these out and asking people to trade cards in order to collect their three favourite ones.

The process of working towards an agreement about the purposes of the group and how it will go about achieving these varies from group to group. Even so, there are key components which it is the groupworkers' responsibility to introduce. Creating space for the group to work on an issue is significantly different from giving the group instruction; though the latter may occasionally be appropriate with some kinds of group, it is the former which is most likely to help people understand what it is to become a group.

Groupworkers, therefore, have an important role in signposting key topics for the group's attention.

GROUP PROTOCOL AND GROUND RULES

The way the group is going to conduct itself is key to its success, yet it is unlikely that group members will spontaneously focus on this issue (how many teams of professional workers take time out to consider the way the team conducts itself?). This means that signposting by the groupworkers is essential. Each individual brings their own behaviour code to the group, a 'protocol' learned from their previous family and social experiences. In some groups individual protocols will be consistent (though that does not mean they are necessarily effective for groupwork), in others there will be considerable individual differences. The group aims to develop a protocol which promotes groupwork and it is a dilemma for groupworkers to decide how much to use their own experience and expertise and how much to stand aside for the group members to find their own way.

Rules are evident in other kinds of group. For example, there is a unique set of values and modes of behaviour in youth gangs, and the many rules and regulations in the gang 'have a protection function that maintains the integrity of the gang' (Lee, Lo and Wong 1996: 293). However, the group offers a unique opportunity for members to develop their own explicit protocol, agreed and negotiated and capable of being changed, an active process which is likely to be a contrast to the passive, implicit 'absorption' of family and social conventions. The group protocol is created specific to the purposes of the group and is an early experience of the group taking positive control of its own development. Having signposted the need to agree group ground rules, there are many methods you can suggest to achieve this (Chapter 7).

The value of ground rules is well documented. 'These groundrules served their purpose time and again, in times of conflict and disagreement, in times of distress, at times when an individual woman might feel that she didn't have the right to take up group time, or that she might be going to shock others with what she needed to say' (Wintram *et al.* 1994: 128). Ground rules help the group to differentiate between group membership and ordinary friendship. 'M', a member of a women's group, writes:

> I have a lot of friends outside of this group but it's really strange that these women that I have now formed a great friendship with I value the most, maybe it's because we have groundrules – something that you just assume would apply with other friends – but it's all too often the case that friends let you down. Not these women, I really trust them. (Wintram *et al.* 1994: 134)

If a ground rule is broken at some later group session, the protocol sanctions group members and workers to challenge the behaviour, by giving everybody a reference point. This includes the individual who is not following the code.

THE GROUP'S KNOWLEDGE: CONFIDENTIALITY

It is the strange mix of public and private which makes a group such a powerful vehicle of change and support. The meeting of public and private also highlights the issue of what happens, or should happen, to the group's 'knowledge'. It is a question which might be uppermost in many individuals' minds, and there is likely to be relief when it is signposted by the groupworkers. Confidentiality is the term used to refer to how the group's knowledge should be handled, but it is important not to assume that everybody has the same understanding of what it means. Confidentiality is not just about how information should be protected, but how it should be accessed and who has the power, or should have the power, to decide what is available to whom.

In groupwork there are several dimensions of confidence to consider.

1 Information about individual members relating to their lives outside the group

The group leaders are likely to have information relating to individuals' situations, perhaps gathered during the offer of service, or from knowledge of the individual as a service user. This information helps the workers to ensure that the group is meeting the needs of the members, but they must treat their knowledge with care. Ken makes reference to Jaswinder's 'loss' (3), but fails to be more specific. He enlists this as an example in order to strengthen his case, but it is likely to have come as quite a surprise to Jaswinder to hear his name at this early stage in the group. Ken's tangential approach leaves it to the group to fantasize what the loss might be and to worry about how the group leadership might use personal information about them.

Of course, individuals' situations are likely to be introduced to the group as a whole, but how much is made public, when it is unveiled, and who decides to make it the group's business is crucial.

2 Information about the processes and content of group sessions

In addition to the privacy of individuals' lives outside the group, there is the question of how information about the group's own processes are safeguarded. If members of the group are to take the risks which are necessary to reveal their thoughts and feelings, they need to have confidence that this knowledge will be respected. Individual members might use very different codes to decide how they treat information about the group; creating mutual understanding and agreement about this as a useful process in itself.

3 Information about other groups

Group members observe the leaders closely to see how they handle information. The leaders plough a furrow for members to follow; consciously or otherwise, the groupworkers provide a model. Moreover, group members will judge how safe they feel it is to let their defences down in this group by the way the workers create a sense of confidence. Information relating to other groups can be illuminating to the present group, but it will sensitize group members to the fact that a leader who talks to them about what happened in a previous group will just as easily talk to a future group about what is happening to this current one. That can have an inhibiting effect. Ken wants to enlist the support of past groups to give weight to his assertion that the present group will enjoy using video (5). 'We've used it with other groups we've run and they've all enjoyed it'. How might group members respond to this?

The question of how information will be handled inside and outside the group must be addressed early on. In most cases group members can rightly expect a policy of complete confidence, but there are limits to this. For example, respecting complete confidentiality could sometimes result in colluding with offending (Cowburn 1990: 162). Confidentiality is especially important, and difficult, when the group members have 'significant others' who are very powerful, such as children in a group from which parents are excluded. Pennells (1995: 250) describes the difficulties which some families have in accepting that what children say in a bereavement group will be confidential, though others understand the reasoning that the children are likely to be more open and honest. In all circumstances, group members and people close to them need to know where these boundaries lie.

Finally, decisions should be taken about whether the group's knowledge will be committed to memory or to paper. Written information has considerable advantages, not least the accuracy and clarity which memory can fail to deliver, but who holds the pen and who has access to the documentation should be part of the group's negotiations with itself and, if it is subject to any non-negotiable rules as described later, these should be explained at the initial offer of groupwork.

Group agreement about outcomes

In the first and early sessions, as the group is forming, the tension between process and outcome is immediately evident. On the one hand it is important to negotiate agreement around the processes of becoming a group and *how* the group will conduct itself; on the other is the need to negotiate *what* the group wants to achieve. Although it is necessary for the group to develop common process goals concerning the way the group will go about its business (in terms of ground rules, confidentiality and the like), it is important to be mindful that people can be members of the same group yet hold different outcome goals. In other words, group members might have very diverse aspirations. So, whereas all groups strive to agree a common group process, some work towards collective goals and others towards individual ones (see Lang 1985 for discussion of individual-, collective-, shared- and mixed-goals groups.) It is important for the groupworkers not to set goals *for* the group or its members, a process described by Mullender and Ward (1989: 9) as 'unfettered' goal setting. To use an artistic metaphor, the groupworkers usually provide the materials and might even show some illustrative sketches to help get started, but it is the group which paints the picture. Some will be keen to finish with a pretty picture and others will derive their enjoyment from the act of painting.

An example of an agreement around individual goals is to be found in a group for adolescent female sexual abuse victims (Craig 1990: 112). The girls had individual agreements which varied in intensity and focus. For example, some identified areas around their feelings towards perpetrators, others to work on preparation for giving evidence in court, and one girl with very low esteem to pay more attention to herself and to give herself treats. In order to help each member to achieve her own individual goal, the group agreed three rules about how it would conduct itself: that material discussed in the group was not for discussion outside the group; that the girls must not harm themselves or each other during the group; and that there would be no smoking during the group.

Not all groups develop explicit goals to frame the agreement. However, the more explicit the goals, the easier it is for the group to evaluate its success (see Chapter 12).

TELLING YOUR STORY

The process of helping individuals to develop their personal goals begins by enabling them to tell their story. Sometimes this can be as immediate as a round early in the first session, at other times a story can be so painful that even by the end of the group it is not fully told. In their desire to help people to 'contract in' to the group, the groupworkers should not underestimate the magnitude of this task for some individuals. Perhaps the story has not been told in this way to anybody before; perhaps it has not been known fully to the storytellers themselves. The group might be composed of strangers and trust will take time to grow. Feelings and subjects which social and family protocols have decreed are taboo might be closely involved in the story (Chapter 3) and it is still not clear what is 'allowed' in this group. It is a long stride from feeling marginalized in society to being the centre of attention in a group.

For all these reasons, then, it is crucial that the groupworker considers the best ways to encourage the individuals in the group to begin to tell their stories in ways which others can hear, to allow escape routes and to enable the whole group to accept that individuals within the group will probably need to move at different speeds. In the next chapter we present a variety of 'action techniques' which can be used at any juncture in the group, not least at those times when you want to help people to tell their own story. As you will see in Chapter 7, the telling does not have to be verbal. Out of these stories will emerge a better understanding of what kind of ending each person would like to see for themselves and how the group can help them to write that ending.

Non-negotiable elements

In this chapter we have been using the term 'agreement' to emphasize a process of negotiation in groupwork. As with any form of practice (individual, family, group or community) there are some elements which cannot be open to negotiation and groupwork methods must be able to accommodate this. Jones *et al.* (1991) describe two kinds of non-negotiable category in a group for women offenders. The first is determined by the co-workers, with a requirement that members commit to an initial series of five sessions (absence from the first session or any two others means the member must leave this group and await the next programme). The second comes from the court at the time of sentence, if a requirement of attendance has been agreed by the offender, and attendance on this basis involves ten sessions.

Groups can work well with non-negotiable elements, even when some members are subject to them and others not as described above, but only if this is made explicit and the underpinning reasoning is explained. The group members need to understand and agree the reasoning which lies behind the non-negotiable requirements.

There may be some aspects of the group which have become implicitly non-negotiable, for example the group's name. In Chapter 3 we saw how empowering it can be for the group to consider what to name itself; groupworkers may not have considered the name of the group as either negotiable or non-negotiable, but opening it up for discussion is one way of creating a greater sense of ownership of the group.

The alpha session

In contrast to those groups where attendance at the first few sessions is non-negotiable, in some groups the first session is one where individuals are finding out whether they actually want to become a group. Rather than the first session, it is more accurate to describe this as the 'alpha', or 'zero' session (Matzat 1993: 40). For example, a group for adolescent female sexual abuse victims met once a week for four weeks before the girls had to make a decision about whether they wished to continue; one of the nine girls in one group decided she could not make a commitment to the group beyond this orientation phase, so continued involvement is certainly not taken for granted (Craig 1990: 111). In most cases, this joining phase of any new group should allow time for members to decide whether they want to continue, unless there is an element of compulsion which has been explained at the offer stage (Chapter 5).

Groupworkers need to be flexible, therefore, about the number of alpha sessions which might be necessary. Only two young women turned up for the first session of a group for white women with black children, but the next week four came, though the following session the number dropped back to three; only by the fourth session, when five of the nine members came, did they feel they had sufficient numbers to begin the programme of work (Rhule 1988: 44).

This kind of flexibility is evident in a group for mothers of children who have been sexually abused:

> It was intended from the very beginning [of the group] that the first six weeks or so would be primarily focused on women introducing themselves to each other and getting experience of a group setting. It was anticipated that there might be a certain amount of coming and going during that period. Once it was over, the groups became closed as they began to address the question of women telling their own stories about what had happened in their family. (Dobbin and Evans 1994: 121)

Portfolio extract

The Opening Statement of Purpose was delivered on a large sheet of flip-chart paper. The title of the group 'Girls just wanna have fun!' was surrounded by musical notes which we thought was rather clever (later in the group the girls told us that it wasn't!) We reiterated the few rules and detailed possible future activities whilst making it clear that we were open to suggestions and alteration to the programme.

Following the opening statement I introduced some ideas that we intended to run throughout the group. These included individual folders which they could decorate and use to collect material, photos, info; a paper banner which they could decorate or graffiti; photos to be taken of individuals and group as and when they felt like it, and evaluation sheets. We had also intended to introduce the video at this point; however, this had fallen through (because of technical problems).

We then conducted a warm-up game which with hindsight, was ill-chosen because it required them to offer opinions and this they clearly felt unable to do so soon into the group.

Following this we moved into the activity which was jewellery making.

At the end of the session we asked the girls if they had any ideas to add for sessions and these were added to the flipchart. We then encouraged them to be photographed in their new jewellery and complete the evaluation sheets.

Notes on power and oppression

It now occurs to me that the whole concept and ethos of the group could be described as oppressive! As workers we had agreed to 'sell' the group as a 'fun' thing; however, we had underlying aims. Whitaker (1985: 92) describes this perfectly: 'Deception occurs when the conductor misrepresents to the potential member the nature of the group in the hope that once the person is in the group he [sic] will be able to make use of it as the conductor hopes. A not infrequent form of deception is that in which the group is represented as a social club or an activity programme while the conductor privately intends that it should have a therapeutic character.'

In our defence I would say that we had nothing more terrible in mind than self-esteem raising; however, perhaps we should have made that explicit to the girls.

JA (1998)

CHAPTER SEVEN

Action Techniques in Groups

About 'Kaleidoscope'

This activity prompts you to consider the broad range of activities which can be used for many different purposes in groupwork. Kaleidoscope presents a multitude of action techniques, organized into six categories, with the intention of helping to extend your responses to the opportunities and dilemmas which you face when groupworking.

Purpose

This chapter reviews the enormous range of methods which can be used to plan and run with a group session. It aims to help dispel the notion of the 'talking circle' as the norm for groups, introducing you to a wide repertoire of techniques. This breadth is an essential aspect of creative groupwork.

Method

- Consider a 'sticky moment' from a group or meeting in which you have participated recently. Review what made the situation sticky.

- Look through the kaleidoscope. Once you are familiar with the six categories and some of the action techniques named in each category, return to your sticky moment.

- Consider how you might use one action technique from each of the categories in turn in order to work with the sticky moment.

Variations

It is always important to consider the 'how' for each activity; in other words, what kind of 'shape' best fits the action technique you are using? Consider the implications of the different shapes for the particular group or meeting.

Kaleidoscope

1 Spoken word

Discussion (structured or open) Role-play •
Rehearsal • Drama
Simulation • *Storytelling* • Guided fantasy •
Meditation • Reminiscence • *Oral history* •
Life scripts • *Decision making*

6 Movement

Play • *Mime* • Games • *Dance* • Crafts •
Relaxation exercises • Sculpting •
Goldfish bowl • Activities (e.g. Fruit
Salad, Group Tangle) • *Tea/Coffee
breaks* • Trips • *Recreational outings* •
Visits •
Outdoor pursuits

2 Written word

Minutes • *Logs* • Reports • *Summaries* • Let-
ters • *Questionnaires* • Quizzes • *Press cuttings*
• Statistics • *Articles* • Handouts • *Novels* •
Stories • *Diaries* • Homework • *e-mails* •
Critical incident analysis • *Task analysis* •
Contracts • *Evaluation sheets* •
Recorded observations • *Official
documents* • Leaflets

5 Props

all those articles brought in to support an activity, e.g:
Money • *Food* • Smells • *Clothes* •
Clay • *Tokens (conch)* • String •
Wool • Puppets • *Dolls* • Masks •
Projects • Objects • *Furniture* • Music

3 Graphic

Flipcharting • *Posters* • Mapping •
Quick-thinks • Drawing • *Cards* •
Cartoons • *Sketches* • Artwork • *Chalk* •
Painting • *Photographs* • Charts •
Calendars • Plans • *Family tree* •
Diagrams • *Montages* • Collages •
Metaphors • *Dreams* •
Guided imagery

4 Hardware

Audio • *Video* • CD-TV • *Tape Slides* •
Video-conferencing • *Film* •
Photography • OHP • *Computer* • Internet •
One-way screens

'Shape'

individually

in pairs

in trios

in small groups

full group

or any combination of these

hot-seating

goldfish bowl

Notes for the groupworker

Planning a session

> The purpose of a good programme is to give the groupworker something from which they are able to divert. (Ross and Thorpe 1988: 137)

As we discovered in Chapter 4, groups vary in their format from those which are relatively loose to those which are tightly structured (Line 11 of the continuum, see page 89). Although the notion of programming will differ accordingly, some kind of planning is essential. Even in groups where the direction is deliberately uncharted and groupworkers take a distinctly back seat, a consideration of the variety of ways members can spend their time together in the group is always beneficial. The significance of programming is not necessarily to know exactly what you are going to do, but to know what you have omitted to do if the group moves off track! In almost all cases, groups gain from a conscious plan, even if it is only something to reject in favour of its opposite.

Clearly, it is important to have a programme which can be flexible. There are so many variables in groupwork that it can be predicted with confidence that something will not go according to plan. The numbers arriving may be more or less than anticipated (so an exercise relying on groups of four will have to accommodate threes or fives); the mood of the group members may be more upbeat or more subdued than expected; the room you hoped to use is locked; there is distracting noise from an adjoining room; one of the group members arrives drunk; your co-worker is ill. The list of potential changes of plan is endless.

Even if the programme is one you have run before, the chemistry of the new participants is such that the tempo and mood of the group can feel very different. The groupworkers' plans for the speed at which members might feel able to disclose, for example, is exceptionally difficult to judge in advance of the group sessions themselves. For example, the participants in a group for people bereaved by suicide wanted to move much more quickly towards sharing their experiences and feelings about the suicide than the co-workers had planned for in their ten-session programme (O'Connor 1992: 80). At other times, the converse is true and groupworkers can feel frustrated by the reluctance of members' progress.

Just as one individual session can be carefully scripted or loosely conceived, so the entire groupwork programme falls along this same continuum. To what extent does each session fit into an overall plan for all the group's sessions? Open groups may resemble a series of single sessions rather than a coherent programme, especially if membership varies considerably, such as in a drop-in group (Henry 1988). In contrast, Peake and Otway (1990) use the term 'curriculum' to describe the programme for their group for girls who had been sexually abused – a programme of 35 sessions, with detailed, planned content for each one. 'Previous experience with groups has shown that where the topic is painful and the workers are unclear exactly what they are going to do with the children, this only leads to chaos. The group members would sense the uncertainty and respond with diversion and ambivalence' (Peake and Otway 1990: 128–9).

'Patterning' and sessional design

Most groups develop patterns which give a recognizable shape to each session, a 'wave' flowing from order to relative chaos and back to order again (Manor and Dumbleton 1993). In very structured groups the pattern is likely to be in place from the first session, in looser groups the pattern may evolve over a number of sessions. Developing a sessional pattern gives a group a sense of security, which is important not just for the completion of group tasks but also for the emotional wellbeing of the group. It is rather like making a meal – if the kitchen is familiar, you are able to cut corners and save time because you know where everything is and how it works, and the same is true of groupwork. Even for groups where it is more important to 'be' than to 'do', a familiar environment is the most conducive.

CHECKING IN AND OUT

Part of the pattern of most group sessions includes a spot for everybody to 'check in'. This helps the group to reorientate itself and fill the gap between this and the previous session. There may have been specific actions which group members want to report back; perhaps there is news to share; maybe there is some 'baggage' from the previous session which needs to be unloaded before the group can continue its journey. For example, in a group for female victims of child sexual abuse each session began with a 'how we are' spot, in which each person would say something about how they were feeling at that point and pick up on anything from the previous session (Craig 1990: 113).

A similar process is useful at the end of each session to give members a chance to say a few things about how they have found it and to summarize the ground that has been covered and any agreements that have been made. Once this has become established as a regular pattern, group members will increasingly take ownership for the various items, reminding the groupworkers if they happen to overlook them.

'Patterning' and programme design

In addition to establishing patterns for individual sessions, it is important to consider the overall shape of the group (see Figure 7.1). Of course, there is no single pattern which all groups will follow. To take an example at one end of the time spectrum, a long-term (four-years) support group for people with chronic schizophrenia in the community had an initial six-month stage, 'Fighting for group survival', followed by another six-month stage, 'Developing a group identity', with a third stage lasting two-and-a-half years, 'Working through life's problems', and a final stage of 'Closure, separation and group disintegration' over the last six months (Cwikel and Oron 1991: 169–70). These stages were identified retrospectively, so in this case the group's shape could not have been safely predicted when it started.

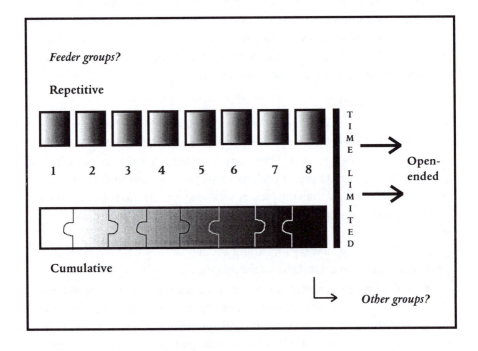

Figure 7.1 The overall pattern of the group

Towl (1990) describes the two distinct phases in his work with culture groups in prisons, in which the first part is set in the safe territory of 'the other' (for example, group members watched the film *Educating Rita* to discuss cultural influences on our values and beliefs), whilst the second part moved closer to home with exercises like 'Fathers and sons' in which group members draw on their own personal accounts in order to generate rules for such relationships and discuss them.

OFF-THE-SHELF PROGRAMMES

If a group has run well a number of times, it is not surprising that others want to learn about the formula in order to use it successfully with others. This formula might be adopted by the agency; indeed, in some probation services, there are service users who may be required to enter the agency's groupwork programme. Off-the-shelf packages, in which the pattern for the whole group programme is determined from the beginning, are increasingly common. The following 'kit' from a motoring offenders' group is typical (each number represents a separate session).

1 *Introduction*: rule setting; confidentiality; Highway Code – road use.

2 *Attitudes*: input from police; video quiz; discussion.

3 *Documentation needed for legal driving and responsible vehicle ownership*: fact sheet; input from police on road safety and police equipment.

4 *Personal offending analysis*: costs to self and others; victim perspective; trigger videos.

5 *Insurance, uninsured driving and driving whilst disqualified*: input from insurance assessor on why you need it; what it does and does not cover; how the costs are worked out; how to get it; consequences of uninsured driving for self and others.

6 *Alcohol and driving*: quiz; influences on driver ability; try out breathalyzer equipment.

7 *The role of the courts*: input from magistrate; discussion of what they take into account; sentencing exercise based on video and anonymous social inquiry reports; sentencing exercises and discussion.

8 *What to do after accidents, and course review*: where do we go from here; future plans; personal target setting; follow up Highway Code quiz; client feedback (written and in discussion for the less literate)

> on how they found the course; helpful/less helpful parts, likes and
> dislikes, comments, etc. (Hutchins 1991: 244–5)

In these circumstances, when somebody has done the creating for you, it can
feel difficult to be innovative yourself. However, action techniques can be
used creatively not just to plan a group from new, but also to customize an
off-the-shelf programme.

What is an action technique?

> The value of activities lies in the process of pursuing them together …
> (Heap 1985: 146)

The key to an understanding of an action technique is the sense of purpose.
All groups include activities of some kind (they do not have to be physically
active – quiet meditation is an activity) and most activities in a group will
have a purpose. However, some activities are done uniquely 'for themselves'
and without another purpose in mind – indeed, sometimes with *no* particular
purpose in mind ('watching television'). In contrast, an action technique is
deployed as a vehicle for other purposes as well. This is not to say that the activity at the heart of an action technique does not also have intrinsic value; indeed, it has its greatest impact when all the various purposes – extrinsic and
intrinsic – are in balance (see Figure 7.2).

The boundary between activity and action technique is blurred. When
does 'preparing food' in a group become not just an activity but an action
technique? A range of activities in a residential setting – bingo, community
singing, domino drives, knitting, etc. – might 'succeed or fail in fostering a
group spirit' (Mullender 1990: 290), but are not necessarily action techniques as we use the term here.

Tempo: selecting an action technique to meet the occasion

> When activities are developed primarily as means to keep people busy or
> happy, they have the anaesthetic effect of deterring individuals from
> taking the kind of action that produces significant changes in their lives.
> However, given the opportunity to participate in meaningful activities,
> the opposite is true. (Breton 1991: 41)

The challenge for the group is to discover what is 'meaningful'.

One of the groupworker's concerns is to help the group achieve a balance
between understimulation and overstimulation. The right pace for the group
is difficult to gauge, so it is important to seek feedback from group members
about how they have found the tempo, especially since your own feelings as

the group worker are not always the best measure. Apart from bringing a different style or change of tempo into the group, an action technique can provide a sense of 'distance' which, paradoxically, can often help group members get closer to difficult topics and to each other. Addressing a taboo issue head-on might result in embarrassed silence or defensiveness, whereas an action technique with a relevant theme can often provide the kind of horizon necessary to put the topic into perspective (Drower 1991: 122).

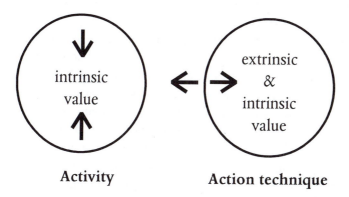

Activity   **Action technique**

Figure 7.2 Activities and action techniques

It is important to consider the focus of an action technique. Is it intended to help individuals in the group, or is it centred on the group as a whole? The action technique might centre around feelings, thoughts, problems, strengths, aspirations, etc. in the group. The change from one to the other, such as from a feelings-based action technique to a physically based one, is part of the variety of tempo we have been describing.

Groupworkers need to avoid employing an action technique just for the sake of it and must consider how the action technique chimes with the group's purposes at any one time (Phillips 1989; Vintner 1974). If it becomes a gimmick it is being misused as an entertainment, or perhaps a prop for groupworkers and members wanting to avoid other kinds of work. The distancing described earlier can prove too distant, so that the action technique becomes a shield against difficult feelings or taboos in the group. Reid (1988: 128) describes it thus: 'with a flick of the wrist the [group leaders] can do a "trust walk", have members fall backward and caught by the group, and do sentence completions like a pro'. Group members should not be left with a stronger memory of the worker's magical skill than a sense of the meaningfulness of the activity for themselves.

Group culture

One of the principal blocks to any new approach with an existing group or meeting is a sense of what is considered 'normal'. The assumptions which are made about groups in general and this group in particular produce a mindset which can take considerable confidence and skill to shift. Even the physical set-up of a group or meeting, its topography, can become fossilized, with each individual staking claim to the same territory at each session. Group culture is the best way to describe this constellation of assumptions, expectations and established patterns.

The members of any particular group are likely to join with a restricted idea about what happens in groups. It might be difficult to generalize from other experiences because we operate in a large number of groups which are not necessarily recognized as such. Sally does not necessarily see her family as 'a group', nor the work team, the choir, the neighbourhood committee, the running club. She may hold a stereotypical view of groups as being 'touchy-feely' or 'discussions', quite separate from anything she experiences in her everyday life. These views of what groups are like can be held so strongly that they become an obstacle to a person joining.

The various action techniques outlined in the kaleidoscope reveal the considerable choice available, so it is important to give proper consideration to the range of different action techniques for the following reasons.

- *Achieving the group's purposes*: the first method you think of may not be the most appropriate to achieve the group's purposes at any one time. A careful consideration of alternatives is likely to ensure that an action technique is being used to suit the specific purpose and not out of habit.

- *The interest of group members*: do not underestimate the element of 'performance' in leading a group – warming it up, encouraging involvement, maintaining attention and interest. If you rely heavily on one mode or style (constant discussion, interminable video-watching, a succession of flipchart brainstorms) your audience will tire and the group will become increasingly ineffective. The benefits of kinetic activity – movement of some kind – are well proven; even standing up and changing seats in the group can break inertia. The tempo usually needs to change in order to sustain concentration and interest.

- *Your development as a groupworker*: although the primary purpose in leading the group is to benefit its members, the group is also helping you to develop your skills as a groupworker. In this sense, each group is a rehearsal for the next. The group should stretch you so that your skills are developed in new directions; if you find yourself feeling that you could run the group in your sleep this is the time to take a serious review of your group leadership – or, perhaps, to move on.

We have been focusing on the dangers of repetition and of over-reliance on one particular kind of action technique. There is also a risk of using too many different kinds of action technique in too rapid succession. Particularly in the early stages, group members may have a limited view of what groups are capable of, so they need a careful introduction to different activities, especially ones which seem to involve an element of risk (for instance, through personal disclosure). There may be suspicion that group leaders are going to be 'tricksy' and an unwillingness to be led down a particular path without a transparent explanation as to where it leads. For all these reasons, it pays for groupworkers to be clear about why they are using a particular action technique, to have considered its appropriateness with these particular group members at this particular time, and to have rehearsed the rationale for its use.

Categories of action technique

The six categories of action technique in the kaleidoscope provide one way of grouping the various possibilities. The categories, defined by 'kind', are not watertight and action techniques can often be used in combinations which cross categories. However, we hope it will prove a useful framework for groupworkers, novice or seasoned.

We will review each of the categories, looking at selected examples within each category. As we have already emphasized, the appropriateness of a particular technique lies in its relationship to the purposes of the group at that time and in the context of what other action techniques have been used and are intended.

1: SPOKEN WORD

Many of the action techniques in other categories involve 'talk', so what is different about the action techniques specific to this one? Basically, these activities are centred around the spoken word as the exclusive or primary medium. Although the techniques in this category are very useful, there can be an unthinking reliance on spoken word activities (especially discussion) without consideration for the way they can disadvantage people who are less than articulate or have hearing impairments. Good talking relies on good listening.

Discussion

One caricature of groupwork is 'talk therapy'. It is one of the dominant mental models of groupwork; people sitting in a circle, talking. Over-reliance on discussion discriminates against less articulate, less confident members in just the same way that an all-writing group would disadvantage less literate members. In a mixed-gender group, discussion is often dominated by the men. 'Discussion', then, may need to be structured or guided (in conjunction with other kinds of action technique) in order for it to be used in an anti-oppressive manner. For example, members of an anger management group in a prison 'talk through their partner's story to the rest of the reconvened group', and everybody is then invited to comment on the particular anger incident (Towl and Dexter 1994: 258). This is an example of talking which generates good listening.

The 'group dialogue' method relies on talk, but has no fixed agenda or topic of conversation. The method focuses on shared meanings in an attempt to develop a therapeutic community in the most unpromising of settings – a prison (Garrett 1995: 54).

Role play, simulation and drama

Groups provide a valuable forum for people to rehearse their life problems. The rehearsal can be at a general 'talking it through' level or as a more formalized practice, in which the situation is recreated to enable participants to replay it, with different inputs and outcomes.

The value and extensiveness of role play, in which individuals take on certain parts and act them out, is evident from the groupwork literature. For example, in a large-scale survey of groups for adults with learning difficulties in Ireland, Schonfeld and Morrissey (1992: 46) found that role play and drama were the most commonly used aids. Role play was combined with video in a women's group to review and discuss the tapes the group members made of themselves role playing problematic situations (Breton 1991: 35). Dramatic techniques can be put to powerful effect, be it a quick vignette to rehearse a difficult incident or a profound psychodrama to release deep feelings (Williams 1991).

We tend to assume that role play is used to rehearse situations which have gone wrong, but it can also be used to replay situations which have worked well, as reinforcement and learning for the whole group; for example, when an offender has been successful in managing his violent feelings (Canton *et al.* 1992: 48).

The difficulty of introducing role play to people who are unfamiliar with it should not be under-estimated. The idea of role play can be fearful and might be quite outside the previous experience of group members. Conversely, others may have experienced role play used badly and without safeguards. The response of a group to the request for a volunteer role player can, itself, be used to look at group processes and to promote growth. What goes on in people's minds when the group is asked for a volunteer to role play? Craig (1988: 53) describes how two chairs were used to help bring out a role play volunteer's dialogue with himself before deciding to volunteer ('you should volunteer' when sitting on one chair, 'you shouldn't volunteer' when sitting on the other). This was instructive to those who had not volunteered (that their fears were shared by the volunteer, too) and had a very positive impact on the use of role play in later sessions of the group. It relates well to the notion of risk-taking, which can often be a theme in groups, and it is a good example of how one action technique, in this case role play, may need to be approached carefully by the use of others.

Finally, it is important to create opportunities for people to generalize from role play into 'real' play. In order to make sure that role play and drama are not just time-fillers, links should be made between how changes in behaviour or attitudes experienced in the context of the role play in the group might transfer to similar situations outside the group.

Decision making

Decision making is a very structured form of discussion, in which group members' powers of reasoning are developed. For example, the prisoners in a Families and Imprisonment group participated in an action technique called 'Not in front of the children', described as 'an action maze in which inmates have to decide how to handle difficult issues relating to the imprisonment of a parent and subsequent dealing with children' (Ashe 1991: 282). The increased ability to reason can be experienced as very empowering by individuals who have habitually resorted to other methods of making decisions. Gangs, for instance, are an especially tight-knit kind of group and notoriously closed to outsiders. Nevertheless, even in these inauspicious settings, Lee *et al.* (1996) have described a process of encouraging rational decision making in ways which have lessened the criminal tendency of youth gangs in Hong Kong.

Guided fantasy

If 'spoken words' had a physical weight we would expect that a well-functioning group would have a fairly even distribution. There are times, however, when a monologue from the group leader can be very effective and appropriate. A powerful example is the guided fantasy, in which group members are encouraged to imagine themselves into a situation by following the group leader's story. To reinforce the power of the words, group members are usually asked to close their eyes, so that there is no distraction. For example, a Keeping Your Head group for offenders explored the process of 'losing it', becoming out of control. Members were invited to 'imagine an escalator moving you quickly upwards. The danger signals become obvious to those around you. Your chances of being sidetracked in a sensible direction decrease, but you are not beyond control at this stage' (Mackintosh 1991: 269). The guided fantasy provides a strong verbal and visual image, strengthened by the fact that it returns to the listener when he or she is in an actual situation where they are beginning to 'lose it'.

2: WRITTEN WORD

The spoken word is often fast, transitory, spontaneous, subject to misinterpretation and – unless linked to a strong visual image – difficult to recall precisely. These constitute both its strengths and weaknesses. When there is a need to slow the pace, to be more exact and definitive, to capture thoughts, feelings and decisions on record, it is appropriate to consider action techniques centred on the written word. The written word also affords good opportunities for 'homework', in which the work in the group is taken out of the group into the substance of the group members' lives.

Just as the spoken word benefits articulate people, so the written word can advantage literate people. The spoken word can discriminate against those with hearing impairments, and the written word those with visual impairments. All of these factors need to be taken into consideration when deciding the balance of action techniques in any particular group.

Questionnaires / evaluation sheets

When individuals complete questionnaires on their own, it is a rare opportunity for privacy within the group, and allows access to opinions and expressions which are unaffected by the groundswell of the group; in other words, it can be a useful way of giving an equal voice to all members rather than listening to the loudest. A questionnaire or written evaluation also allows people time for reflection as they complete it at their own pace, and it captures information which can be digested later in everybody's own good time. The time taken to complete a questionnaire in a group is a rare occasion for 'soft silence' – silence not experienced as stressful.

Diaries

The precision and reflection of the self-generated written word is particularly evident in the use of diaries. Diaries are likely to be completed outside the group, generating material which can be used in the group itself, and making links between what is happening in the group member's life outside the group and what is occurring in the group. Robertson (1990: 252) describes how parents who were experiencing nights with sleepless children were asked to keep a diary in order to examine the weekly pattern of sleeplessness. This helped the parents to understand what factors might be influencing the sleeplessness, and helped to build a more precise picture of the size and nature of the problem. It is interesting that some parents were able to make good use of the diaries, but others were incomplete, largely due to the degree of chaos in their family, sometimes drug or alcohol related. The sleep diaries were also used in follow-up individual work. Diaries stay behind long after the group itself has finished.

Letters

Letters have changed the course of history (the alleged Zinoviev letter toppled the first Labour government), and most individuals can remember a letter or two which has changed the course of their own personal histories.

Writing a letter is an action technique that most people can instantly relate to because it is a part of everyday life. It is an opportunity for an uninterrupted statement to another person, with the decision whether to share the final statement remaining in the hands of the author (unlike spoken words, which cannot be swallowed back). The letter can be an exceptionally private affair to release feelings, or a powerful public statement intended to influence larger events. An example of the former is a group for people bereaved through suicide where each member wrote a letter to the person who had committed suicide and read it out loud to the other group members (O'Connor 1992: 80). An example of the latter is where the withdrawal of funding from two long-term groups galvanized the members into writing a communal letter 'to the case managers' to save the group from ending (Gobat 1994: 217).

Letters can be especially effective action techniques at the ending of a group (Chapter 13). Writing a letter to the group members and workers is one way of helping the individual to assess how far they have come with the aid of the group, and formally saying 'goodbye' and perhaps 'thank you' to people who have helped (Davidsen-Nielsen and Leick 1989: 196–8).

Group agreements

As we saw in Chapter 6, an agreement or contract is an important way of formalizing the aims, purposes and codes of conduct of the group and its individual members. A number of different action techniques might be deployed in order to achieve the agreement, but the final product is a significant marker for the group. Making reference to the group agreement (perhaps to exercise a sanction or remind the group of its purpose) is the easier because it is in a written format; it can be stuck to the wall and everybody can have their personal copy.

Critical incident analysis

Apart from a greater understanding of how and why critical incidents arise, this action technique enables group members to appreciate the effects of their actions on other people, to recognize and control physical symptoms associated with feelings such as anger and to practise self-statements which help them to avoid escalating situations.

Henchman and Walton (1993) describe their use of a pro-forma with a group of probationers to help them and the group as a whole to understand how a particular incident (usually the offence) occurred. The pro-forma consists of four columns, as shown in Figure 7.3. The juxtaposition of the thoughts, actions and feelings on the page encourages the writer to consider how the three are linked and the extent to which they are consonant with each other. Using the written work rather than the spoken enables the groupworkers to frame the members' responses more precisely, and lets the writer return to the action technique later for further reflection.

Thoughts	Actions	Feelings	Time

Figure 7.3 Analyzing critical incidents

Public documents, leaflets, reports

We are told we live in the 'age of information' and, certainly, we are beset by public documentation of all kinds. Exercising proper discrimination, it is possible to introduce some of this into the group as part of an action technique. A particularly imaginative example of the use of documents in the public domain was the way cases reviewed by the Criminal Injuries Compensation Board were used in a group of violent offenders. The group was asked to assess some actual published cases and award a sum of money. Their 'assessment involved careful and demanding reflection on the many ways in which violence can be damaging' (Canton *et al.* 1992: 50).

Look out for leaflets, brochures and the like which have a particular relevance to the themes arising in the group and consider ways in which this public information can be developed into an effective action technique.

Press cuttings

The private troubles of individual group members are often mirrored by famous people in the public spotlight. Making use of these parallels by introducing newspaper or magazine cuttings relevant to the group's concerns can provide that degree of distancing which can be a significant factor in the success of many action techniques. Reading how a soap star handled a problem is preparation for group members to consider their own situations. A variant on the press cutting is the self-generated item, when individuals each write a piece for the group's own 'newspaper'.

Novels

The parallels between fictional lives and group members' lives can be very poignant. Though novels, autobiographies, fairy tales and the like must be well chosen to be effective, there is no doubting their potential impact. Transactional analysis, a therapeutic method used in both individual and group contexts, makes skilful use of fairy tales and 'life-scripts' to enlighten people (Berne 1964). Weinstein (1994) reports some useful suggestions about novels and autobiographies capable of having an impact on groups.

3: GRAPHIC

There are, of course, overlaps between the categories we have constructed to help us make sense of the many different kinds of action technique. For example, graphic techniques frequently use the written word. The flipchart sheet may be composed of words, but they are often written by different hands, in different colours, dotted around the sheet at angles to each other, with lines and squiggles to represent the way they relate to each other, so that the effect is much more one of display than of prose. For these reasons, we categorize the use of flipcharting as graphic.

Flipcharting

One of the most effective of action techniques in groups is the use of the flipchart. The chart, placed in a position where all can see and have access, is a very democratic tool. A dramatic illustration of its power came in a group for people with learning disabilities, held in a day centre. The co-workers had been reticent about using the flipchart, but were encouraged to experiment by their groupwork training course. They found that one of the group members, a woman who was not capable of speaking to other people, was able to use the flipchart to communicate with the group, albeit it in limited, phonetic English. It is difficult to know why the flipchart liberated her in this way; perhaps she found it less stressful to write than to speak, easier to address the group than a specific person. It is not easy to take in all that is being said, especially at the beginning of a new group. The spoken word disappears into the air, perhaps misheard or misunderstood, the written word (in the sense of a handout) can be over-formal. A flipchart enables a picture to be built up, step by step, mirroring the build-up of the group's processes at the group's own pace.

The flipchart can be brought into play from the very beginning of the group, when people are introducing themselves. Names are often misheard, so it helps everyone to have a visual reminder of others' names, which can be written on the flipchart in such a way as to mirror the group itself (Figure 7.4). This is a useful memory aid for everybody and a symbolic representation of the group's togetherness. The circle within the names might become filled with information from the next part of the group's session; people's hopes and fears for the group, for example.

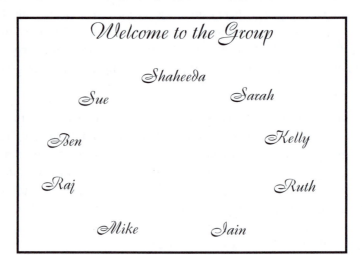

Figure 7.4 Flipchart introductions

Other graphic representations of the group's work and the interrelationship of the members could include the use of a jigsaw pattern, with each person in the group having their own 'piece'. Each individual piece can be filled with that group member's expectations, until the whole group 'fits together'. As you can see from Figure 7.5, no-one should feel a need to have any special expertise in graphics!

Quick-thinks / brainstorms

An effective method of eliciting ideas and opinions is to ask members to do a 'quick-think' (brainstorm) and gather the responses on the flipchart. This can free up a group that has become stuck, and can generate material for more

Figure 7.5 'Jigsaw' flipchart

careful consideration later. It encourages whole-group participation and helps group members to spark off each other's ideas. The flipchart conveys group ownership of all the material generated.

One of the most unusual brainstorms described in the literature is that of a detached youth worker who realized that the young people on the estate where he worked would be unattracted to a formal group in an indoor location, so produced a piece of chalk and held a quick-think session with the youths there and then on the paving stones (Mullender and Ward 1989: 19).

Group calendar

Graphic representations of the group can include an overview of the plans for the group, or the timescale available to the group. For example, a group for boys who had been sexually abused was preoccupied with time, and anxious that they would not be able to fit in everything they wanted to do. 'A group calendar was made outlining the length of the group, leaving space on it for outings, activities of choice etc. This gave the boys some visual idea of how long they would be coming and helped them to prepare for an eventual ending' (Dixon and Phillips 1994: 87). The graphic representation of the time available to the group had more impact on the boys than a verbal explanation or a written handout, in the same way that a 'pie chart' can convey statistical information in a more accessible fashion than a table of figures or a paragraph of prose.

Artwork

In the examples in the groupwork literature, art therapy is usually described more as a treatment model than merely an action technique – in other words, it is used systematically and as a primary technique throughout each session and for the duration of the group.

Art therapy groups have been used in many different settings. Otway (1993: 210) explains the power of art therapy to help people externalize thoughts and feelings that may have remained unexpressed, and she counters misconceptions that this kind of therapy is only for the artistically gifted. Two different studies describe the use of art therapy with people with eating disorders; one for young people with eating difficulties (Fitzsimmons and Levy 1996) and another for 'women who use food' (Ball and Norman 1996). Although Otway's group was not specifically for women with eating disorders, there was an anorexic member who used the painting time to explore her body image and eating patterns. The expressive potential of artwork is also evident in a family service unit group where children were given the opportunity to 'paint their feelings' and to do combined or group 'messy' paintings (Clerkin and Knaggs 1991: 54).

Drawing can be equally expressive, as in the 'dream house' action technique, where paired group members hold one pen together and, without speaking, draw their dream house. Afterwards, discussion focuses on how the activity was experienced, how conflicts were resolved, and whether a partnership was achieved (Preston-Shoot 1987; Reynolds and Shackman 1994).

Family tree

A significant benefit of many action techniques is their ability to help people to approach a difficult subject in a way which is not too threatening, often in an oblique fashion, coming at the topic from the side. The subject of families is not likely to be an easy one for female sexual abuse prisoners, but preparing their own family trees individually or in pairs, before sharing these with the group, is a way to trigger discussion about early family experiences (Barnett, Corder and Jehu 1990: 196). The process of 'doing' acts as a kind of warm-up, helping group members to prepare for the coming discussion, reminding them of the inter-relationships in their family and letting them practice how much and how little they wish to disclose.

Mapping

As a way of 'checking in' when a new group begins, each individual puts themselves on the map – this can be as local as a neighbourhood map or as large as the world, depending on the size of the constituency of the group. Individuals should be helped if they find it difficult to locate themselves – the action technique is not designed to be a test of cartographical skills!

Photographs

One of the most important of social skills is the ability to 'read' people in order to complete the feedback circuit which allows us to understand our impact on other people, and to attempt to avoid dangerous situations (Canton *et al.* 1992: 49). A technique called 'photo-language' uses photographs of commonplace social situations to explore the stereotypes and myths which we use about other people and other groups (DeVere and Rhonne 1991). It can also help group members to disclose more about themselves by choosing a photograph with which they can identify and then describing how they relate to the characters or situation in the photograph. The technique is based on evidence which suggests that pictures can be more readily stimulating than verbal language; in other words, 'a picture is worth a thousand words'.

Conceptualizations

The interactions in a group of people seated in a circle could be graphically displayed using a ball of wool as a prop (see Category 5 below), throwing the ball from one speaker to the next and holding on to the end of the thread so that a complex weave develops. The same idea of a group interacting with itself could be conceptualized as, say, a spider's web. This kind of conceptualization produces mental imagery of a graphic nature which can be every bit as powerful as the actual sight of a web of wool. In addition to the physical graphic there is also a kind of mental graphic, comprising imagery, metaphor, visualization and conceptualization.

Groupwork is an ideal medium to introduce mental maps or frameworks to help people to make better sense of their situations. Complex inter-relationships are readily portrayed and understood in graphic ways. An example is the self-identity diagram (Figure 7.6) used with male offenders 'to help make sense of the wide range of confusing and often contradictory factors involved in establishing [male] identities' (Bensted *et al.* 1994: 43). The group members use it as a template, contributing their personal responses which builds a picture of the most important factors in their identity formation. Presented first as a physical graphic on the flipchart, the diagram becomes internalized as a mental graphic, a conceptual framework to carry outside the group meetings themselves.

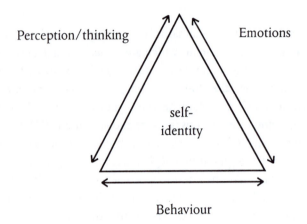

Perception/thinking   Emotions

self-
identity

Behaviour

Figure 7.6 The self-identity diagram

Metaphors and dreams

We use metaphors as a way of elaborating our experiences and as a kind of shorthand to enable others to acquire a better understanding of a particular dimension of our experience. For example, we might liken someone's temper to a volcano, with all the imagery of explosiveness, unpredictability, heat and danger that this conveys. We might extend this metaphor which links feelings to temperature by describing a 'feelings thermometer', calibrated from 1 to 5, to rate how angry certain situations make us feel (a 'feelings seismograph' would continue the geologic metaphor). The thermometer could be discussed as an image, or it could be drawn as an actual sketch on a flipchart. Indeed, participants in a group of violent offenders were presented with exactly this and asked to calibrate their responses to various situations (Canton *et al.* 1992: 47). Interestingly, the apparent failure of this metaphor with one of the participants in fact exposed an important reality for him; he marked everything '3' because he did not have the sensation of anger rising, but more of anger as a switch, on or off – a frightening sensation of powerlessness, made graphic by the use of a different, more apt metaphor, that of a light switch.

Within the general notion of metaphor are other kinds of visualization such as dreamwork, in which dream images are seen as unopened letters to oneself, in other words an important key to self-discovery (Edgar 1992). Groupwork promotes joint puzzle solving, as the possible meanings of different group members' dreams are investigated and linked to their current situations and problems.

4: HARDWARE

> Most people who talk about new media think of single users, individuals
> sitting in front of their personal computers and televisions, one person
> communicating with many others. But it is very important to create a
> structure for entertainment, for learning, for political debate, for *groups*.
> (A cinema operator discussing the new digital technology, quoted in the
> *Guardian*, 21 May 1998)

This fourth category of action technique has considerable potential but can
cause the most angst and is perhaps most open to misuse.

Prerecorded video

The most common action technique in this category is probably the use of
prerecorded video. A well-chosen piece of video which speaks to the group's
essential concerns can be extremely effective; it involves the whole group in a
common event, focusing the attention of the group on the same experience
and it speaks directly to the audience – ten seconds of video can be worth ten
minutes of explanation.

However, prerecorded video also carries dangers. First, its very directness
can be offputting if the video is off the mark. It is crucial that group leaders
review any video that they intend showing to the group to check its likely
effect. Second, the notion of audience can be a passive affair, so that what the
groupworker considers 'use of video', the group interprets as 'watching the
telly'; in other words, the group settles into entertainment mode, in which the
video induces inaction and even sleep. The third problem is one of the high
expectations which professional videos have produced in video audiences;
the poor quality of anything short of this can be a distraction, causing mirth
rather than engagement.

It is better to use video sparingly with a demand for a high level of
concentration; for example, five- or ten-minute vignettes, perhaps as part of
an exercise so that the group members are focused on what they need to be
considering whilst viewing. Canton *et al.* (1992: 47) describe how an extract
from a television comedy, in which a series of misunderstandings led to an
exchange of blows, was used to trigger discussion amongst a group of violent
offenders about how the incident arose and how it could have been
prevented.

Very occasionally, longer viewings might be appropriate, perhaps even as
an outing to the cinema. A women's group wishing to assert the value of
single parenthood might, for instance, watch Sandrine Veysset's film, *Will it
Snow for Christmas?* (Y'Aura-t-il de la Neige à Noel?), in which a mother and
her seven children live happily in their father's absence in a remote area of

rural France. Upon the father's return, a tyrannical regime of manual labour is imposed on the children. Although the setting is distant from most people's experience, the human issues are not, and the film is a powerful exposé of the foolishness of the belief that two parents are always better than one. Weinstein (1994) analyzes a number of films of books for the groupwork learning they offer, including *One Flew Over the Cuckoo's Nest* and *Lord of the Flies*, which gave us 'the conch' – a strong symbol in much groupwork.

Live camerawork

Another form of video is live camerawork. This is such a powerful medium that it needs to be handled with care; although the camcorder has become relatively common, there are still many people who have not seen themselves on video and for whom the cosmetic effect of watching their own image can overwhelm any other purposes which the groupworkers might have intended. Groupworkers, too, need to feel familiar with the equipment, so that anxiety about the technology does not eclipse the main purposes. With these caveats in place, there is no doubt that capturing group processes on video provides the most direct and transparent feedback possible. Moe (1989: 272) describes its use to record family interactions not just in the group setting, but also with the families in their own homes. Feedback was focused on positive interactions, to increase parental awareness of behaviour which furthers development. In this way, the camera gives the family, the group and the groupworker an invaluable eye on behaviours and interactions which otherwise would only be available second hand through reported memory.

E-mail

An assumption made about groups is that the members must be in the same room at the same time for it to be a group. However, advances in technology allow degrees of interaction between individuals which have not been possible before, so that groups of people who are in communication via electronic communication like e-mail might create conditions we would recognize as groupwork, even though separated by thousands of miles.

Telephone and video-conferencing

In addition to e-mail, other advances in technology, such as the use of video-conferencing, open up the possibility of groupwork between people who are not in the same room together. We have little documented experience of how this might feel to group members compared with those in a conventional arrangement, though Regan (1997) has described teleconferencing group counselling as having a different sense of time than occurs in a face-to-face group, and there are a number of accounts of telephone group support programmes (Ritter and Hammons 1992; Trang and Urbano 1993). There is no doubt that the development of the video group (and, indeed, the 'virtual reality group') has considerable potential.

5: PROPS

Some action techniques rely on items or objects brought into the group's activity for an express purpose. These 'props' might be familiar objects used in a new way, such as chairs, or brought into the action specially for the purpose. So, the chairs which group members sit on are not props until they are used for another purpose, such as positioning one in the centre of the group as a 'hot seat', or rearranging a set of them in order to act out a ride in a car. It pays to be opportunistic in the use of props, so that everyday items not normally considered part of the group might play their part in helping group processes. For example, an old tent was discovered by chance in the corner of a room where a group for emotionally disturbed boys was meeting, and the tent became a punch bag at a highly charged point in the group (Clarke and Aimable 1990: 43). Below we outline other examples of the use of props.

Money is a very powerful symbol and is already widely used in games such as Monopoly. 'Loose change' is an example of the use of small change from group members' pockets being used, with imagination, to decide how the £200,000 on the floor (since each 1p is worth £100) would be spent (Silverlock and Silverlock 1995).

Wool became an important medium in 'knitting groups' for older refugees in Croatia (Ajdukovic, Cevizovic and Kontak 1995: 38), helping the members to engage in practical activity and also earn a little income. Ross (1991: 64) describes an action technique to help the process of ending a group, in which a *ball of string* is thrown from member to member, with each person holding onto their end of the string and saying 'goodbye' to the person on the receiving end and saying why they will particularly miss them. The web of string at the end of the activity represents some of the network of affection within the group. The goodbyes finished, each person symbolically cuts themselves out of the web with a pair of *scissors*.

A *satchel* helped to provide a group of female mental health providers with a 'sense of connectiveness and playfulness', using it in pantomime (Holstein and Addison 1994: 142). A *puppet* called 'Plonker the Rabbit' helped one boy who found it hard to verbalise his sadness, by telling the group what he wanted and how he felt (Badger 1988: 265). Puppets played an important part, too, in helping a boy tell his own story of sexual abuse (Dixon and Phillips 1994: 83). In the same group, the co-workers pointed to the link between *food* and trust, and the boys' refusal to accept any of the snacks or drinks offered to them. This changed later in the group's life, when three of the four boys indicated that they had accepted sweets from their abusers and, by this act, felt they had somehow given permission for the abuse.

Props can be used to create a sense of safety and security, something tactile and concrete to act out or through; they can divert or focus, soften or sharpen the mood of the group. An example of props used in an exceptionally challenging way was a group for motoring offenders, in which 'a chilling reminder of the consequences of unsafe driving or casual attitudes to safety is brought home by handling *motorbike helmets* from fatal accidents' (Hutchins 1991: 245, our italics).

Sometimes a particular prop can acquire a status as the embodiment of the group, either in a planned or unplanned way. The *conch* in *Lord of the Flies* became the embodiment of power, allowing the holder the power of speech. Many groups acquire their own talisman, even if it is not such a recognizable physical object as a conch. For example, a *box* attended each meeting of a Who Cares? group. The box came to contain all of the group's memorabilia as each session progressed, so that it gradually came to represent what the group had been and what it had done (Mullender and Ward 1989: 13). Indeed, props are particularly effective if they have a special meaning for the nature of the group – such as the fantasy of the *magic carpet* where the use of legs did not matter in a group for brothers and sisters of children with physical disabilities (Badger 1988: 265).

Projects

The term 'props' suggests the relatively brief introduction into the action of an object or objects to help the group's purposes, with some props acquiring a special status. However, if the props become central to the group's activities, we might describe them as projects. For example, Paulsen, Dunker and Young (1997) describe an activity group for emotionally disturbed children in which a carefully constructed group programme is built around the planning and construction of individual projects in the group, such as bookends, teddy bears, string art and constructing a catamaran. The projects are used to help the children progress through various developmental stages.

6: MOVEMENT

The tendency to inertia is strong in many areas of life. The desire to sit in the same place, whether it is the bench in a park or the seat on a bus, seems irresistible against the patterns which seem to steady and fix our activities. This is just as true of a group, where it is highly likely that whatever positions the members of the group took in the first session they will resume in the second and will maintain until the end (especially if they are adults); unless, of course, you use your position as groupworker to 'unfix' the members. Movement might be whole body or as simple as laughter.

Games are useful because they involve a high degree of interaction and are highly structured in a way which involves prescription from 'outside' (the objective rules) rather than the leaders. For these reasons they are particularly favoured in work with adolescents, introducing rules given by the game and not by the groupworkers.

The benefits of movement are considerable. Movement, and its absence, affects our mood. Lordan (1996: 65) describes the use of group *sculpts* in social work education, with a belief that images can be closer to our true feelings than words and that sculpting techniques can act as a counterbalance to the 'technician approach' to social work training. Rowland (1995) explains the use of a technique called *storylining* to help students at school make the transition to the adult world of employment by means of a challenging, physical, outdoors experience, structured around a complex, step-by-step story.

Drinking tea, or whatever refreshments are made available, should rightly be seen as an action technique. It can provide a very important period of reflection on work which has just been completed, or a release to be able to talk quietly about things outside the group. Smokers will appreciate the break as an opportunity for a cigarette if the group has a no-smoking policy.

The question of arousal is an important one in successful groupwork. So far, we have been considering how to stimulate group members into a state of alertness, but there are times when the focus is on the negative effects of arousal. For example, anger management groupwork with prisoners emphasizes the development of 'an awareness of signs of increased bodily arousal and practising relaxation techniques' (Towl and Dexter 1994: 257). Quiet time, in which the absence of physical movement is in itself 'physical', can be a useful technique to provide a mood of calm reflection.

Trips

A day's outing can have an extraordinary effect on a group and a residential trip is even more powerful, though it is not always a suitable or practical option. A women's probation group secured funding for a three-day residential trip to a Butlin's holiday camp for nine women and six children, and the experiences which this generated (including a racist attack by a group of white women holidaymakers) provided 'an important focus for group discussion in the next twelve months in the group' (Mistry 1989: 151). Trips can be used for rewards or as turning points or to say goodbyes.

GROUP SHAPE

The groupwork mindset so often sees 'a group' as a circle of people in mutual discussion. We hope that particular perspective has now been broadened, especially by this chapter's discussion of the enormous variety of action techniques available. In addition to the action techniques which might engage the full group, it is possible to see how the group can be broken into pairs, trios or small groups for any part or parts of the action. This allows huge scope for groupworkers to tailor the action technique and its shape at any particular time in the life of the group or the particular session. So, at points of intimacy, shyness or privacy, it might feel right for the group to start an action technique in the closeness of pairs; at points of creativity, challenge and diversity the preference could be for full group activity.

Even when the whole group is involved there are a number of options and alternatives to the circle. One of the best-known full-group arrangements is the *goldfish bowl*, in which one group looks on another by physically surrounding it. Sometimes each member in the active inner group has a particular shadow in the observing outer group. The crucial aspect of the gold fishbowl technique is the different roles which group members have. In the gold fishbowl, one set of group members are actors and the other set are observers. In the *hot seat* technique, it is one individual who has a singularly different role from the rest of the group. To a certain extent, whenever an individual in a group speaks, it becomes a hot seat, which is one reason why some people can find it very difficult to speak in the group. The formal hot seat physically places the individual in the centre of the group's gaze.

It is important to consider the most appropriate shape for the group at any particular time; sometimes this will be planned outside the group session and at other times it will arise out of a response to the particular needs and opportunities in the group at the time. We have already noted the need for changes in tempo and, similarly, variations in shape are usually a factor in creative groupwork.

Mixed modalities

The categories in the kaleidoscope have provided a framework to consider the countless possibilities for action techniques. Certainly, in the course of a group's life, or even just one session, it is likely that action techniques in several categories will be in evidence. For example, Mullender (1995: 84) describes the content of group sessions for children who have lived with domestic violence as including the writing of stories by the children (Category 2), which can then be read out (Category 1) or acted (Category 6) or videoed (Category 4).

The categories are not watertight and at any one time the group might be engaged in a raft of different modalities. Though listed as a spoken word activity, reminiscence work is a good example of a mixed modality action technique. For example, in addition to props (Category 5) such as memorabilia, music, smells, clothing and food, Gibson (1992: 32) also describes the use of magazines, books and newspapers (Category 2), and photographs (Category 3) to trigger older people's memories. Multisensory triggers (smells, sights, sounds, tastes, touches, etc.) mean that people with severe visual and hearing impairments can actively participate.

One activity, therefore, is often comprised of a variety of action techniques. For example, the five- to eight-year-olds in a group for children who had been sexually abused used dolls and puppets (props) together with video camera and play back (hardware) to role play (spoken word) situations such as going to court and seeking help (Lebacq and Shah 1989: 126).

If you look back over the life of a group as a whole you should be able to list the different action techniques which have been used and the variation in category.

Order and chaos

Just as the tension with which the wool is held affects the quality of knitting, so a group requires the right degree of 'tension' for effective groupwork. Too slack and it is under-stimulating and benign, too taught and it is over-challenging and unsafe. The art of the groupworker, like that of the knitter, is to feel for the right tension. Experience plays its part in developing this feel, but we have no wish to mystify this process; this book is designed to make explicit the factors which encourage effective and creative groupwork so that they can be observed, identified, learned, rehearsed, adapted.

One of the tensions which you face as a groupworker is that between order and chaos. Of course, this is a universal tension, but it is highlighted in the public forum of a group. Manor and Dumbleton (1993) describe an activity as promoting ordered, relatively predictable responses and a growth game as necessary to produce creative chaos (as opposed to random chaos). The balance between order and chaos is an important indicator for the group to help groupworkers select action techniques related to the group's developmental needs. In Manor and Dumbleton's terms, an activity relies on rules, collaboration and patterns of behaviour and so tends to reinforce the sense of order. A growth game intensifies a disturbance in the group system which, in turn, can lead to a revision of the underlying principles governing the system. They illustrate this difference by taking a prop such as cardboard and describing how play with cardboard could be used on the one hand to construct a house (an activity) or, on the other, to be flattened and destroyed (a growth game).

Portfolio extract

In the first session [of the Womens Group] we used the Continuum Line Game [in which everybody strings themselves along an imaginary line from 'love' to 'loathe' in relation to various topics. We used it] in a light-hearted way, as an icebreaker and to get members moving around. Both me and my co-worker joined in with the game and it was interesting to find that the women either followed me or my co-worker on the imaginary line, regardless of what they thought of the topic themselves ... This demonstrates issues of powerlessness. I think the women initially found it awkward to be asked to make a decision, perhaps because this is so rarely done in their lives. It was also unusual for them to have us, as workers, join in with the activity and as a result they may have copied us because they felt it easier and assumed it might be the 'right answer'. It may have been because they wanted to please us or they felt safer stood next to us ... In later sessions they did not appear to have any difficulty expressing their opinions even if they varied from ours or from the majority's.   LW (1998)*

Because we wanted to finish this session in a light-hearted way, we concluded with the Knitting Game. This was very positive and great fun. I took care to explain that although each strand of wool on its own was very flimsy, when woven into a web it became strong. The web we had woven with the wool was symbolic of the strength of the group and the way members supported one another within the group.   JP (1998)*

*LW and JP are co-workers with a group for women. They are prequalified mental health support workers in a community mental health team.

In critical incident debriefing, which occurs after major accidents and disasters, it is essential to create an extremely safe, ordered and controlled environment for people who are traumatized. For this reason, the debriefers are highly prescriptive in laying down rules for the session and determining the physical set-up (Parkinson 1993). To begin with, participants are prompted to describe the trauma with a set of very specific questions which they each address, and they are asked to frame their responses as though they were at a distance from the event, 'above it' (emotions and closeness to the scene follow later). Sensory experience – what people saw, heard, touched, tasted and smelled – are investigated in turn, because this 'helps individuals to understand such memories if they emerge at a later stage and to control them when they do' (Parkinson 1993: 147).

It might seem that highly prescribed activities are likely to engender safety, since they reinforce the sense of order, and highly unstructured ones would encourage risk-taking. Paradoxically, very structured activities can promote more risk-taking, in the way that a safety net encourages a more daring performance on the high wire.

CHAPTER EIGHT

Interactional Techniques in Groups

> **About 'Full house'**
>
> Successful groupwork relies on a broad range of interpersonal skills. The communication skills necessary for work with an individual are a good foundation for the more complex communications in groups. 'Full house' presents the dialogue from part of a group in which each of the types of interactional technique described in this chapter is illustrated.

Purpose

There are many ways in which the communication skills in groups have been identified and clustered. This chapter takes the interactional skills identified by Bertcher (1994) and modifies them slightly in order to present 14 categories of technique. This framework will help you as a groupworker to consider which techniques you use more than others and whether there are some techniques which you need to include more frequently in your repertoire.

Method

- Take a blank piece of paper and number from 1 to 26 down the left-hand margin. Draw a line down the middle of the page, separating it into a left and a right half.

- Read through the full house exercise before turning to the rest of the chapter. At this stage you will be making untutored notes in the left half of the sheet against each numbered dialogue. What communication skills do you think are being used at each stage?

- Familiarize yourself with the notes for groupworkers in this chapter. Return to the Full house exercise and reread it, using the right half of the sheet to make fresh notes. Each of the 14 interactional techniques described in the chapter are illustrated in the exercise – can you recognize them? How does this compare with your notes on the left side of the page, made before you read the rest of the chapter? ('Answers' are given in the box on page 164.)

Variations

If the group in which you are working gives its permission, it is a valuable experience to audiotape or videotape a group session and use the Bertcher framework in order to analyze the communication patterns in the group and your own use of interactional techniques.

When you are familiar with the 14 interactional techniques discussed in this chapter, identify two which you think you use most frequently in your groupwork. With a co-worker or colleague, check your understanding of what the techniques mean and identify specific examples of when you have used them. Now consider two techniques which you think you use least frequently in your groupwork. Again, check out your understanding of these techniques with your partner and consider why you seldom use these techniques.

Full house

It is towards the end of the third session of a women's group led by Selina and Yasmin. There are nine women members of the group and they have just completed the First Person exercise (see page 196), in which everybody is asked to write an 'I' on the same piece of flipchart paper. The Is are written in the shape of the group itself (for example, in a circle, if that is how group members are sitting), and each person chooses how to style their own I.

1   Selina (*sitting down, with the flip paper on a stand in view of everybody*): So, now that we've all written our Is on the flipchart, let's take a look at them. Maybe each person could say a few things about why they chose their particular style of I. Yasmin you agreed to start us off …

2   Yasmin: Yes, this is the first time I've done this, and it wasn't easy. In the end I decided on that particular shape (*points at her I on the flipchart*); it's supposed to mimic the shape of a human being, but I'm no artist! (*A little laughter.*) And the reason it's shaped like that is because I like to see myself as very approachable and, well, human.

Silence, as people are reluctant to follow suit.

3   Selina: Of course, these things are very personal and people may be feeling that talking this way is rather different for them, so –

4   Manjit (*interrupting, coming in quickly and nervously*): I hadn't realized how hard it would be to do this exercise. It's really so difficult to think about I, me. It's not been encouraged – it goes against grain, you know.

5   Selina: Is that why you put a question mark by your 'I'?

6   Manjit: Yes, it's easier to be 'we', you know … (stalls)

7   Selina: In what way, Manjit? Can you say more specifically why?

8   Manjit (*thinks*): When it's 'we', it doesn't feel like there's spotlight on me.

9   Julie: I thought it was difficult, too. In the end I played it safe and just did, you know, a line. Just a plain, straight line – I (*writes it in the air*).

10 Selina: What do you think that means about how you want to be seen, Julie?

11 Julie: Well, I suppose I want to be seen like that, straight up and down and sort of 'fitting in'; I'd feel embarrassed if it was any different. But I'm not sure that's how I *really* want to be seen. But I do know that I'd die if somebody thought I was like that fancy I on the sheet you gave us!

12 Yasmin (*looking around the group*): Did everyone find it difficult?

There is agreement.

13 Yasmin: I wonder if this is something to do with our gender, the fact that we are all women? Perhaps we are not encouraged to consider our own needs – who I am, who we are.

14 Susan (*defensively*): I know I'll be told it's not fashionable to say it, but I think it's right to be thinking of my family's needs. That's what makes me feel good about myself.

15 Selina: No, you're right to express your feelings, Susan, and it's important we all respect them – but what about those feelings of being trapped you talked about in the session last week? Do you think sometimes you pay a price to feel good about yourself?

16 Gill (*comes in urgently*): I'd paid the price for a long time, too long. I know that for a fact. It became so as I couldn't think who I was.

Everybody seemed to have shares in me, except me! I'm not saying it's been a doddle since I left, but at least I feel I am me. I know who I am.

17 Susan: Yes, but you can't just walk out on your responsibilities. Your family's dependent on you and they expect you to be there. You can't all of a sudden become the big 'I AM'.

Susan and Gill continue in this vein and start to become heated …

18 Yasmin: I think we're each going to come to different solutions and conclusions. What's the right thing to do for Gill is not necessarily going to be the right thing to do for Susan, and vice versa. That's the value of this group, to hear other people's views. Just look at the amazing variety of Is on the flipchart (*turns to the circle of Is*) – lots of different sizes, shapes, expressions – but all valued equally and deserving our respect.

19 Selina: Yes, Yasmin's right. It relates very much to the first session of the group – do you remember when we drew up the group contract and agreed that the important thing was to learn from each other and for us to use the group to help each person find their own solution?

More group members go on to share what their particular I means to them. There is a pause when all the group is looking at the flipchart.

20 Julie: It's funny, but I hadn't thought about it before, but one thing we have in common is that we're all Is. I mean, you think of I as being individual and separate, but in fact, writing it down like that – I, rather than each of our names – we didn't even know that Mary hadn't written her own I … because we're all I's together!

21 Selina: Julie, you've said something really deep there! I think that's taken us all on by a good mile.

All nod their heads and laugh, except Mary.

22 Yasmin: Does what Julie said make sense for you, Mary?

Mary smiles sheepishly.

23 Yasmin: It's to do with earlier when we were looking at how there are some things which are similar for group members and some things which are different. Remember how we spoke about the group moving from nine Is towards one we – in other words, we are beginning to share things and to do things together. We're

even using the word 'we' more often than 'I'; that's how groups develop – if they're working well together, like we are. But then Julie's just pointed out something we'd all been missing – that being an individual – an I, if you like – is something we all have in common.

Mary still seems puzzled.

24 Selina (*looking at her watch*): Maybe that's a good note to end on. We all promised to end on time and it's been a good discussion – not easy for any of us to do the I exercise, but it feels to have put us all in touch with a challenge – how to be true to ourselves, even when being true to yourself means different things to different people. Well, as you know, there's always a piece to do at home! This week's 'homeplay' is to make a note of a time when you feel that your needs are being met.

25 Julie: This group's the only time I think my needs are being met!!

Laughter.

26 Selina: That's good news for the group – but see what you can do about having your needs met outside the group – at least once, anyway! And we'll start the next session with a round, so we can all hear how everybody's got one.

As the group gets ready to leave, Yasmin talks quietly with Mary about how she is finding the group.

Examples of interactional techniques in the Full house dialogue

Starting: 1

Attending: 22 (10)

Responding to feelings: 3

Giving information: 23

Seeking information: 5, 10, 12 (22)

Negotiating, etc.: 19

Gatekeeping: 18

Focusing: 8, 13, 20, (24)

Modelling: 2

Rewarding: [individual] 21; [group] 23, 25

Confronting/challenging: 15 (10)

Mediating: 18

Summarizing: 23

Ending: 24, 26

(Numbers in brackets refer to paragraphs that include some indication of the technique; the categories are not water-tight and some communications can use more than one technique.)

Notes for the groupworker

What is an interactional technique?

There are several layers to groupworking. At the broadest level is the group's overall purpose and direction, often suggested by its name: a *reminiscence* group; an *activity* group; a *therapy* group. At the next level are the methods which are used in the group to achieve the overall purposes. These, too, might be apparent in the group's name – an *oral history* group; a *drama* group; an *art therapy* group. More often, a wide variety of methods is deployed, both in the group programme as a whole and in any one session. In Chapter 7 we described these methods as 'action techniques' and explored how the same action technique can be used in groups with very different purposes, and how different action techniques can be used together to achieve diverse results.

A further layer of groupwork is the communication within the group. These interpersonal skills are essential in order to enable group members to communicate effectively with each other and with the group as a whole. They help groups to build support, foster belonging, challenge obstacles, focus energy and make use of all the other ingredients of successful groupwork. Without these abilities the group is unlikely to progress beyond the everyday experiences which people have when they gather together, often pleasant and sociable, but not what constitutes groupwork. In this chapter we cluster these various communication skills into a set of interactional techniques, based on the work of Bertcher (1994).

Another way of looking at the three levels which we have described (the macro, mezzo and micro) is to think of the overall group aims as *roads* which take the group to its destination, to see the action techniques as the various *vehicles* which the group uses to travel the road, and to view the interactional techniques as the *fuels* which keep the vehicles moving on the road. Thus, each aspect is dependent on the others and a successful group is one where all three are properly serviced.

Any categorization of interactional techniques cannot escape being shorthand. In the same way that the 26 letters of the alphabet simplify the vast range of available sounds of pronunciation, so the 14 interactional techniques below cannot reproduce each person's individual signature. They overlap, leave gaps and shade into each other, but they provide a rudimentary language to describe what is happening in groups. They provide a lexicon of common 'phrases' – made up from sets of smaller communications (sounds, looks, non-verbal gestures and postures) which, taken together, convey a purpose or meaning. They can be used skilfully and unskilfully, appropriately and inappropriately, by groupworkers and by group members.

Of course, there will be some groups where the lexicon of interactional techniques used in this chapter is not especially pertinent. For example, in many self-help groups of the Alcoholics Anonymous type, 'participants hold a series of monologues rather than dialogues or discussions' (Matzat 1993: 33). It is the catharsis of the confessional which carries most power in this context, not the usual interactional techniques employed by groupworkers.

Some techniques may be emphasized at the expense of others, according to the orientation of the groupworker. For example, a psychodynamic groupworker might consider 'interpreting' and 'diagnosing' as key interactional techniques. Setting, too, has a big impact on the kinds of technique which are appropriate. Lo's (1993) description of the streetworkers' task to neutralize group control in youth gangs in Hong Kong relies on techniques such as 'diversion', 'protection' and 'direct squashing', unlike many group settings.

Fourteen interactional techniques

Of course, there are many ways in which interactional techniques can be described and clustered; for example, energizing and facilitating techniques (Ward and Mullender 1991: 143); harmonizing, expressing group feelings, evaluating the emotional climate and building trust (Douglas 1976: 71); diagnosing and giving directions (Brown 1992: 71); 'dialoguing', in which group leaders have a discussion in front of the group, enabling feelings and processes to be named in a safe manner and in ways which the group members themselves would not consider (Crown and Gates 1997: 64). In Chapter 6, we discussed the importance of signposting as an important technique.

In the following lexicon of techniques we use Bertcher's (1994) framework, with some adaptation. Many of the techniques are relevant to individual one-to-one communications, as well as groupworking.

1: STARTING

Starting refers to the activities and behaviours used to begin a group meeting or to introduce a new topic during the session. Thus, there are many startings in the life of the group, not just the obvious 'big bang' of the initial session. We refer you to Chapters 5 and 6 for a more detailed introduction of starting techniques.

2: ATTENDING

Attending is letting a group member know that you are paying close attention to what he or she is saying or doing, so that he or she will be encouraged to continue ... it also involves selective *ignoring* of certain kinds of information, when that information is judged by the groupworker to be irrelevant to the topic at hand or likely to shift the focus of the group's activities. (Bertcher 1994: 19–21)

Attending is a strong form of listening. Listening might be taken for granted, but 'surprisingly, we found most people have never discovered how to listen, and instead spend most of the time whilst another is speaking working out what to say the moment he or she stops [and] we found almost nobody listens to themselves speaking' (Garrett 1995: 55). This observation was made of prisoners in groups, but rings true for many other situations.

Attending is, therefore, letting group members know that you are listening very carefully indeed to what they are saying or doing. It has the effect of inviting them to continue and is usually reinforced by steady eye contact and 'minimal encouragers' such as head nods and verbal 'hmmm's. There is little to match the power of attention; for example, when somebody is speaking in the group but giving you sole eye contact, glance repeatedly at somebody else, and you will find that the speaker will divert their attention from you to the other person.

There are times when it is proper to focus your attention on one specific group member – perhaps they are discussing something very personal or need special encouragement to speak in the group. At other times it is good practice to scan the group so that your attention does not land on any particular individual. This will feel inclusive and reinforce a sense of group membership.

All attention is selective, which means that there are some communications which will be ignored. It is important to be aware of how you make these judgements, especially the way they are related to your own biography as a man or a woman, a black person or a white person, etc. The power of attention must be used in ways which are inclusive for the group as a whole.

3: RESPONDING TO FEELINGS

An ability to sense how people feel and to articulate this awareness is crucial to effective groupwork. The technique of responding to feelings is the verbal and non-verbal action by which groupworkers and group members communicate their empathic understanding.

This technique involves an ability not only to sense feelings at an individual level, but also to be able to take the emotional temperature of the group as a whole. It also requires the groupworker to understand how to act on this awareness, whether to verbalize it ('it sounds like you're feeling very confused about what's been happening, Manjit'; 'the group seems to be happy with that decision') or not (putting a gentle hand on the individual's shoulder, or suggesting the group breaks for a coffee break, etc.).

There is often a degree of risk when responding to feelings, because something which has been unspoken is made explicit. You risk being mistaken or, indeed, being too painfully accurate, with the individual or group not yet ready for the exposure. Nevertheless, there are risks in not responding to feelings, as group members might well know from their own life experiences. The consequence of avoiding feelings may become one of the group's themes (see Chapter 10 for more discussion about group themes).

Two particularly important feelings in groups are identified by Bertcher (1994: 88), who cautions that they should be anticipated by groupworkers:

- the fear that your participation might be rejected

- the disappointment associated with an attempt to participate that is ignored.

It is especially important to plan for people's apprehensions about participating, perhaps by creating opportunities to build up to full participation via the safer ground of pairs and small subgroups, and by tuning in to those feelings before the group starts (see Chapters 5 and 6).

Finally, it is important not to pathologize by responding only to negative feelings. Be aware of positive feelings and respond to these, too.

4: GIVING INFORMATION

Although this technique and the associated one of seeking information are self-explanatory, they are often poorly handled (Bertcher 1994: 31). Information is a difficult commodity to handle, since there are infinite amounts of it and the supply can be erratic.

Your opening statement of purpose (Chapter 6) will have been an opportunity to give information in a way which fits with the group: in some cases tight and purposeful, in others loose and open-ended; in detail with this group, sketchily with that one. Whatever manner the delivery of your opening statement, it is likely to be taken as a template for the way in which information in the group can be given. It should, therefore, set the tone as an acceptable example of information-giving.

Giving information can seem a deceptively simple process, too often clouded with opinions. 'Giving' information can also be a very passive exercise. It is important, therefore, to consider different options, especially those which are more creative and which engage others as much as possible. 'Rather than giving information in a lecture format, a set of specific questions related to the topics are asked of both parents and children' writes McKay *et al.*

(1997). In this multifamily therapy group the responses from parents and children to requests such as identifying rules in their household are compiled in order to develop a set of guidelines for all families to implement. The end result is the giving of information, not in a conventional handout format which would probably have little impact, but by making a 'demand for work' (Shulman 1984). This is also a good example of the way in which the giving of information can entail the seeking of information.

The difference between 'you' as groupworkers and 'them' as group members has already been explored, using the themes of authority and intimacy (Chapter 3). A strong signpost for difference is the use of language in the group, not just individual words but the language codes and patterns which are used. Giving information in ways which are honest to the differences yet inclusive of all the group is an interactional technique worth rehearsing.

5: SEEKING INFORMATION

Just as the opening statement provides a template for giving information, seeking information from individuals at the beginning of the group can set the tone for the rest of the group, possibly resulting in a wide variation in the amount and kind of information elicited. Some people are inclined to reveal the barest minimum whilst others spill their worries at great length all over the other group members. Setting a standard by giving information of the nature and scope that you are expecting can provide a model for other participants and save them the embarrassment of inappropriate self-disclosure.

The most significant factor when seeking information from group members is trust (Bertcher 1994: 42). Participants need to know why the information is being sought – what is its purpose? Is it needed in order to get to know one another better, to solve problems, to receive feedback or some other purposes? Giving the reasons for seeking information and being sensitive to the likely impact of your request is important. In addition, group members need to know *how* information is going to be used. This involves issues of confidentiality and the boundary between the group and the outside (Chapter 6), but also the respect that is shown for information within the group. A further factor is who is seeking the information? Groupworkers are powerful, even if they do not feel so, and if they are perceived to be very different from group members (in terms of gender, race, age, life experiences, etc.) they will need to work particularly hard to be trusted with information. All of these factors, then, have an impact on the growth of trust and the ease with which information can be sought.

6: NEGOTIATING, RENEGOTIATING AND REINFORCING THE GROUP
AGREEMENT

We have already discussed the importance of achieving agreement about the
nature of the group and ways in which this negotiation can be conducted, beginning with the very first contacts and the groupworkers' opening statement of purpose (Chapters 5 and 6). This process of negotiation can be seen
as a composite interactional skill, involving many of the other techniques described in this chapter (seeking and giving information, mediating, etc.).

The negotiating technique is essential to creative groupwork practice
throughout the life of the group, not just in the early stages. When it is focused on the business of reaching explicit agreement to keep to certain expectations within the group, Bertcher uses the term 'contract negotiation',
though there may or may not be a formal, written contract. The same technique is also used to develop goals 'that the group as a whole and/or its individual members hope to achieve through their participation in the group'
(Bertcher 1994: 44).

Groups differ in their ability to reach a common agreement. The 'spread'
of the necessary agreement will also vary, some groups managing with only
general ground rules, and others requiring cast-iron rules written in capital
letters. It is worth remembering that it is easier to establish ground rules at the
beginning (even if they are rather more formal than needed) than to try to re-
capture lost ground later. Where groups are sanctioned by courts, such as
many in the probation service, the basic contract is often non-negotiable and
the group leaders' focus is on how to help members engage with the imposi-
tion.

Whereas all groups have a purpose (or should have), some will be working
to more explicit goals than others. In some groups it is possible to negotiate a
group goal, which all members subscribe to and are working towards; in
other groups, each person's goal differs from person to person, with a commitment to using group processes to achieve personal goals. Power to influence the nature of the agreement, at whatever level it is pitched, is likely to
increase members' satisfaction with the group overall.

The group agreement needs periodic review so that if it is not serving its
purpose it can be renegotiated. When rewards and sanctions are invoked by
group members or leaders, these should be related to the agreement, and seen
as reinforcing it. It is the group's contract with itself which often justifies a
particular technique, such as a confronting intervention, and ensures that
techniques are used responsibly and purposefully.

7: GATEKEEPING

> Gatekeeping is behaviour that helps all members of the group participate more or less equally by limiting those members who monopolize the discussion and by encouraging low participators to talk more. (Bertcher 1994: 114)

Gatekeeping is a term used frequently in the groupwork and social work literature. As its image suggests, the general meaning of gatekeeping is the power to open up or close off. An intake team gatekeeps access to the agency's referral system, an assessment gatekeeps access to agency resources. In Chapter 9 we explore gatekeeping in terms of the power of group members and the group as a whole to prevent the group from moving on into new pastures, fearful of what might lie ahead.

Although there is a tendency for gatekeeping to be seen as gateshutting, it is important not to lose sight of the positive aspect of this interactional technique. To continue with the literal image, as the whole group approaches a narrow gate or stile, the only way in which it will pass through successfully is one at a time, regrouping on the other side. It is the groupworkers' responsibility to gatekeep to ensure that each has his or her opportunity to participate.

Gatekeeping is not a question of dividing the sessional hour-and-a-half by the number of group members and ensuring that each has equal airtime. It is concerned more with ensuring equal access to the group's time, and enabling group members from social groups who are traditionally seen as lower participators to play their part. In addition to interactions designed to promote this balance, groupworkers should also consider how the action techniques described in Chapter 7 can be used to promote broad participation. The group 'shape' (see page 156) is crucial in encouraging low participators to feel confident to contribute to the whole group, by using pairs and small subgroupings early in the group's life. In addition, the spoken word is easily dominated by high participators, so introduce other kinds of action (for example, graphics on the flipchart) to prevent this kind of domination.

8: FOCUSING

> Focusing means calling the group's attention to something that has been said or that has happened to highlight or clarify it so that the group will be more aware of what has occurred, or to bring the discussion back to the agreed-upon business of the group. (Bertcher 1994: 90)

In order to turn a conversation into a purposeful discussion, groups rely on signposts and signals. Not that there is anything inferior about a conversation; it is just that a conversation does not require a groupworker or a group. If the aim is to enable people to have social contact in order to converse, it is unlikely that a groupworker has a role to play other than perhaps helping set up the initial arrangements.

Individuals in the group, and sometimes the group as a whole, are inclined to drift and wander from the group's central concerns. Group members are likely to consider that the role of bringing the group back to its purpose belongs to the groupworkers; if frequent refocusing is needed, it may mean that the initial agreed focus is misdirected and that the group should reconsider its main aims.

Time-keeping, or at least being aware of the passage of time, is an important function of groupworking. This is not to reinforce the tyranny of the clock, but to recognize that the group has a limited amount of time together and that there may be issues which particular group members, or the group as a whole, want to devote time to. People may have commitments immediately after the group (child care responsibilities, for example) which mean that the planned end for the sessions should be respected. Leaving a group which is in full flow beyond the planned end of the session can feel very excluding and discriminatory, so it is important to see focusing not as an attempt to impose the group leader's timescale, but to help the group keep its contract with itself. So, focusing is not concerned with keeping to the straight and narrow, it is about using some of the available pressures of time and place to help the group to achieve its purposes.

9: MODELLING

> Modelling occurs when a participant in a group demonstrates a behaviour or set of behaviours in such a way that another person can imitate it. (Bertcher 1994: 141)

We are familiar with notions of 'role models', in which particular individuals are seen by others as possessing qualities which they would like to emulate. Often the power of the role model emanates from the fact that the model has certain characteristics in common with the modeller (race, gender, age, etc.) With people coming together in the group because of shared concerns or problems, because they are 'in the same boat', it is not unusual for individuals in the group to provide role models for others; and your own behaviour as a groupworker will be seen as a model for working in groups.

Sometimes it is appropriate to harness these naturally occurring forces and focus them in such a way that they are used in a deliberate and systematic fashion. For example, the groupworker might suggest that group members rehearse how they might handle situations they have been finding difficult; often an individual group member provides a specific example, which is illustrative of ones which the rest of the group can relate to.

When using the modelling technique in this systematic fashion, Bertcher (1994: 142) suggests five specific steps, which are summarized as follows.

1 Determine that the learner wants to learn from this modelling approach.

2 Demonstrate the model to show the learner.

3 The learner attempts to imitate the modeller until comfortable with their own words.

4 The learner is given feedback.

5 The learner practises, then *improvizes* the behaviour to fit different situations.

These steps follow a well-established pattern sometimes described in the literature as coaching, guided practice or rehearsal.

Modelling is, therefore, a conscious focusing of something that is happening in an unfocused way all the time in groups. There is a close link with the technique of rewarding (see Section 10), so that when certain behaviours draw a favourable response from the group and others provoke a negative one, the reward of a positive reaction will tend to reinforce that behaviour as a model for other group members. So, modelling takes place at two levels; at an unspoken, implicit level continuously, and then sometimes as an explicit technique, labelled and named for the group as 'modelling'.

In order to be effective, models have to be credible, so that the group member has a sense of 'if she or he can do it, so can I'. For this reason it can be particularly effective to invite people to the group who have been in similar situations to the group members, but who have come through the experience successfully, though not to such a degree that their success feels out of reach.

10: REWARDING

Rewarding is any action that tells an individual or the group as a whole that they have done something to help move the group towards its goal. Rewarding might be as implicit as giving attention to somebody or as explicit as an affirming statement, drawing attention to the way in which an action or discussion has been helpful to the group. The focus of the reward should relate to the aims of the group; for example, you can reward the act of disagreeing as a sign of the group's growing trust and self-confidence, without rewarding the disagreement itself (Bertcher 1994: 70). However, if rewarding is used idiosyncratically, the group will see it as 'favouritism', which would prove very destructive to the group's development. The effect of rewarding is often to reinforce a particular behaviour or attitude, because the power of reward is considerable, especially when the whole group rewards an individual.

The rewarding technique provides a good illustration of the significance of the cultural context of all groupwork techniques. What a North American group member takes as rewarding, their British counterpart might feel as patronising. Conscious rewarding behaviour is not as evident in British social codes as North American ones, where positive feedback is given more generously and is often unsolicited. It is interesting to speculate why there are these differences, and whether class distinctions account for the fine line which many British people feel they must tread between patronage and deference (depending on the class and status of the rewarder and the rewarded). Making a rewarding remark is a powerful communication, and this is particularly pertinent in terms of who controls the distribution of rewards in the group, and the extent to which group members recognize and use their own power to reward or withhold rewards. Groupworkers may be surprised by the number of group members who are unable to make positive statements about themselves, or to 'hear' them from others, choosing to interpret their rewarding behaviour as manipulative or flattering.

What is particularly significant about the dilemmas which the technique of rewarding illustrates is the need for groupworkers to be aware of the social codes of the group members and how these might differ from themselves; these codes will be influenced by race, gender, class, culture, age and the like. This awareness should inform the use of any interactional technique.

Rewarding behaviour is like a gift, and the way we accept a gift is a good indication of how we might accept a social reward. The 'you shouldn't have' kind of response denies both the giver and the receiver any pleasure from the act; perhaps it is a fear of the rejection of the gift of rewarding behaviour which holds people back from using it.

11: CONFRONTING/CHALLENGING

> Chronic problem situations produce a tendency towards hopelessness and apathy in the people caught up in them. At the same time, chronic situations produce in would-be helpers a tendency to give up challenging people in favour of supporting them – and support without challenge does not lead to learning and does not lead to empowerment. (Breton 1991: 45)

There is some evidence of a reluctance to confront amongst relatively inexperienced groupworkers, stemming perhaps from a fear of not being liked, of being seen to misuse authority, of provoking an over-reaction, or of embarrassing the group. However, for the developing groupworker, it should not be a question of whether to challenge, but *how* to challenge in a way that does not lead to greater barriers (Reid 1988: 132).

Some of the difficulty lies in the breadth of meaning covered by the terms 'confronting' and 'challenging'. Bertcher (1994: 126) uses confrontation to describe the technique of informing an individual, individuals or the whole group of an inconsistency. This inconsistency might exist between something they have said or done and something else they have said or done, or between the facts and something they have said or done. This sense of 'confrontation' makes it a specialized form of information giving. As with other interactional techniques, a confrontation should be related to the achievement of the group's aims, otherwise it will be perceived as a personal attack and the response will be defensive.

We can see how confrontation and challenge are a response more to inconsistency than to conflict and that groupworkers are using their skill and experience to point to these contradictions in ways which group members can hear and can learn from.

12: MEDIATING

> Mediating involves putting yourself in a neutral position between opponents in order to avoid or resolve a disagreement that is keeping the group from reaching its goals. (Bertcher 1994: 153)

Overt conflict is unusual in the early stages of the group unless there is a history to the group, where members are already known to each other. However, at some stage there are likely to be disagreements and conflicts which will require mediation. Group members might take on this role, but more often they will look to the groupworkers, who must take care not to squash conflict by making decisions on behalf of the group (in the mistaken belief that they are shielding one vulnerable person or subgroup from another more powerful one). It is too easy to reach a decision without resolving the conflict that lies behind the need for one.

When a group member makes a suggestion which is likely to meet disagreement, rather than inviting immediate comment on the one suggestion it helps to generate other options and discuss their relative merits before coming to a decision. In this way, individuals do not get wedded to 'their' idea and each is seen to be contributing to the pool of ideas which becomes the group's. Where disagreement persists and escalates into conflict, it is important to help the whole group to look behind the conflict in order to find out as much as possible about it. The information-seeking technique can be combined with mediating to draw heat out of the situation and to generate new options.

The timing of any interactional technique is important, and none more so than mediation. 'The better you know your group, the more likely it is that you will be able to use mediating on time, rather than jumping in too early (which stops a potentially useful exchange) or intervening so late that irreparable damage occurs' (Bertcher 1994: 153). This is especially difficult if you are in strong sympathy with one of the parties. Indeed, if one of the opposing positions is consistent with the group's aspirations and the other is not, it might be necessary to support that position, being clear about relating the reasons to the group's overall purposes; this underlines that your support is based on fact, not fiction. Whatever the conclusion, any individuals who might see themselves as 'losing' must be brought back into the group's processes.

If your neutrality as a mediator is brought into question (perhaps because the conflict is splitting the group along gender lines and your own gender is inescapable) it is sometimes necessary to consider introducing a co-mediator who can satisfy the desire for fairness and balance.

The success of mediation is enhanced if you have an awareness of your own style of conflict management. Fatout (1989: 76) describes subjugation and alliance as the more primitive methods of conflict resolution, and if these are prevalent styles amongst group members, groupworkers need to model less coercive approaches. The Thomas-Kilmann (1974) conflict model considers two behavioural dimensions – assertiveness and cooperativeness – with a possibility of five different responses to conflict, depending on the degrees of assertiveness and cooperation:

- collaborating (high assertiveness and high cooperation)
- competing (high assertiveness and low cooperation)
- avoiding (low assertiveness and low cooperation)
- accommodating (low assertiveness and high cooperation)
- compromising (moderate assertiveness and moderate cooperation).

Although some terms seem negative (avoiding), whilst others have positive connotations (accommodating), all five strategies have their merits. It is important that groupworkers develop the ability to employ different strategies when necessary. For example, if your style is very reliant on accommodating, you might find it hard to adopt styles which rely on high assertiveness even when these styles would be more effective responses to the particular situation in a group.

13: SUMMARIZING

> Summarizing is the process of drawing together and briefly restating a
> number of prior responses into one statement, then seeking agreement
> or correction from the group members until a summary statement has
> been produced that everyone considers accurate. (Bertcher 1994: 102)

Although you may wish to model the technique of summarizing by beginning a session with a summary of the previous one, it is wise to encourage
other group members to summarize, too. If you know that you will be summarizing you attend particularly carefully and take the trouble to clarify what
others are meaning. This careful attending behaviour is important to the
group's development.

As with all of the interactional techniques presented in this chapter, the art
of good timing is essential to a successful summary. A summary must draw together a number of different contributions (otherwise it is merely a collection
of 'attendings'), so it should allow enough discussion to begin to arrive at a
position or a consensus, and not so much that it becomes repetitive and circular. The summary needs to include processes and feelings as well as outcomes
and actions; the best summaries become more than a series of additions in an
equation but make connections for the group which take its understanding to
a different level. This is especially true when the summary draws out an
emerging group theme (see Chapter 10). In formal meetings summaries are
usually written, perhaps in the form of minutes, which makes it easier for the
next meeting to pick up where it left off. A less formal group might make use
of a flipchart to summarize.

14: ENDING

Ending refers to the activities and behaviours used to end the group, a group
meeting or to conclude a topic during the session. Thus, there are many endings in the life of the group, not just the obvious farewell of a final session.
Clearly, the summarizing technique described above is often a component of
ending. See Chapter 13 for more detailed discussion of ending.

Portfolio extract

Technique: Confronting/Attending

Joan (groupworker): OK – now that we've all had the chocolate, are we ready to start?

Una: Yeah – what are we doing this week? I forgot.

Veronica: We're doing make-up. Louise's brought all her stuff. Look it's over there.

Sara: I know what I want on me …

Joan: Hang on, hang on – we haven't done the opening game yet.

Chorus: Oh, do we have to? We don't want to. They're crap.

Joan: But you enjoyed last week's …

Chorus: No we didn't!

Veronica: Do we have to? We don't want to.

Joan: Well hang on a minute. You say you didn't enjoy last week's but that's not what your evaluation sheets say – I'll get them. Yes, look Veronica … and Una … you've both given them 5 – that's the best you can give!

Veronica: Yeah, but that's not because we like them.

Joan: Well, why is it then?

Veronica: Because we didn't want to hurt your feelings. We thought you'd be upset.

Joan: Oh right. So let me get this straight then – are you all saying that you don't like the warm-up games?

Chorus: Yes.

Joan: None of them?

Chorus: Yes / No.

Joan: Meaning none of you liked any of them?

Chorus: Yes.

Joan: What about the close-down games?

Chorus: Them as well / They're worse / No.

Joan: OK – so you are saying that from now on you don't want to do either?

Chorus: That's it / Yes / No.

Joan: OK.

I think that this was dealt with appropriately; however, I can see it lacks any real gatekeeping. Anyone who hadn't wished to go along with the group consensus would have found it difficult to object or offer an alternative. The decision was made. We could have opened up the discussion, involved the other leaders on the 'pro' side to allow support for anyone wanting to voice dissent. We could have flipcharted the pros and cons.   JA (1998)

CHAPTER NINE

Individual Behaviours in the Group

About 'The deal'

When you lead a group it can feel like being dealt a hand of cards; some-times they fall kindly, other times less so. 'The deal' presents nine 'cards', each representing individual behaviours in groups. You are asked to con-sider how these behaviours could show themselves and what they might signify.

Purpose

The creative tension between the individual and the group is evident in the different behaviours exhibited by individuals in the group. This chapter de-scribes a variety of behaviours and their possible meaning, triggered by your completion of the deal activity. It is designed to alert you to a range of behav-iours, and to make a clear distinction between individuals and their behav-iours. The chapter also introduces a general framework to help groupworkers handle difficult episodes in the life of a group.

Method

- Consider each of the eight cards with headings on page 180. (It is best to photocopy them and cut them out.)

- Before turning to the notes for this chapter, write a brief definition of each behaviour. Don't worry if you are uncertain about some of them at this stage.

- On one side of each card write a very brief example of the behaviour in question. Use the blank card, ?, to describe any other group behaviour you would like to identify. It is preferable to use the experience of a current group; otherwise, use one from your previous experience, or a hypothetical example which you think illustrates each behaviour.

The deal

Monopolizing	**Leading from within**	**Challenging**
Keeping silent	**?**	**Gatekeeping**
Joking	**Being different**	**Scapegoating**

Variations

- Review your eight or nine examples. How many present the behaviour as problematic or difficult? How many see it as helpful?

- Turn the card over and write an example which is the opposite to the one of the reverse (i.e. if your first example illustrated the negative effects of the behaviour, write an example that presents the behaviour positively). Again, this can be a hypothetical example if needs be, but it is preferable to draw from current practice.

Notes for the groupworker

Debrief

Were you surprised at the proportion of negative examples you described? Perhaps you were more surprised by being asked to contemplate behaviours like scapegoating in any positive light, as having any potential for a beneficial impact on a group. If you did not manage to complete both sides of each card, try once more before reading on.

Roles and groups

There are many different behaviours in groups, and these have been variously catalogued by groupwork theorists and writers. Even a cursory dip into the literature will reveal 'scapegoats', 'gatekeepers', 'passengers' and the like. However, there are two difficulties with the usual manner in which roles in groups are discussed.

The first difficulty is a tendency to see individual roles as problematic, especially from the groupworker's point of view. The literature alerts us to 'monopolizers' and 'deviant members', but rarely to 'problem solvers' or 'unifiers'. The tendency to focus on the negative has parallels elsewhere – we have lots of words to describe ill-health (fever, gangrene, indigestion, etc.), but the state of good health is undifferentiated. However, this negative focus inevitably points the groupworker in the direction of pathology. That it why it is important to consider how the reverse sides of the cards in the deal activity might appear.

When we read of 'the scapegoat', 'the joker', 'the internal leader', we can immediately see the second difficulty with the way in which role theory has been applied to groupwork. The role is personified. Instead of displaying challenging behaviour, Becky becomes The Challenger; Harjinder's different behaviour makes him The Deviant Member. Imagery which describes members as 'Sherman tanks', 'snipers', 'exploders' and 'clams' is vivid (see Bramson in Lumley and Marchant 1989: 141), but we need to remind ourselves that these are *icons*, not real people in the group. This is not just a matter of semantics. If we see these as role behaviours they become more fluid, so that we can observe that different group members might display the same challenging behaviour without becoming the group's 'challenger'; and Becky's challenging behaviour early in the session might become Becky's 'leading from within' behaviour later in the same session. Of course, there are patterns to each individual's behaviour, and people too readily allow themselves to fall into a regular role. This is notoriously true of scapegoating behaviours which are often directed towards the same person. However, part of a group's purpose is often to help people to break free from these patterns and, as a groupworker, you can give a strong lead to this uncoupling of person from behaviour. So move away from nouns which label individuals towards verbs which describe their behaviours.

Below we explore in detail the eight example behaviours from the activity. What emerges from this exploration is the reality that most behaviours cannot be explained without an understanding of the context – for the individual and for the group. A general strategy for working with the behaviour, whatever its nature, is described in the section following the behaviours themselves.

The eight 'behaviours'

Powers of observation are crucial. Groupworkers may misinterpret, exaggerate or understate the behaviours and their frequency, so always be prepared to check out, test and refute. For example, one groupworker was seriously concerned at the frequent four-minute silences endured in the group and was about to construct an activity designed to counter the problem, until several sessions were monitored and the silences were found to be less than 90 seconds long, and occuring with less frequently than the worker had estimated (Reid 1988: 128).

MONOPOLIZING

Monopolizing behaviour is sometimes personified in the groupwork literature as 'the dominant member'. A person's behaviour is monopolizing if they take up a disproportionate amount of the group's time, to the extent that other members are finding it difficult to contribute. It can be a fine line between a person who has been useful in starting the group off when other members were feeling reticent and withholding, and the next stage when group members are ready to participate but find they have lost the ground and are not being allowed the opportunity to regain it.

Groupworkers need to consider the following questions. Is this a regular pattern for this person? Is the group colluding, by letting this person do all the work? Have the group leaders given mixed messages by encouraging the person to dominate early on because of a fear that nobody would speak?

LEADING FROM WITHIN

The groupworkers frequently have formal authority in the group, but group members can also exercise leadership qualities and functions. There are many possible origins for the authority of 'internal leadership', and it is most effective when it derives from the other group members themselves and when this serves to strengthen the formal leadership of the groupworkers. Internal leaders can been treated as allies or enemies, depending on how secure the groupworkers feel, how in touch with the group they are, and the nature of the internal leadership.

The motivation for leading from within can spring from many sources: an habitual challenge to formal authority; a desire to cosy up to those with power; a confidence in the formal leadership and a desire to bolster it; a commitment to the group's aims and a fear that the existing leadership is not competent to meet them. Each of these would have a quite different feel for the groupworkers and the other members; it is a powerful illustration of how a behaviour in one circumstance can be helpful to the group, and in another can hinder.

In a group with parents of learning disabled adolescents, a mother with an older child was seen as wiser by virtue of longer experience and was 'able to challenge denial by the parents of younger children' (Gobat 1993: 224) in a way that would have been difficult for the groupworkers.

CHALLENGING

The very act of setting up a group and acting as its leader can evoke a challenge. Whether you are comfortable with it or not, and no matter how much you have softened your leadership style to empower members, you are usually different from the group members. Often, your value to the group stems from your difference (perhaps the access which your position in the agency gives to group members is useful), and the way in which you handle your difference will be seen as an exemplar by group members as to how they might handle difference in the group.

Sometimes, then, a challenge is an expression of the individual's discomfort with the perceived difference in role and power between group member and groupworker. It may be a way of testing what will be acceptable and what is beyond limits in the group. A challenge may stem from a very deep misunderstanding or disagreement about the purpose of the group, or the methods which are being proposed to achieve those purposes.

A challenge often feels uncomfortable, not just for the groupworker, but for other members, too. It may be heavy-handed and unaccomplished; it may reach to the heart of the groupworker's insecurity; it may encourage others in the group to join a bandwagon. The outcome of the challenge, and in particular the way the groupworker responds, is usually of intense interest to the rest of the group, for it signals how disagreement will be handled in this setting. How safe is it to challenge and be challenged in this group? How accepted will it be?

Challenge can provide groups with an opportunity for growth in a way that is difficult to achieve in groups where there is no challenge. Groups which fear challenge, or ones in which there is a cosy consensus, are unlikely to encourage the risk-taking which many people hope to gain from being a member of a group.

KEEPING SILENT

> Silence is often related to the operation of power and is a sign of the existence of conflict. (Batsleer 1994: 198)

There is perhaps no other behaviour in a group which causes such immediate consternation as silence. This is reflected in the pages devoted to it in the literature, which is far from silent (Batsleer 1994; Brown 1992: 128; Butler and Wintram 1991; Heap 1985: 87; Shulman 1984: 286). Whether it is the silence of an individual over a period of time ('the quiet member') or the group as a whole, silence can feel unsettling. Whereas silence in a one-to-one session can serve to emphasize the intimacy and closeness of the encounter, silence in the group as a whole can feel very public and expose the loneliness of individuals.

It is not easy to understand what is being communicated by the silence, since the possibilities are so diverse. A sense of warm intimacy, or a cold, hostile distance? A reflective, thoughtful musing, or a switched-off, 'wish I was somewhere else' boredom? Groupworkers will tune into their own responses and try to read the group's non-verbals, but these are not always reliable, especially if clouded by their own embarrassment, doubts or panic about what to do.

There is always a need to make the links between the dynamics in the small group and the wider, societal forces outside the group, and nowhere is this more evident than in the meaning of silence in groups, where 'the institutional location of groupwork determines or shapes whose voices are privileged and whose speech marginalized' (Batsleer 1994: 203). 'Having a voice' in society and the experience of being listened to are not common for many people; Weinstein (1994) reminds us of the symbolic authority of 'the conch' in *Lord of the Flies* to impose silence on others.

There was a fashion in therapeutic circles for tolerating long silences, but it is important to consider the potential oppressiveness of prolonged silences and the responsibilities of leadership. Noticing the silence and enquiring what others think the silence might mean can be an honest way of using and breaking the silence at one and the same time. The groupworker has a responsibility to listen, hear and speak. Ignoring the silence by introducing a new topic in order to fill air space is what you might expect of someone at a tea party, not of a skilled groupworker.

Keeping silent can be a powerful way of not sharing, which can be resented by group members who have taken the risk of putting themselves in a vulnerable position, so some groups might not allow silence as an option. The rules in a group for girls who had been sexually abused were that every member would take turns and share their experiences, because 'for one girl to opt out and not share would leave her with a knowledge of others' experiences and lead to imbalances of power in the group' (Peake and Otway 1990: 125). However, the options offered in 'turn-taking' were not just to speak, but also to write or draw, or have a peer or groupworker to speak for them. It is important that the ground rules for the group have considered silence, because there are times when keeping one's counsel is an important act of self-preservation which needs to be respected.

The term 'keeping silent' suggests a deliberate act of retention. There is a difference between keeping silent and *being* silent. Being silent implies a sense of restful security derived from just being here in the group, rather like the safety which a child feels when dropping off to sleep in adult company, the sound of voices and the mere presence of others providing a physical and emotional comfort which does not demand active participation. A member of a group for refugee women spoke virtually no English, no-one spoke her language and she did not want an interpreter, 'yet she continued to come, sitting silently, smiling occasionally. She was always warmly welcomed by the other women ... she apparently gained some comfort and support from the group' (Tribe and Shackman 1989: 163). We can all appreciate the comfort to be derived from just being in a group and the very different quality of this kind of silence.

GATEKEEPING

When the group gets close to something difficult, a group member might try to divert the discussion. A variety of strategies can be used, such as lingering on a previous topic, asking lots of factual questions, keeping quiet, introducing red herrings, etc. There may be occasions when the whole group takes part in this gatekeeping behaviour; witness the sophisticated techniques deployed by training groups to edge away from a proposed role play! It is as if the group, having braved itself for the plunge, suddenly becomes fearful when it nears the edge. 'What exactly did you say the depth of this particular plunge was? … Perhaps we don't need to take it after all – let's go and sit on that comfy bench over there.' The effect can be to shake the groupworkers' confidence so that they, too, start to question whether the group is really ready; alternatively, the workers might become exasperated and want to shout, 'just do it!'

There are times when it is right to respect the gatekeeping behaviour, and there are other times when the group needs the groupworkers' confidence and trust to move on. Pointing to the gatekeeping behaviour can help to dispel the fears which lie behind it, though it can also provide fodder for further diversionary tactics!

In a group for children of divorced and separated parents, composed of six sets of sibling pairs (in effect, six subgroups within the group), one pair of siblings acted as the group's gatekeepers, providing an escape route for the rest of the group when things got intense. 'While the focus was on them the group was superficial and non-threatening' (Regan and Young 1990: 32). They were not scapegoated, but provided breathing space to retreat when the going was tough.

It is important for groupworkers to be observant in order to notice any patterns of gatekeeping behaviour. Often it is only in the time for reflection after a group that the behaviour is recognised for what it is, and a discussion can take place about whether it helped or hindered the group and how to respond if it reoccurs in the next session.

JOKING

> The humour was rich, raucous and sometimes very very funny. (Dobbin and Evans 1994: 122, of a group for mothers of sexually abused children)

Humour is the group's salt and pepper. It often makes palatable what would otherwise be unpalatable. Even in groups where the content matter is distressing and painful – perhaps especially in these groups – humour is an essential element and can provide a catharsis. We need to remind ourselves of the obvious; that people will return to a group and give it their support if they enjoy it, and humour plays a significant part in this. Those with a gift for humour can be very influential in the group and they can use this position in ways which bind or ways which divide. When we focus on the behaviour, in this case using humour, we can see how it is an essential ingredient for group success; if we personalize this into 'the joker', we can see clearly how it assumes a pejorative meaning.

Humour in the group can be entertaining, amusing, diverting, playful, sarcastic, witty, facetious, and sometimes all of these at the same time, depending on the context and the group members' mutual perceptions. If patterns develop so that humour is used regularly in ways which inhibit the group's progress, such as a gatekeeping function which blocks the group from exploring difficult territory, then it is necessary to signal the effect which the humour is having. It is possible to acknowledge the value of humour in general in the group (and an individual's special wit) whilst pointing to any detrimental effect it is having at a particular time.

The use of humour can bond the group together, helping to demonstrate the common humanity of the whole group.

BEING DIFFERENT

Sometimes people in groups behave in ways which are very different from the general behaviour in the group. This is more likely to happen in the early stages when the group is forming, and the social rules are still uncertain. Differences may persist throughout the life of the group where individuals are not able to modify their behaviour in relation to the rest of the group. This kind of behaviour may present a challenge or a problem, but there are times when the person may be articulating a concern shared by others:

> A community meeting was called jointly by the staff of the neighbourhood social services and a local general practice, in order to involve citizens (and not just 'clients' and 'patients') in the work of the health and social services. The introduction took care to frame the issues around health and social care, and then questions were invited. The first question was: 'what are you going to do about the dog dirt on the pavements in our neighbourhood?' It appeared to be 'deviant' because the professionals who had organized the community meeting had expected to focus on health and social care issues. However, the questioner met a chorus of approval, and it became evident that the state of the pavements was the most immediate concern of the assembled citizens.

When different behaviour is highlighted by other differences in attribute (for example, the person behaving differently is also the only man in the group, the only Asian, etc.) it becomes problematic to separate the behaviour from the person. The cause of the different behaviour becomes (and is) inextricably bound with the difference in attribute; the very oldness of an older person is a challenge to the 'normality' of a group of young people, and groups do not manage this kind of challenge easily.

The person who is different in a group can often be a catalyst for change. In the groups for parents of learning disabled adolescents, Gobat (1993) identified a person who was 'the most needy and most vulnerable' and who drew the group into more painful feelings. Deviant behaviour can also be a source of strength for a group. In youth gangs, for example, the punishment which brings many deviants back into group conformity reinforces the importance of conformity for *all* group members and serves to increase group solidarity (Lo 1993: 58). However, the person who is different can also inhibit the group's development. O'Connor (1992: 81) describes how the absence of 'Sue' from a group session liberated the other members to share very deeply about their bereavements by suicide; Sue's level of vulnerability was so deeply different that it had prevented them from travelling that far during previous group sessions.

The difference which an individual represents to the group resonates with the difference which group members feel in the wider society, and this brings us to the last of the behaviours we are exploring in this chapter.

SCAPEGOATING

> Whether it is overt scapegoating in children's and teenage groups or the more subtle type experienced in adult groups, the impact on the group members and the worker can be profound. (Shulman 1984: 267)

Scapegoating is the collection of strong feelings of hostility often directed towards one person in the group on a regular basis by the other group members. This is probably the best-known and most-feared social and group role and at some time in our lives we have all had experience of this behaviour and been aware of its potential destructiveness. Once again, we use the term 'scapegoating behaviour' rather than the label 'the scapegoat' in order to acknowledge the shared responsibility in these situations.

The difficulty for the groupworkers is compounded by the strong feelings which scapegoating arouses in them. Often this is a strong distaste for the behaviour of the group members and a desire to protect the scapegoated person, but it can also be a considerable sympathy (and possible collusion) with the group members faced with a person whom everybody finds hard to like.

There is much written in the groupwork literature about scapegoating, so we will focus not on what it is but rather consider it as an example of how groupworkers can learn to treat behaviours in the group as messages rather than problems. In this chapter we have been looking at these behaviours in groups not as disfunctional problems, but as communications to the group members and workers, capable of helping or hindering the group's work, and sometimes both at the same time. Whichever side the card is dealt, the behaviour is sending a message which needs to be read. If it remains unread it can assume a disabling grip over the group, growing in power the more it is ignored. The single most significant action the group leaders can take is to point directly to the behaviour and name it. This breaks the spell and allows the whole group to check it out: 'How do we each see it?' It brings power back into the centre of the group and away from the behaviour.

In training groups, we have characterized this as 'the elephant shit in the middle of the group': though everybody can smell it, no-one is acknowledging it. It won't go away on its own; indeed, it will continue to grow and to smell, and to become even more powerfully foul because no-one is able to deal with it. Only when the group acknowledges its existence can it be swept up and dealt with (and, as one person with a gift for positive reframing noted, 'used as fertilizer on the garden'!). In terms of scapegoating, for example, the groupworkers' task is to help the whole group look at the processes at play, not by putting the spotlight on the person being scapegoated, nor by condemning those who are active in the scapegoating, but by helping the group to tease out the messages and themes which lie behind this behaviour (Chapter 10). Moreover, pointing to behaviours which are halting the group's work creates an opportunity for problem solving by the group as a whole, rather than seeing the situation as a tough nut for the intrepid groupworker to crack.

One of the principle roles of the co-workers is to enable the group to discuss issues of *power*. Frequently, the individual behaviours outlined above, will be an entrée to the question of power, its use and its distribution in the group. This will be especially noticeable when behaviours fall along certain fault lines: the only man in the group is seen to monopolize; the person whose behaviour is different from the group norm is also different in other ways (the only black person, the only young person, the only person with a speech difficulty – Chapter 3). Recognizing and challenging oppressive behaviours in groups requires skilled interactional techniques and an ability to use all of the techniques detailed in the previous chapter.

Other behaviours

What other behaviour did you identify for the blank card in the activity? Subgrouping is frequently mentioned, and we explore this group phenomenon in the next chapter. However, there are two kinds of behaviour which fall outside the range normally associated with groups.

The first of these is *absence*. It is not difficult to see why the impact of absence can be insidious, because we are less likely to notice the *lack* of something (Whitaker 1985: 340). A headache makes its presence felt, but we are often unaware when the headache has stopped. The most difficult kind of absences are those which are sporadic, because it is difficult to build a sense of continuity in the group and members have to catch up, both in terms of content and process. In common with the eight behaviours we have already explored, it is important to consider what lies behind the absence. Are the reasons practical, structural or emotional; are they within the group's power to alter or not? It can be complex; for example, are absences from a group for people with cancer due to their finding themselves not well enough to attend some sessions, or unable to face some of the emotional pain involved? In these kinds of circumstance, where uncertainty is unavoidable, it is useful to have a system to lessen the uncertainty; for example, telephoning the group membership earlier in the day of the group meeting to check on likely attendance (Daste 1989: 63).

In contrast to absence is *steady presence*. There are those in a group whose behaviour is not noteworthy but who provide 'ballast' to the group. It may only be on later reflection that groupworkers are able to see the calm base which such members provide. In a group for children of divorced or separated parents, Regan and Young (1990: 32) noticed that one pair of siblings 'in retrospect ... seemed to provide a kind of stability for the group as a whole by remaining low-keyed'. This kind of behaviour can be taken for granted; it is different from silence, which can make its presence all too felt, but it is a significant factor in groups.

Sticky moments in groups

What inhibits groupworkers and group members from pointing at the elephant shit and naming it? One of the common fears is that pointing at it will raise its status and significance, thus highlighting the problem. For example, if 'it' is a person's difference in the group, then pointing at 'it' only serves as a reinforcement, making 'it' all the more exposed and different. In these circumstances the groupworker may need to find less direct ways of addressing the difficulty – perhaps to come up alongside it by opening up discussion about how people respond to difference first, rather than moving straight to the difference in question. There is more than one way to scoop up elephant droppings!

Allan Brown (1992: 123–6) suggests a number of different options for dealing with difficulties in groups:

- do nothing
- indirect responses
- direct implicit responses
- direct explicit responses
- contact outside the group.

Each of these responses has its merits and the skill of groupworking is knowing how and when to use them. Whatever your particular response, it is important that it is a considered one and that it is made with both the individuals-in-the-group and the group-as-a-whole in mind (Chapter 10). You need to be sure that your particular response was made because it was the most appropriate to the occasion, and not because it is the one you feel most comfortable with or use habitually.

Most groups have incidents which put groupworkers on their mettle: an action which leaves you not knowing what to do; a comment which leaves you speechless. As a groupworker, you need to consider how to use these sticky moments as valuable opportunities for your development, rather than experiences which frighten you away from groupwork. Preparation is an important factor, so that you make use of the information you gained when you offered the groupwork (Chapter 5), and the experiences you have had during any previous sessions of the group. These will help to you to anticipate potential 'stickiness', and rehearsing these will mean that you have a number of considered responses already available should they be needed.

If you were not able to prepare for the sticky moment before it occurred, revisit it and rehearse what you might have done. Re-playing it later in a discussion with yourself, your co-worker or mentor will help your analysis of what exactly made the situation 'sticky' and why it proved so difficult to handle. This, in turn, helps to understand what the group was communicating to itself and why you found it hard to respond. Following these steps will increase the odds that your sticky moments will accelerate rather than block your learning.

Groupworkers who do not seem to have any sticky moments should consider the following possibilities. The first is a failure to recognize sticky moments for what they are. At first sight, this seems an unlikely possibility, since the definition of a sticky moment is, surely, an acute consciousness of self; however, it is possible that there are such occasions for group members but, as group leader, you are not being sensitive to them. A second possibility is that the group is playing safe and avoiding risks; this may alert you to the need to encourage the group (including yourself) to stretch itself. The absence of testing situations may feel comfortable, but could be letting the group off the hook. Perhaps you are colluding with the group in gatekeeping behaviour?

In Chapter 10 we introduce a framework drawn from systems theory designed to help develop your analysis of how to work with obstacles to group functioning which are often experienced as sticky moments.

Formal roles in the group

Some behaviours in groups are institutionalized into formal roles ('roles with names') which a group can choose to confer on its members. For example, a group with a very explicit purpose and a high division of labour may have a chair and vice-chair, a treasurer and a secretary. The way these roles are allocated are a strong indication of levels of participation and democracy in the group.

Some roles may continue in the same hands for the life of the group, whilst others change from session to session (such as the tea-maker), or are agreed for just part of a session (for example, the time-keeper for an exercise). These semi-formal roles can be important in enhancing group commitment, cohesion and task-completion. They provide a way to build on people's particular abilities and interests, underlining how individual contributions make the whole group stronger.

The manner in which roles are assigned in the group and the decision about whether they should rotate or not is a reflection of the style of that particular group. For example, a group for people with disabilities in Ireland has an action group of five members, within a broader membership of twenty, to carry on the work of the group between meetings. 'This action group rotates its membership on a regular basis so that everyone gains experience at this level' (Chorcora, Jennings and Lordan 1994: 71). The role of chair in a group held within a hostel for girls evolved to a state where the position was rotated around the girls and 'in time, the person in the role was accorded considerable respect' (Duffy and McCarthy 1993: 155).

There is no doubt that social roles in groups are an inescapable and potentially valuable part of the groupwork. The groupworker's own role includes an awareness of the impact of these behaviours and roles, and a willingness to help the group become 'unstuck' when they are hindering the group's progresse. We will look in more detail at co-working behaviours in Chapter 11.

Portfolio extract

Claire became an outsider. She was not scapegoated, but she never became part of the group, no matter how hard she tried. When she was absent from the group she was not missed, no-one asked where she was. When she was present she struggled to be heard even though she had a lot to say and did try to say it. She was often ignored and it would be left to leaders to pick up what she said and draw it to the attention of the group. [In an all-white group] I think it was Claire's obvious difference in class, lifestyle and academic achievement that marked her out as different and her absences that confirmed her as an outsider ... she talked about second homes and other things that reinforced that particular difference ...

I think the other girls, as they felt more and more part of the group, experienced her absences as a lack of commitment to the group, a rejection of it and as part of the process of drawing together, rejected her. In some ways, I feel that Claire helped to accelerate the process of forming the group amongst the others – she was the 'them' to their 'us'. In common with the other groupworkers I felt great sympathy for Claire as we knew enough of her personal background to know that she is very unhappy and that she was desperate to do something normal. Ironically, the group seemed to reinforce her feelings of not being normal. I think we all felt a bit powerless about Claire and I certainly worried that the group was one more negative experience for her.

Her social worker expressed no surprise when she dropped out and although we followed it up, we accepted her decision not to come again – and then she turned up two sessions later.

When she did come we continually attempted to facilitate her integration into the group and to a degree, in the end, she achieved a measure of success. I think this was partly due to the group's confidence in its own identity and the consequent capability to allow more diversity. For Claire's part, I think she used her absences as 'a device for diluting an otherwise too intense experience' by 'accurately assessing [her] capacity to tolerate the group' (Whitaker 1985: 341).   JA (1998)

CHAPTER TEN

The Individual and the Group

About 'First person'

A person's choice of pronoun ('I', 'we', 'you', 'they', etc.) is significant. It signals the way they locate themselves in relation to the people around them. It is especially significant in terms of a group, where the movement from I to we is a metaphor for the development of a group identity. The First Person activity helps to develop your powers of observation in groups, as well as alerting you to a technique by which to measure the movement from a collection of individuals to a group.

Purpose

This chapter considers the balance between individuals in the group and the group itself, and the particular place of subgroups. This balance or tension between the need to consider two separate sets of needs – those of the individuals in the group and those of the group as a whole – has been a strong theme in groupwork theory (Schwartz's 'Two Clients', 1976; Shulman 1984). The chapter helps you reflect on the nature of group culture and to consider how the notion of group themes (sometimes explicit, sometimes implicit) can help the group's progress. The chapter also offers a framework drawing from systems theory to help groupworkers to analyze and work with perceived obstacles to the group's progress.

Method

- You will need access to a group meeting where you can be an observer, such as a team meeting or a video of a group session. On paper, draw the group with a small circle to represent each individual; write each person's initials by their circle and I/we by the side of their initials.

- During a period of observation of between fifteen and thirty minutes take a count of the number of times each person uses 'I' and how many times they use 'we'. At the end of the period of observation you should have two scores for each person: an 'I' count and a 'we' count.

- Consider the scores. What is the balance of 'I's to 'we's? What differences are there between individuals in the group? Do these seem related to any other attributes (gender; role in the group; power in the group, etc.)? How well did you feel the group was functioning, and does this tell you anything about the significance of the I/we tally?

Variations

There is a warm-up game which begins 'If you were an animal, which animal would you be?' For animal, it is possible to substitute day of the week, country, room in a house, etc. The activity is an oblique and creative way of helping people to disclose information about themselves without having to be concrete or direct. It appeals to feelings and impressions rather than logical thinking, and it reveals as much about a person's self-image as it does about their self.

In the First Person example on page 196 we have used various type fonts to indicate the different ways in which individuals might express their I-ness, their sense of self. So, the activity could be used to ask 'If you were an I, what kind of I would you be?' You could consider asking group members to do this graphically on a large piece of paper, reproducing the shape of the group on the paper (circular, horse-shoe, haphazard, etc.), with each individual marking their position with an I of their choice. Each group member would discuss what they wished to convey by their choice of 'I', followed by how the group is progressing towards a sense of 'We'.

The discussion might continue to consider the notion of group themes and an exploration of whether there are any group themes emerging.

First person

Successful groups move from first person singular to first person plural without losing sight of, nor respect for, the individual differences.
How would the 'I's in your group style themselves?
How often do group members use 'I' and how often 'we'?

Group themes

What group themes have you noticed?

Notes for the groupworker

When is a group a group?

    First there is the individual.

        Then there is a group of individuals.

        Then there is the group.

This, at its barest, is the kind of progress which group leaders hope to achieve. As we saw in Chapter 1, the common usage of 'group' is inexact, so that a collection of individual items is often termed a group. A stand of trees is merely a number of individual trees whose close proximity leads us to group them together. The proximity of a dozen people huddled together in a shelter whilst they await a bus leads us to describe them as a group. However, like the trees in the stand, they are a group of individuals. They are not a group in the sense in which we use the word in this book.

'When does a group of individuals become a group?' is a bit of a 'how long is a piece of string?' question. It is better to think of a continuum, where one pole is characterized by a very atomized assortment of individuals and the other by a group where the members are in tune with each other and, together, amount to much more than the sum of their parts. Few groups will achieve the ultimate, and most groups will vary from session to session, appearing to be more collective in some sessions and more atomized in others. This can be a disappointment to group leaders, when a session in which members have acted very much in consort is followed by one where their divisions are dominant. However, this is common in the life of a group.

Lang (1986) has used the terms 'aggregate', 'collectivity' and 'group' to signify a continuum in the degree of interaction of people who are gathered together (see Figure 10.1).

Figure 10.1 Individuals becoming a group

Group identity: from 'I' to 'we'

> The knowledge of the certainty of the group's existence, its weekly regularity, serves in itself to provide a sense of collective activity and experience that is not achieved elsewhere. (Butler and Wintram 1991: 80)

Trust, reciprocity, open self-disclosure, positive feedback and mutuality are identified by Butler and Wintram (1991) as key to the development of group identity in women's groups, and these factors can safely be generalized as significant in other groups, too.

In more simple language, the movement from individuals to group is from a focus on 'I' to a sense of 'we'. In fact, the count of 'I's and 'we's in a group session is probably as good a measure as any of the progress along the continuum. Group leaders make deliberate use of 'we' in order to engender a sense of togetherness and when group members start to speak of 'we', real progress is being made.

The sense of I should not be neglected; indeed, the group might enable each member to undertake a journey of self-discovery which increases each individual's own awareness of the I. Writing about the power of feminist groupwork, Butler and Wintram (1991: 80) state that 'the power of the group can be discovered through each woman's *self*-discovery'.

In her capacity as a researcher, finding out whether reminiscence work would be possible, Atkinson draws an illuminating picture of the movement from working with a collection of individuals to a whole group in her work with older people with learning disabilities. She 'addressed group members rather than the group: asking questions, seeking clarification and reflecting back their answers. Not surprisingly, then, this first phase was characterised by group members speaking, on the whole, directly to me rather than to one another' (Atkinson 1993: 203). The first 14 one-hour sessions of the group continued in this vein, led by the needs of her research rather than the needs of the group and resulting in a process often referred to as 'switchboarding'. Tribe and Shackman (1989: 163) noticed the same phenomenon in their work with a group for refugee women: 'we encouraged the women to speak directly to each other, but at first they directed their contributions through us'. At the beginning of the group the leaders are seen as the chief 'I's.

The search for commonality

A group of individuals might make unaided progress along the continuum from atomized to collectivized, but the role of the groupworker is to accelerate this process. How can people who, in most cases, pursue their own individual lives outside the one or two hours of many groups be helped to use that time in ways which are significantly different?

A good example of the creative exchange between individuals and a group is a response to the 'Christmas present dilemma'. Who buys what for whom in a relatively close-knit team can be problematic. One such team of 12 people realized that for each to buy 11 presents for all the others was expensive and time consuming and would amount to an exchange of 131 presents (whether people celebrated Christmas or not, they all liked to give and receive at this time of year). The team decided to set a spending limit of £5, and to buy just one present each. To emphasize the fact that the present was on behalf of the whole group, it was given anonymously; this was achieved by each team member putting their name in a hat and drawing out another, unseen. During the following week each bought a present for 'their' person, adding it to the 11 presents chosen by colleagues for other individuals. The presents were opened communally at the office party. This is an excellent example of the needs of group and individual being met creatively.

One of the factors which bring individuals together is a sense of commonality (Heap 1979; Sarri and Galinsky 1967). In first contacts commonality is frequently connected with physical attributes. At a party where you do not know anybody, you are apt to pick out somebody you perceive as being like yourself. This provides a toe-hold until you have surveyed the larger gathering in order to make a more informed choice (the small group who seem to be laughing a lot, the person who looks like they want to be as quiet as you do, etc.).

The nature of conversation reveals the strength of the urge to search for commonalities, those things which bring us together. Strangers sharing a conversation will look for connections and find considerable joy from small coincidences, such as the fact that they lived in the same city ten years ago or discover they have a mutual acquaintance, no matter how tenuous. There is evidence to suggest, therefore, that the search for commonality is a human need like the need for affection or respect.

However, this process does not necessarily occur spontaneously. In a group of eight individuals, it may not occur to the other seven how the problems of the eighth relate to their own situations. In these circumstances it is crucial that groupworkers help individuals to make these connections. The following sequence is adapted from Kurland and Salmon (1993).

1   An individual *raises a problem* or issue which is concerning them.

2   The problem is clearly *identified* by the individual and the group.

3   The problem is *explored* in considerable detail before any solutions are offered. A flipchart is useful, if literacy and visual impairment are not in question, in order to build a clear picture of all aspects of the difficulty. Other individuals in the group can understand the situation from the point of view of the individual raising the concern, but can also begin to think about it in terms of their situation.

4   *Others recount* situations and dilemmas they have faced that are relevant to the problem; this could be begun in pairs, if it is likely that group members will find it difficult.

5   *Options* are developed which might alleviate the problem raised by the individual, drawing on the experiences of the full group.

6   The group as a whole helps the individual to *choose a course of action* and help to develop a plan to implement it.

7   The workers ask group members what they have *taken from the discussion* and how this might relate to their own problems.

This process is often described in the groupwork literature as 'using the group process' (Heap 1988: 18) or 'building a system of mutual aid' (Shulman 1984: 163). It is concerned with the subtle interplay between the many 'I's in the group and a developing sense of 'we'.

The search for commonality is not without its problems. First, it requires social skills to reach a satisfactory conclusion; without the skills to make connections, people can seem too distant, too fast, too curious. Groupwork can provide an opportunity for people to practise the skills of engagement with others. Second, the search for what is held in common can be a denial of what is different. This denial can be the result of fear or ignorance, but it will hinder the proper development of the group and, inevitably, feel oppressive to those who are seen as 'different'. So, the movement from 'I' to 'we' should not be a steamroller; there is nothing intrinsically better about 'we' and it has the potential to be oppressive if its inclusiveness denies differences.

Group themes

We have established that part of the groupworker's role is to help a variety of individuals to become a group. Fortunately, there is a powerful tool to aid this process, and this is the *group theme*. (See McCluskey and Miller 1995, for a related discussion of theme-focused work with family groups.)

EMERGENT THEMES

We have already highlighted the importance of the group's name and the way in which this is finally decided (Chapter 3). In many ways, the name of the group is the most public and direct 'theme' of the group. The fact that group members are coming to a group called the Young Offenders Group points directly to one thing they share – they are all young offenders. Sometimes the group has a euphemistic name which disguises its purpose from the public world (the Tuesday Group), though the focus is known well enough to insiders.

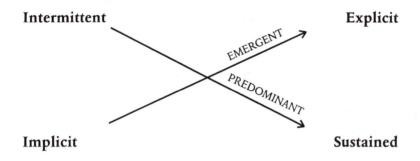

Figure 10.2 Different kinds of theme

The upfront reason why people are in the group, whether it is enshrined in the name of the group or not, provides an immediate and given theme. It will have been discussed openly in the offer of groupwork to individual members and is likely to be pivotal in the first session of the group. Even if it is a theme which is taboo outside the group, inside the group it is sanctioned. It provides an immediate, distinct connection between group members similar to the 'you look like me' connection at a social gathering we referred to earlier. Like a group of individuals who have 'come out', this mutual connection might be the stronger because it is the first time they have made a public acknowledgement. This is the power of the 'I am Sally and I am an alcoholic' format of Alcoholic Anonymous groups. The given theme is, therefore, an extremely important tool to encourage the development of a sense of 'we'.

A theme is not necessarily a description of what everybody has in common. All of the group members may have been abused as children, indeed this might be a criterion for membership of the group and it might constitute a given theme to start the ball rolling. However, there are likely to be group themes which are not evident at the first stages of the group and it is the mutual discovery of implicit themes which can have a powerfully unifying effect. Indeed, this has the potential to be more powerful than a descriptive term like 'abused'.

One of the tasks for the groupworkers is to help the group discover or uncover the implicit themes and to help them become explicit. Sometimes they are implicit because the links have not been made, in the way that a ball of wool has not yet become a scarf, but at other times these themes are hidden, even forbidden, and deliberately buried. In these circumstances, the groupworker's task is to help the members to tell their stories safely (Williams 1991) in a search for possible common theme. The very 'forbiddenness' of the story, and the reasons behind this, might be a common theme. DeVere and Rhonne (1991: 134) describe how the photo-language technique can be used to help hidden agendas to emerge in groups, by asking participants to reflect on photographs of everyday social situations. The distance which group members can put between themselves and the photograph can, paradoxically, help unspoken issues around stereotyping, attitudes towards other group members and the like, to emerge.

In general, the very process of discovery of themes is an integrating force, a part of group building. However, the co-workers might take a deliberate approach to the introduction of a theme which they consider significant yet unstated. For example, the leaders in a group for juvenile sex offenders introduce the theme that there are links between non-offending 'feeling states' and offending 'feeling states'; 'it is an introduction to the concept of their offences having to do with a feeling about something else in their lives' (Crown and Gates 1997: 60). This can be a legitimate and creative use of the groupworkers' experience to introduce new ideas and to accelerate the understanding of themes which might otherwise lie unfound, yet remain influential.

Of course, there is a fine line between helping the group to expose common themes and intrusive delving. Digging for themes 'on private property', especially if there are none to be found, is destructive to the individuals concerned and to groupwork processes. Moreover, the unhappy association between professional expertise and this kind of interpretative delving increases the power of the leadership at the expense of the members. In short, it is very disempowering.

PREDOMINANT THEMES

Some sessions might develop their own theme, without it necessarily recurring at other times in the group's life. Other themes might make subsequent appearances on an intermittent basis, and yet others might be sustained throughout the group. The musical meaning of 'theme' serves as a metaphor for the group's understanding of these different kinds of theme.

Themes might arise from topics, but they are different from them. For example, a Social Action Women's Group touches on a number of topics, such as sexuality; relationships with male partners; Black identity, racism and bringing up dual parentage children; money management, poverty and politics (Butler 1994). Out of these topics, Butler (1994: 169) identifies a number of themes which included *disappointment*, certainly in relation to sexuality. Food, too, might be an encompassing theme, linked as it is to nurturing, giving and receiving, and poverty. Management of the food budget when 'running out of money was a ubiquitous experience for women in the Social Action Group' (Butler 1994: 175).

Ball and Norman (1996: 56) describe these themes as emerging in their group with women who use food:

- the inability to take in and retain anything good
- the potential for the 'good' to be damaging or to be destroyed by the bad
- a fear of endless and overwhelming need within the self
- the desperate desire to eat which may then be replaced by guilt and self-reproach
- the need to get rid of food.

Norman (1994: 228) describes how the two themes of male power (both explicit violence and abdication from parental responsibility) and of consent to intercourse recurred in a group with young mothers.

ABSTRACT THEMES WITH CONCRETE EXPRESSION

Themes are often identified at the level of an abstraction, such as: trust; power; fears; anger; loss (themes identified by Dixon and Phillips (1994) as emerging in a group for boys who had been sexually abused). Similarly, self-blame, racism and sexism, body image, and shared experiences were seen as themes emerging in an art therapy group for women (Otway 1993). Expressed at this level of abstraction, a theme can provide a common denominator from which each individual can build their own concrete experiences. Sometimes a theme becomes 'actual' in the group itself; in an unusual circumstance a tiny baby became a kind of theme in a group for mothers of sexually abused children: 'one member's baby ... was used by all as comfort and reward as well as distraction and, occasionally, shield' (Dobbin and Evans 1994: 119). The baby served to bond the group together.

Themes may not become evident to group workers until after the group has finished. The latent theme of homophobia only became apparent to the group leaders of a group for male offenders when they later prepared a paper for public presentation (Bensted *et al.* 1994: 46).

In addition to common themes, the progress from 'I' to 'we' is achieved by the experience of common feelings. The activities which you use in the group are, by definition, commonly experienced. Sometimes they will generate common feelings in all members at the same time (good humour, sadness, reflectiveness, etc.) and at other times, members might be moved in different ways. The feelings level, thought not necessarily articulated in words, should not be underestimated as a powerful factor in helping individuals to become a group.

Obstacles

Progress from 'I' to 'we' is not guaranteed and it is useful to consider how and why groups can stall. Your recognition and analysis of the kind of obstacles that can prevent the group from functioning well is influenced by the general theories you use to explain how and why groups work, whether you hold these explicitly or intuitively. For example, a systems approach such as the one introduced in Chapter 1 will frame a groupworker's actions in very different ways from the psychodynamic one evident in Grindley's (1994: 59) view that 'it is important (to) learn about defence mechanisms in general, what they are, how they operate and why they come into play, [in order to] deal with other types of destructive behaviour when it arises'.

If groupworkers are to identify an obstacle as an obstacle, they need to be aware of the framework they are using to recognize them as such. The groupworkers' failure to recognize a pattern of difficulties as an obstacle can, in itself, be a block to the group's progress.

The systems framework helps to locate obstacles by providing a mental map of the group which can guide analysis and subsequent action. Figure 10.3 below presents a group as a series of concentric circles, with the leadership at the centre, individual members in the intermediate orbit (with possible subgroups of individuals) and an outer band representing the whole group. Beyond the whole group system lies the wider context – group members' families, communities, and the like, which have a considerable impact on the systems within the group. It should be emphasized that the central position of the leadership system is not to suggest that it is the most important, but to acknowledge the reality that it is often the most significant, at least initially. Moreover, although the groupworkers are often seen as 'Central Person' (Heap 1979: 49), the leadership system does not automatically mean the groupworkers. Leadership qualities and role will emerge from within the membership, especially in self-directed groups.

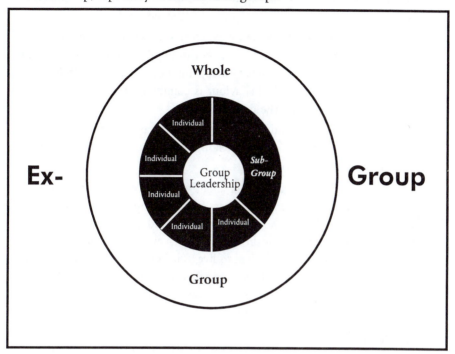

Figure 10.3 Group systems

We explore the group leadership in the next chapter, so let us consider a potential obstacle located in each of the remaining systems.

1: INDIVIDUALS IN THE GROUP

An individual in the group is behaving aggressively.

Each of the eight common behaviours described in the previous chapter can, along with a number of other behaviours, become obstacles to the group's progress. For example, an individual can monopolize the discussion in a group to such an extent that other members lose interest and the group fails to achieve its purposes. In addition to these behaviours there are others which can hinder the group's work such as violent, aggressive and disturbed behaviours. These are immediately challenging for the group and its leaders, but there are more subtle ways in which an individual's behaviour can inhibit or disrupt the progress of a group.

With all kinds of obstacle it is important first to recognize the obstacle as such. This is obvious with an in-your-face behaviour such as a person who arrives drunk to an alcohol management group, but less so with someone whose behaviour only slowly emerges as influenced by drink.

Even more complex is the situation when an individual's behaviour arises not from happenings outside the group, nor from physical reactions to drug intakes, but from a response to what is happening in the group itself. In these circumstances the individual's behaviour is communicating something beyond themselves and about the group itself.

The groupworker might focus on the individual as the obstacle to group functioning, yet this person can be speaking for a better group that could be, as opposed to the group that is:

> The women only want to talk about what men should do, what men don't do, what's wrong with men, it gets boring. They talk about the same things all the time ... I just sit there and listen ... I'd like to say, 'How would you like to be stuck in a flat with no furniture for four months?' That's how I've had to live. But I don't feel able to say these things. Every week it gets back to the same topic, men ... I'd like us to talk about us, women and our ordinary problems. (African-Caribbean woman quoted in Butler 1994: 172)

2: SUBGROUPS

> Three group members always sit together and giggle subversively during sessions.

Individuals find strength within the group by finding an anchor; note how often group members (and yourselves as groupworkers) sit in the same position in the group. Group-building exercises often deliberately forge subgroups, pairs, trios, etc., so that individuals can gain confidence in smaller groupings as a stepping stone to playing a full part in the group as a whole. We must not underestimate how difficult it can be for people to learn how to use groups, especially when they are not used to participating in groups, or have poor experiences of them (such as their own family group). A small grouping such as a pair, a trio or a foursome can provide a home base from which to explore the rest of the group. The Groupwork Project (Chapter 2) requested paired participation in the training programme because of the evidence that the learning in the workshop is more readily translated into practice with the support and reinforcement of a partner.

Subgrouping is an essential component of groups that are working well, but it can also be seen as a threat to the group's progress. Sometimes this is as an issue of control; if groupworkers feel it is their prerogative to establish groupings, those which arise spontaneously will be viewed with suspicion, even when it is clear that the subgroup arises from those individuals' need for security within the group. Difficulties can also arise if there is an imbalance so that some individual group members develop strong bonds with one or two others, but other individuals do not. It is not uncommon to see someone glowering across a group at the discourtesy of two members who are whispering together, only to witness them indulging in the same behaviour with their neighbour five minutes later. This can be an irritant, but if it becomes persistent and is reinforced by other alliance behaviours (such as an unwillingness to form new pairings) there is cause for concern that the group's purposes will be undermined and incoherent.

Small groups of two or three persons who develop their own communication system and their own subculture are almost invariably seen as a threat by the larger group. The allegiance to the smaller grouping seems to threaten the main group's identity or purpose. There are many possible different kinds of dynamics at play, not least of which is the power which accrues to subgroups, with their own information network and their privileged communication. Three group members sitting together and giggling during the group session is likely to press many negative buttons for other group members and the workers. Even though the subgroup may be laughing about something outside the group, the rest of the group can feel that it is they who are being laughed at. The power of the subgroup is seen to be at the expense of the whole group, which feels weakened by the experience.

There is something 'sibling' about a subgroup, especially since subgroups are frequently composed of people with similar attributes (race, gender, age, etc). The subgroup often shares a language code and a sense of humour from which the larger group feels excluded, in the same way that outsiders can sense their isolation from a close family group. This can provoke jealousies, especially if the closeness which the members of the subgroup feel towards each other spotlights other group members' lack. The feelings of exclusion experienced in the group might be intensified because they mirror similar encounters in the wider society.

The challenge of subgroups is to enlist not resist, so that they are working *for* the whole group and not against it. How can the subgroup represent itself to the whole group, and vice versa, in ways which are beneficial to both? (Turkie 1995). For example, what qualities does the subgroup bring which the whole group can benefit from? Perhaps it is its energy and good humour, its questioning of conventional thinking, its sense of loyalty and belonging. The same question needs to be asked of the whole group; what qualities can it teach the subgroup? It is the task of the groupworkers to establish a dialogue between subgroups and whole group. This is even more important in those circumstances when the whole group is missing because *every* individual member's primary allegiance is to a subgroup.

One of the more difficult situations is when the group splits fairly evenly into two camps. Kohli's (1993) Asian women's deaf group split into two subgroups because of a variation in communication abilities, each group having clear and distinct needs. In these circumstances it can be best to recognize the split and to consider the need for two groups, if resources allow.

We tend to think of subgrouping as the characteristic of large groups as if, jelly-like, they are unable to support the whole mass, but even small family groups can exhibit subgrouping, such as Finlayson's (1993) description of groupwork with four siblings where a split between the older two and the younger two was evident. Indeed, the presence of subgroups in families can be very challenging for family workers. However, Regan and Young (1990) describe how one natural subgroup in the family, the sibling group, was used as the basis for a successful group for children of divorced or separated parents. Indeed, this group was composed entirely of subgroups, six sets of paired siblings. The strength of the ties in each sibling subgroup seemed to help group members tolerate a greater age spread than usual (7-year-olds to 12-year-olds of different genders), and to move more quickly from the initial phase to the work phase of the group. Interestingly, a subgroup of the older siblings developed, arising from the theme of the conflict between the time spent at their fathers' home curtailing available time with friends. The younger siblings also formed a subgroup around the issue of leaving their toys in two different homes. What united both, a common whole-group theme, was a desire for more control and security and an emergent theme, a subtext, of 'I wish dad could come back home'.

Other whole groups can be similarly composed of established subgroups, such as couples groups and groups for families with different generations participating (McKay *et al.* 1997). Subgroups composed of family groupings can be used positively, for example by breaking into individual family units to discuss family rules which are broken and returning to the full group to share these with each other. The advantages of having groups composed of family subgroups are obvious; in particular, the problems which in many other groups have to be described at distance are often physically demonstrated in the group itself. There are many sources of immediate feedback on parenting when whole families are present together, and the presence of the whole group can also intensify feelings of closeness within the subgroup of each family unit, as each represents their own family to others in the group. It is these processes which groupworkers can seek to replicate in the positive use of subgroups even when it is not so well defined as the family unit.

3: WHOLE GROUP

The whole group refuses to do an exercise which it has been asked to do.

There are occasions when the obstacle to a group's progress is identified at the whole-group level. Groupworkers can find this kind of situation very isolating and frustrating, with the consequence that the message is not easily read and they ask themselves whether it is genuinely an expression of the whole group's sentiments or one individual is subverting from within. Is it an indictment of the leadership or a powerful expression of the group's solidarity?

There is a tendency for groupworkers to become defensive when they identify an obstacle to group functioning at the whole-group level. This is largely because of the threat to the power and expertise of the leadership which this kind of obstacle can be seen to represent. It is difficult for groupworkers to make a considered response when they feel their own competence or judgement is at issue. However, the same analysis applies to difficulties at whole-group level as at individual and subgroup levels, i.e:

- in what way is this an obstacle?
- is there a pattern to the obstacle?
- at what systems level is the difficulty being expressed (its manifestation)?
- how are other systems involved?

These processes cannot take place in an instant and the group will not 'freeze-frame' whilst you deliberate with yourself. Sometimes it is necessary to let your immediate judgement guide your response. However, if you and the group are to learn from this experience, why not take the group through the above analysis so that you can all explore the difficulty together? It is important that this process is seen as a genuine engagement with the group, not as a punishment or a search for the guilty.

In the example given at the start of this section, 'the whole group refuses to do an exercise which it has been asked to do', this means stopping the action and 'stepping outside' the current group processes to survey what is happening. If this is the first time that you have stepped out you need to explain what you are doing; the group will soon become familiar with this process once you have introduced it two or three times. You see this as an obstacle to the group's progress and this is an opportunity to share your perception with the group. You need to check this out with your co-worker, too. Group members will probably wish to explore the content of the situation, whilst you are asking them to focus on the process; in other words, they want to debate the pros and cons of doing the exercise, whilst you want to look at why the refusal.

The analysis should clarify the nature of the difficulty and whether it is, indeed, an obstacle to the group's functioning. It should help progress to the next stage, which is whether there is any discernible pattern which might explain what is happening, and clarify which systems are involved (ex-group, whole group, subgroup, individual, leadership). This careful process is designed to help the group move forward on the basis of self-awareness and shared understandings. If this process is followed diligently, the obstacle should become an opportunity for the group to learn more about itself, and the whole group means members and workers together.

A group of five- to seven-year-old girls, siblings of children with special needs, refused point blank to participate in an activity planned by the workers which was designed to lead into a role play about disability. They suggested 'their own alternative which was much more about having fun' (Ferraro and Tucker 1993: 48). Fortunately, the groupworkers saw this not as an obstacle or a rebellion but as a communication; they changed their approach, looking at disability issues via the concept of difference, which proved to be very effective. In effect, the children were saying 'this may be a group for the brothers and sisters of children with disabilities, but we are not "brother and sisters", we are individuals in our own right!' By focusing on disability, the group leaders were reinforcing what the children already faced in their everyday lives, a tendency to be overshadowed by their brother or sister with a disability, and they took action to move the group in the direction they wanted.

Sometimes the norms of the groupworkers and the members collide, and all the other systems seem pitted against the leadership, or antithetical to it (Kurland and Salmon 1997). In other words, the ideas that members use to guide and sanction behaviour in the group are very different from those of the workers. This is particularly evident in groups of adolescents, where the communication norm may be the put-down, but it is also evident in more subtle ways when the culture of group members is at variance with the culture of the workers (for example, not to talk about taboo subjects). These differences might also be reflected in a conflict between the agency's norms and those which the workers are attempting to establish in the group. The worker needs to decide where the conflict is best addressed, inside the group or outside it. Often it is unfair to put group members at odds with others, such as their families, by expecting them to discuss issues (for example, sex) of which the others would disapprove. It may be necessary, therefore, to work with people outside the group to ensure that work inside the group can progress.

4: OUTSIDE THE GROUP

> A group member doesn't turn up to the session.
>
> Even when [the members of a group for people with Aids] could not attend because of severe illness or hospitalization, members told us that they would recall the time and place of the meeting, in an effort to reach the turbulent, life-giving atmosphere of the group. Some men who have dropped out still maintain contact with the workers and ask about other members of the group. Members of the group visit one another in hospital, have dinner or go for drinks and an evening at the opera together, and attend a relentless series of funerals and memorial services – the tribal rituals of life in the time of AIDS. (Getzel and Mahoney 1989: 95–6)

The exchange between the group and its 'outside' is very important and we have already explored in detail the significance of context for successful groupwork (Chapters 1 and 2). The absence of an individual group member can illustrate the insecurity generated by the relatively 'unseen' area outside the group, though the quote above also illustrates the considerable impact a group can sustain even on members who cannot be present.

The non-attendance of a group member might be seen as a private affair for that individual, but it helps link members to the theme of 'the group's out-side'. Each individual group member's scope for change is affected by the different opportunities available to them outside the group, not just by their response to the environment created within the group. An understanding of the diverse life experiences and opportunities of the individual group members is an essential part of the movement from 'I' to 'we', especially if the re-sulting 'we' is to be unoppressive and inclusive. The absence of a group member can be the result of the pressures of their particular circumstances and, as such, is a useful message about the different opportunities of all members.

The boundaries between the 'inside' and 'outside' of a group are especially blurred in residential and day centre settings. Whatever the setting, though, groupworkers must consider the nature of contacts with members outside the group itself. One of the workers of a group for 'high-risk' families regularly visited the homes of families in the group at the actual times, such as bedtimes, when problems described in the group were most likely to occur (Moe 1989: 272).

Whatever the obstacles to a group's progress, it is important to consider their relationship to the various systems which have an impact on the group and to understand them as messages for the whole group rather than as challenges to the group leadership. In this way, the resources of the whole group can be brought into play to help to move it beyond any particular obstacle.

Portfolio extract

An example [of the 'Two Clients'] was when my co-worker was talking about a sensible diet. Tracey, who feels she is overweight, spoke about how she felt, and other people's comments about her weight made her feel. Tracey went on to explain her efforts to lose weight and, although members tried to contribute to the discussion, Tracey once again expressed her feelings and how these were tied up with how her father had viewed her (she is still coming to terms with her father's death). I was pleased Tracey felt comfortable within the group to share these feelings, but ... also aware that Tracey was enjoying a 'one-to-one' situation.

Other group members were not having an opportunity to express their views and feelings ... and I was aware that Dawn felt uncomfortable as she was desperately trying to put weight on. She had been anorexic in the past and says she doesn't want to be like that again ... I tried to address this by pointing out to Dawn that the diet sheet addressed weight gain as well as weight loss. Dawn brightened up when she was made aware of this, and when my co-worker related some of her own experiences, this encouraged the rest of the group to join in. I felt I was more aware of Dawn's needs, as I was more able to observe the group as a whole while my co-worker was talking.

... Although Dawn seemed happy with the information which I had pointed out to her, it may have been more effective to have said [to the whole group], 'for some people trying to gain weight can be just as much a problem as trying to lose it'. This would have made the whole group aware that other people have problems with their weight in a different way. A whole new discussion may have arisen then.   JP (1998)

CHAPTER ELEVEN

Co-working and Leadership in Groups

About 'So you think you want to co-work?'

The idea of co-working can be more rewarding than the reality if you fail to take the necessary precautions. The best way to ensure that you and your prospective co-worker are singing in tune is to be open and explicit about the expectations you have of each other. 'So you think you want to co-work?' provides a framework for you to confront your hopes, fears and expectations together.

Purpose

Co-working in groups is one of the most rewarding professional activities you can undertake. The opportunity to work with a colleague in a shared venture, to plan together, to learn from observation of each other in a live setting and to give and receive direct feedback, is all too rare in social work and social care. Co-working in groups can provide all of these opportunities and more; but the greater the potential gains the greater, too, can be the pains. For the sake of the group, it is essential that you and your proposed co-worker are confident that you can work together.

Knowing your co-worker as a colleague in a team is not the same as joint work in a group. Even if you think you know each other very well, you will find it enlightening to complete the questionnaire on page 216 as a prelude to further discussion about your expectations. You may find that there are significant differences in your motivations, methods and styles.

Method

- Before you complete the questionnaire, have a preliminary discussion about how you both feel about completing it. For example, how honest do you think you can be? Ironically, this can sometimes be more difficult with somebody you know well. What is the status of the questionnaire? Have you already decided to co-work a particular group and you are using the questionnaire to refine the co-leadership roles; or is the questionnaire a way of helping you decide whether you can co-work together?

- Complete the questionnaire independently, then come together to share your answers. If you have access to a mentor, seek their involvement in the questionnaire. Take time to debrief (are there any responses which surprise you?) and consider the implications of your replies for the group and for your relationship as co-workers.

- Keep sight of the positive responses. Don't gloss over the differences. Differences in themselves are not problematic, but they need to complement each other, and you and your co-worker need to be comfortable with them.

Variations

You may wish to add questions or adapt them (for example, substituting other ABCs for please/intimidate/irritate in Questions 5 and 6). Consider making a written agreement out of your responses, including your line manager or mentor.

Keep the questionnaires to hand, so that you can use them as part of your regular review process; indeed, before you leave this activity you should decide how you will review your co-working, and how any differences will be handled. 'Let's wait and see' is a risky policy.

Sentence completion activity

'So you think you want to co-work?' is only useful if it elicits specific responses. For example, if one of the responses to 'three things I want most from my co-worker' just states 'support', this is unhelpful. One person's support is another's neglect and yet another's overdependence. Examples of what this means in practice will give you a much better idea of what your co-worker sees as support. The sentence completions below are designed to draw out more specific, concrete replies:

- If a group member deliberately broke a rule which had been agreed by the rest of the group (such as not interrupting somebody else), I would …

- If a group member was speaking about something that had a strong parallel in my own life (such as the fact that she was adopted and I was, too), I would …

- If a group member spent the whole of a session in silence, I would …

- The thing that would most 'throw' me in the group would be if …

- I tend to think that what people who are members of this group can benefit most from is …

- I think that what has to be most avoided in groups for the people we will be offering this group is …

- If my co-worker answered a question that had been directed at me, I would …

- If my co-worker said something misleading to the group, I would …

- If I get somebody's name wrong in the group, I would expect my co-worker to …

Add your own trigger sentences, making them particular to the group you are planning.

In Chapter 7, we described the 'dream house' as a graphic action technique which could be used with group members to explore issues of partnership. This technique, in which the partners together hold one pen and draw their dream house without speaking, could be used by prospective co-workers to explore the balance of dominance and passivity in their own relationship (Reynolds and Shackman 1994).

✓

So you think you want to co-work?

A questionnaire for co-workers to complete together

1   Why I want to be involved in leading this group:

2   Three things that I am good at, which will help make the group successful:

3   Three things my co-worker is good at, which will help make the group successful:

4   Three things I want most from my co-worker:

5   What might ABC my co-worker about me:

    A   please

    B   intimidate

    C   irritate

6   What might ABC me about my co-worker:

    A   please

    B   intimidate

    C   irritate

7   What scares me about leading this group?

8   What other supports do I want for this group?

Notes for the groupworker

> Co-working is a preferred way of working for many if not most groupworkers in Britain. (Mistry and Brown 1991: 101)

Co-working a group can be a bit like parenthood; as a twosome everything has been going fine, but when the children come along you suddenly discover you have very different views about how to raise them! Choosing a co-worker is important, if choice is a possibility. In addition to the skills and personal qualities of your potential partner, this chapter also considers how attributes, such as gender and ethnicity, also figure in these choices.

Co-working or co-leading?

The term 'co-working' is often preferred when there is a philosophy that group leadership is shared with all members of the group. However, this is not always the case, nor is it always realistic to expect that this should be the group's aim. Leadership is sometimes properly located firmly with the groupworkers for much of the life of the group. Although there is a different emphasis between co-worker and co-leader, we use the terms interchangeably in this book to recognize that we are addressing a wide range of groups and groupworkers.

There are many views of the group leader's role, such as Whitaker's (1985) 'conductor' and Heap's (1988) 'central person'. In most cases it is the workers who have taken the initiative for a group, so members tend to look to them to clarify aims and purposes; they may be the only people who know each individual member. Furthermore, the groupworker has recognized skills in groupworking; just as we do not consider it autocratic or oppressive for radiographers to use their radiography skills, so we might reasonably expect groupworkers to use their groupwork skills. An essential part of that skill is, of course, to encourage participation and confidence in those not designated as 'groupworkers'. Unlike radiography, the hope is that the participants in groupwork will, themselves, increase their own skills in groupworking.

In addition to your skills as a groupworker, who you are makes you a central person. There is, of course, the power of your position and the access this gives you to resources. There is also the emotional strength and solidity which you can bring to a situation in which you are not hurting, grieving, angry, etc. So the very aspects which might make you feel uncomfortable about your difference and distance from group members (that you have not been sexually abused, you are not caring for a child with a learning disability, etc.) can be a source of strength for group members. Conversely, there is the danger that, as central person, groupworkers might be seen as a representative of the 'authorities' and therefore the focus of feelings intended for others. Either way, the position of groupworker is undeniably different from the position of group member, even though groupworkers are, in one sense, members of the group.

Benefits of co-working

A survey of groups in probation settings found that 87 per cent of the 1463 groups in the survey used two or more facilitators, and that in two-thirds of the groups, paired co-leadership was the favoured approach (Caddick 1991: 207).

Hodge (1985: 1) puts the early development of co-working down to the need for mutual support in the uncertainty of the statutory social services, and concludes that it has 'much to commend it as a means of enhancing the work of a group'. He identifies the following benefits.

1 Leadership resources available to the group are enriched.

2 Leadership tasks can be shared.

3 Group members experience the interest or concern of at least two people in authority.

4 Group members have more than one person in the leadership to test themselves against or identify with.

5 Specific social and interactional skills can be modelled by the leaders (especially true when a male-female leadership can exemplify mutual respect).

6 Co-workers can support each other and give feedback to each other about their conduct of the group.

7 The leaders can test out their views of what is happening in the group.

8 Difficulties presented by group members can be shared, and if one leader is 'thrown', the other can provide direction for the group.

9 Co-working provides training opportunities for a less-skilled groupworker.

10 A session does not have to be cancelled if one of the co-leaders is unable to be present. (adapted from Hodge 1985: 2–3)

The way in which issues of balance and equality are handled in the co-leadership is a model for the way they are handled in the group. As with all partnerships (business, marriage, professional, etc.) there are inequalities. An equal partnership is a reference to the value and the worth which each individual places in the partnership, but the skills, the interests, the attributes and the experience which each brings will contain differences.

Co-working is without doubt an important tool for professional development, enabling colleagues to learn from one another in a live setting. Agencies often balk at joint work with individuals, but when there are many service users involved, as in groupwork, an agency may be more willing to release staff time. Co-workers learn about group management from each other, as well as observing each others' interactional skills (Chapter 8), and they can share the different functions of 'maintenance' and 'task', the former focusing on processes in the group and the latter on outcomes and progress. Ross and Thorpe (1988: 138) suggest that a worker who has prime responsibility for the maintenance function should intervene over the one with the task focus; for example, if a group member is feeling hurt by something that is being said in the group and this goes unnoticed by the worker focusing on task, the co-worker should intervene.

Difference and compatibility

There are several dimensions to the notion of difference in groupwork. In Chapter 3, we focused on the themes of intimacy and authority arising from the difference between being a group leader and being a group member. Then, in Chapter 4 we looked at the mix of group members, using notions of sameness and difference, returning to this theme in Chapter 9 to explore the impact of different group members' behaviours. In this chapter, we turn to the question of differences in the group leadership.

The groupwork and social work literature often emphasizes the need for shared values. For example, the self-directed groupwork model of Mullender and Ward (1989, 1991) is firm about the need for co-workers to 'thrash out' a common value base. However, this is only one interpretation of the notion of 'shared'; in addition to shared as 'same', it can also mean 'made known to each other', as in sharing ideas or feelings. The key question is how much territory separates the positions and whether they are compatible. For example, there would need to be a shared commitment to the belief that racism in the group should be tackled, even if there were differences about how this should be done.

So, this sense of compatibility is paramount. It means being able to work with each other's differences and holding these differences in mutual respect. Indeed, these differences may well be a greater asset to the group than the similarities, for it is possible to see how two co-workers singing the same melody line do not produce such a rich sound as when they are harmonizing two different lines. The ability to work together whilst respecting differing value bases could be a good model for group members, themselves likely to have differences. A commitment to sharing, in the sense of being open about values, is critical but even here there are pitfalls. Co-workers might talk about values in the same language, but the way they translate them into action in the public forum of a group can differ radically. A common adherence to the notion of empowerment might hide very different views about how to put it into practice. Most people are 'for' empowerment, but what does it mean in concrete terms to you and your co-worker?

One of the best ways to check compatibility is to take two or three hypothetical situations and consider what you would each do in those situations (the sentence completions on page 215 can be used as a prompt). Giving an explanation of why you each think the situation in question has arisen is also a useful guide to your respective theoretical orientations. What do you each consider to be the causes of group members' problems and what are the possible methods to help them? Do either of you hold committed beliefs or have strong feelings about the kinds of circumstance in which group members find themselves? This helps to look at compatibility and difference in a variety of situations.

In contrast to values, where there is often an assumption that common is best, the attributes of co-workers are sometimes felt to benefit from difference (male-female; black-white co-leadership). It is necessary to consider whether there is the luxury of choice about the attributes of the co-leadership, and also what the ideal would be in respect of the particular group being planned (Cowburn 1990; Muston and Weinstein 1988).

A life outside the group

There are two kinds of boundary which co-workers must consider. The first relates to boundary behaviours within the group and these are related to the notion of ground rules about what is acceptable and not acceptable (see Chapter 6). They encompass the co-workers' views on confidentiality, how self-disclosure will be handled in the group, and respective attitudes to sanctions, rules and rule-breaking. Making a list of the kinds of behaviour in the group which each co-worker thinks would justify considering a group member's expulsion is illuminating and will provide further evidence of your compatibility (not that your responses must be the same, but that you should be able to negotiate through the differences).

The second kind of boundary relates to the 'outside' of the group. The group is not an island, as we have emphasized several times. Context is just as significant to the co-leadership as it is to the group as a whole and to the individual members. As well as the 'inner' boundaries of each co-worker's values and beliefs, there are the 'outer' boundaries of each worker's relationship to the other systems which have an impact on the group (see Figure 11.1 below).

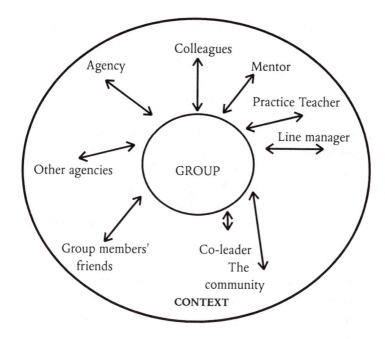

Figure 11.1 The group in its context

> Initially I had two co-leaders, one for each group. They were staff members of the day centre, who had offered to work with me. Keeping boundaries for them was always a problem, and if called upon to cover the work of the centre they would have to be absent from the groups, so I was often alone. (Gobat 1994: 214)

Your relationship as co-workers in the group is influenced by the relationship you have outside the group and will affect the way in which group members see you. A co-leadership composed of two close female colleagues who are friends outside the group will have a different face to a co-leadership of two people from different occupational groups who have come together solely to lead the group. Leadership has a different face in residential and day centre settings because of the greater intimacy of these settings, where 'the worker and the user are both more accessible and more vulnerable' (Brown 1990: 283). Other factors to consider are whether there is any formal relationship between co-workers, such as supervisor and supervisee, or practice teacher and student social worker, and whether you are both accountable to the same or different people. All of these components can be especially significant if the group goes badly; the consequences of failure for two close colleagues in a residential setting is likely to have appreciable fall-out when compared with a co-leadership of relative strangers.

The issue of authority is one we have raised elsewhere in connection with the relationship between group members, group leaders and the group itself (Chapter 3). However, it is also worth considering from what source the authority of each co-worker derives. In addition to your formal roles, you might derive authority from your expertise in the areas of concern for the members (alcohol abuse, community development, etc.) Your groupwork skills may not be an explicit factor initially but they, too, will generate authority. In all these matters it is important to consider how similarly or differently you are perceived by group members. For example, what have your mutual responsibilities been in getting the group off the ground? Has it been a joint enterprise from the outset, or is it the brainchild of one of you who persuaded the other to join? Have tasks been distributed evenly? As Gobat (1994: 214) notes very honestly: 'I did the recording and most of the detailed planning for the groups, and the groups remained 'my' groups'.

Differences in status and occupation must be considered alongside the differences in attributes (gender, race, age, class, sexuality, etc.) mentioned earlier. How do these all add up? How do they reflect the likely composition of the group?

When co-working fails

The size of the potential benefits of co-working is matched by the scope of the possible pitfalls of one which is not working well. As we have suggested, unexplored differences in theoretical orientation, in style, in commitment, in opinions about appropriate methods, techniques and ground rules, etc. can give rise to a co-leadership in distress. Even if early differences have been identified and resolved (for example, as a result of completing the co-worker questionnaire on page 216), new conflicts can emerge if regular reviews are not held. Unanticipated splits in the group membership can result in unhelpful subgrouping which, in turn, feeds any disagreements between the co-workers.

It is important to consider how much choice you exercised, either about leading the group or about working with each other. For example, a group for sexually abused girls had been formed out of expediency and a similarly pragmatic approach had been taken to the leadership of the group; in other words, the answer to the question 'who should lead the group?' was answered in the same way as 'who should be allocated this case?', more on grounds of availability than skill (Allum 1990: 142).

One facet of the co-workers' relationship is competitiveness (Reynolds and Shackman 1994: 25). All relationships have a degree of competitiveness; for instance, no matter how much we appreciate the positive feedback being given to a partner, it is only human to wonder whether he or she is more 'popular' with the group. What can eat away at the co-leadership is not the competitiveness, but the attempts to deny it. We are taught to feel ashamed of competitive feelings, so we try to pretend they do not exist. Only when competitiveness is recognized and acknowledged can it be handled, tamed and redirected positively. There may be strong feelings of competitiveness within the group, too, but the difficulty of being honest about these feelings should not be underestimated.

Another area which can lead to difficulty is opposing theoretical orientations. If your co-worker believes that symptoms of bulimia 'are known to arise in the main from early infantile oral fantasies and awesome pre-verbal imaginings' (Fitzsimmons and Levy 1996: 285), whilst your groupwork consultant considers them to be the result of a genetic malfunction of that area of the brain which governs self-perception and cognition, and you view them as behavioural disorders, you could all be in for a rough time if you cannot achieve the compatibility we discussed earlier.

In Chapter 10 we considered obstacles which manifest themselves at different levels; individual, subgroup, whole group and ex-group. We introduced a systems approach to identify the appropriate location for action to work on the problem. This same approach helps with obstacles which are manifest in the co-leadership system. The obstacle may be evident in the co-worker system, but it is important to consider whether this is the best place to take action. As we have seen, the various systems are interconnected and the most effective response is not always in the same system as the manifestation of the problem. If the co-leadership is in difficulties it is important to consider all the systems involved before deciding how and where to act.

Support for the co-workers

In addition to the co-workers, there are other roles important to the group. For example, a group consultant or mentor can provide advice and support to the groupworkers. This is usually from a position outside the group, but sometimes the co-workers' adviser might provide direct teaching within the group session itself. Describing groupwork with depressed women, Trevithick (1995: 17) writes that 'each depression group has three workers: two group leaders and a group coordinator, with each undertaking different roles'. The coordinator has the role of creating 'a setting that gives confidence' and continuity between one group and the next by taking brief notes during the group, mainly acting as an observer.

Group members need to know in advance about the possibility of outsiders' involvement and to have the opportunity to give or withhold their consent. Groupworkers who are studying for a professional or vocational award might expect an assessor to visit the group to observe their practice. This cannot be an entirely neutral activity, since the assessor's presence has an impact both on the co-workers and on the members, but the impact could just as well be beneficial (inducing a keenness) as detrimental (inhibiting openness). Garrett's (1995: 58) Dialogue Groups had a member of the prison's board of visitors in attendance without any apparent detrimental effect on the way the group functioned. However, the group's attitudes to visitors might be instructive of their general response to 'others' outside the group.

We have presented co-working with an implicit model of a partnership of two workers, but it is possible to have more, depending on the size and purposes of the group in question. A large programme of groupwork courses might require a complex leadership. In this case there is another group to consider and that is the leadership group. A programme for male sex offenders run by probation officers consisted of a number of different cohorts of offenders, each in a group with four leaders, with individual officers brought in to help with two-hour interviews with individual members. Cowburn (1990) describes the role of the consultant in helping to resolve the problematic dynamics of the group leadership as new workers not initially involved in setting up the groups came on board. In the years over which the course developed, several new groupworkers joined the leadership. Other formats might include a group leadership which rotates in the way described by Dobbin and Evans (1994: 119), whose group for mothers of sexually abused children had a leadership of three women; 'all three were present for important events in the life of the group but other meetings were generally attended by only two (rotating).' The authors recognized that this was not ideal, but that by spreading the workload it made it possible for the group to run over a long period of time and be 'invincible against the demands of a busy social services department on its staff'. In fact, they felt that group members made little differentiation between the three workers.

Sole leadership

> Over the past ten to fifteen years co-leadership rather than single leadership appears to have become the norm in British social groupwork practice. (Hodge 1985: 1)

The prevalence of co-led groups is even harder to know than the occurrence of groupwork itself. Of the 48 learners who completed a group in the Groupwork Project (Chapter 1), 46 were involved in co-leading (96%); only two of the 27 groups were solely led. This is not surprising given the Project's active promotion of co-working. Readers will have detected an assumption that co-working is desirable, especially in the context of teaching and learning groupwork practice, but it needs to be recognized that groups also run with a sole leader and that they can run successfully. There are three kinds of reason for sole leadership:

- *An active decision not to involve a co-worker:* based on considered reasoning, such as the style of the individual groupworker or the particular group in question.

- *A desire for co-leadership but an inability to achieve this:* no-one else with the appropriate skill, time, interest, is available. For example, Gobat (1993) made a deliberate decision to be sole leader rather than work with someone she did not know or who did not share her theoretical base. She describes the flipchart as becoming her co-leader!

- *A failure to consider the possibility of a co-worker:* it is important to avoid this kind of decision by default or ignorance.

In the first instance, you should make sure that you are very clear what exactly justifies sole leadership; put yourself to the test by asking others what they think the group might miss by not being co-led. Is there an issue of control (and your desire not lose it); if this is so, how are you likely to respond to group members who wish to exercise leadership from within the group.

In the second case, thinking laterally might bring people into the frame who have not been considered, a volunteer who showed leadership skills in a previous group, for example. In the Groupwork Project, one of the co-workers in a group for people with mental health problems was, herself, a service user. Ultimately, you will need to decide how much the success of the group is likely to rely on co-working; perhaps it is a question of quality, that the group can work with a sole leader but it would work better with two.

The third reason, an act of omission, should not arise, now that you are alerted to the significance of co-working.

Leadership denied: lessons from Zin

A proper concern to provide an environment which is empowering and egalitarian, a group which is participative and owned by its members, can prompt groupworkers to deny the equally proper concern for the functions which add up to leadership in the group. Ambivalence and discomfort are common responses to the power of leadership, and these feelings can lead to an abdication from responsibilities and a denial of the power of the groupworker. It is important, therefore, that groupworkers have an opportunity to explore their attitudes to leadership, because the consequences of this denial can put the group at risk.

One way to explore leadership is to take part in a group simulation. The Zin Obelisk simulation helps people to explore issues of leadership by asking seven or eight people to work in a group on a specific task (to discover which day the building of the Zin Obelisk was completed) within a tight time limit. They are instructed that that no formal leader must be selected and that the 33 pieces of information which have been distributed around the group can only be shared verbally.

One of the themes which emerges from the Zin experience is the difference between a formal leader (a person) and the exercise of leadership (a quality). In the feedback which follows the simulation, the lack of leadership in the group is frequently identified as a key problem, commonly expressed as 'it needed somebody to take leadership'. Yet the group is often caught in a bind, because no member of the Zin group sees the possibility of providing this leadership themselves. This paradox is explained by the almost universally negative view which learner groupworkers seem to hold about leadership. It carries authoritarian associations which are felt to be contrary to the participative and egalitarian aspirations of groupworkers. Leadership is power and that is 'a bad thing'. The risks involved in assuming leadership are, therefore, huge. Not only does a would-be leader fear being labelled as disempowering, but there are strong cultural messages warning those who take one step up that they invite being brought two steps down, to suffer shame and embarrassment if their leadership fails to deliver the right answer. Men, in particular, tend to keep their heads down. In these circumstances it is thought to be better not to try than to try and fail.

Leadership is also caught up with 'expertise'. Zin groups frequently define the group's task as a mathematical problem, so that all those who see themselves as hopeless at maths shut down. In most Zin groups there is a 'Mary' whose mathematician's desire to crack the puzzle motivates her to begin to assume leadership; in fact, her expertise at maths is a handicap because she becomes so caught up with the puzzle that she ignores the group. Mesmerized by her maths, the group are nevertheless unconvinced that her attempts are made on their behalf and, like Mary herself, they become beached on the task.

Zin demonstrates a common confusion over notions of leadership. Namely, that it is best avoided if possible and that it is located in a person with technical expertise in the group's 'subject matter' – maths, alcohol abuse, homelessness, etc. In fact, leadership is not a hat which somebody in the group puts on, but a quality which can and should, in most circumstances, be shared amongst the group. Any individual or individuals in the Zin group could demonstrate this quality, for example by asking the group as a whole to consider how it might proceed with the task in hand and to consider what might prove to be an obstacle. An agreed programme of problem solving in which all play some part would prevent the apathy, task rejection, suspicion and cynicism ('I reckon it's all red herrings') which otherwise arise. The quality of leadership encourages a group to challenge the power of rules, perhaps arriving at a rule-bending formula such as 'OK, we're not supposed to show each other our cards, but it doesn't say anything about writing down all our information on this flipchart!' Zin group members reject the power associated with leadership as undesirable and a threat to 'equalness', yet they are nevertheless extraordinarily compliant and submissive to the greater power of The Rules, which symbolize the social and cultural norms which govern our behaviour because we permit them to.

The consequences of denying leadership as a necessary and desirable quality in groupwork are, therefore, considerable. Co-workers' commitment to principles of empowerment and participation are enhanced and not diminished by an equal commitment to the proper exercise of this quality of leadership.

Portfolio extract

Our [group leaders] working arrangements have often been thwarted by lack of time. If I could change the way we worked (in an ideal world) I would build in from the start more time to reflect and plan, and time simply to mull over the group dynamics and how we worked as a pair. We already know that this is imperative but other things crowd in. I do not necessarily think that pre-group co-leadership exercises would have been very productive other than to highlight differences in style. I am pleased with the way in which the relationship had developed in its own way, becoming mature and having depth. We are able to 'fall out' and reconcile once more.

I would change the way that the probation service resources this kind of group, as a number of group leaders dip in and out over the length of the programme. This has been incredibly disruptive, various groups have responded differently. Some have become withdrawn, others aggressive. I believe that if just one pair of group leaders were left to run the programme it would benefit that pairing and the group.　　　　　LE (1998)

CHAPTER TWELVE

Recording and Evaluating Groupwork

About 'Locating the group's success'

An essential aspect of groupwork practice is the careful recording of its progress and an evaluation of the process and outcome. 'Locating the group's success' makes the evaluative process as inclusive as possible, involving all those who have a stake in the group. It reminds us that different people are likely to have different perspectives on what 'success' means.

Purpose

This chapter asks you to consider the purpose and activity of recording in as creative a light as possible. Traditional methods of recording can be dull and procedural, in contrast to the possibility of interactive and creative ways of recording the progress of groups. The chapter also helps groupworkers make links between the ways in which groups are recorded and the manner in which they are evaluated.

Method

- The 'map' of the Sea of Groupwork on page 231 serves as a template, a prompt to help you consider how you will find out whether the group has worked. The first question in the planning stage of the group is who should be involved in the evaluation of the group. You and your co-worker and the group members all have sight of the group's progress from the 'inside', but who might have sight of the group's success from the 'outside'? Who has a stake in the group?

- Once you have decided who should be involved in evaluating the group's success (that is, naming the 'land masses' around the Sea of Groupwork), it is necessary to consider how success is to be identified. In other words, what methods will you use to discover the many perspectives the stakeholders have about what counts as a successful outcome for the group? How might these be 'triangulated' so that there is some common view of where this group is to be found; in the area which has been agreed as defining successful, or beached somewhere else?

- Finally, how will you measure the notion of 'travel', the distance from where group members started to where they are finishing?

Variations

The map in the activity poses rather than answers the vital questions necessary to discover the extent of the group's success. There is no pretence that these answers can or should be objective, but they can and should be based on real changes which are evident to a number of people. Only in this way can everybody who has been involved in the experience learn from it.

Notes for the groupworker

Begin at the beginning

> Evaluation should not be relegated to the position of postscript, a retrospective and anecdotal look at the group. (Butler and Wintram 1991: 185)

It is necessary to start the process of evaluation and recording from the early stages of planning the group, even if the conclusions cannot be drawn until beyond the group's ending. The evaluation at the end of a group can only take place when there is something to measure potential progress against, so an effective evaluation depends on systematic recording.

Just as it is not possible to take a photograph of the past, so attempts at retrospective recording will be less accurate. Of course, reflections on past events are very valuable, but they cannot replace the immediacy and accuracy of accounts written at the time. Specific incidents and illustrations tend to blur into general feelings and impressions so that a statement such as 'it was a breakthrough when Aisha said "no" to Ronnie's view that the group could accommodate a new member' is likely, over time, to translate to 'it felt like a constructive session with people able to express their feelings'. The richness of the detail turns sepia over time. In particular, it becomes 'easier to remember what occurred rather than what failed to take place', as O'Connor (1992:

Locating the group's success

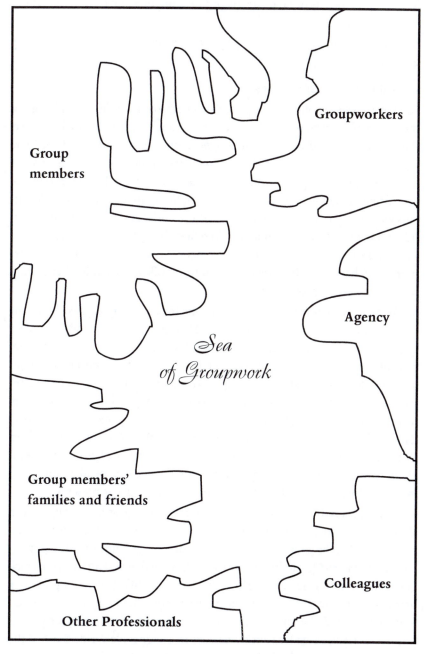

Adapted from *Triangulations* in Doel *et al.* (1996: 17)

79) notes in connection with a group for people bereaved by suicide. If an honest evaluation is to be made, record keeping must be thorough and immediate.

Before setting up any recording system you need to address the following questions.

WHO ARE YOU RECORDING FOR?

You have a responsibility to the group members to record the life and work of the group. If the progress of the whole group and of the individual members fails to be remarked on, a valuable opportunity to recognize and celebrate people's development is lost. Some groups lend themselves to more precise evaluation (for example, a group where the outcomes are framed in terms of specific behaviours), others less so (for example, a support group for sole parents which might be more concerned with attitudes and feelings). The methods and nature of the recording should reflect the style of the group, within a framework which recognizes the differences between the 'I' and the 'we' explored in Chapter 10. It is crucial, therefore, to follow each individual's progress as well as the group as a whole.

Agencies which have clear requirements for recording casework may be less prepared in respect of groupwork. This can be an advantage, for your style and system of recording may be less bound by procedures so that you can tailor it to the group's particular needs. However, it is important that your groupwork does not fall off the edge of the map, and that it is seen to be reviewed in the same way as other aspects of the agency's workload. Apart from its responsibility to individual service users, the agency may wish to collect data in order to evaluate the quality and effectiveness of the services it offers. Whether the group is a relative success or not, the agency has much to learn about this method of working, and this intelligence is dependent on senior managers being aware of your work and the alternative it presents.

Finally, there is the need to record your own progress as a groupworker. Whether it is a matter of curiosity about your own development as a professional, or whether your groupwork is part of a programme of study (for example, for a Post-Qualifying Award), it is essential that you find ways to track your own practice learning. How will you identify your strengths as a groupworker, and those areas which need strengthening? How will you know what you do better now than you did when you first started the group? It is necessary to consider your own needs as a learner alongside those of the agency and the group itself.

In addition to these three major players, there may be others who should be taken into account. Perhaps there are other agencies who have a legitimate interest in the group? Sometimes 'significant others' in the lives of the group members should also be included.

WHO WILL HAVE ACCESS TO THE RECORDS?

The task of recording could easily become more onerous than the groupwork itself, so it is useful to reconcile all these different purposes and consider who might be involved in keeping record.

Sometimes the same recording can serve a number of purposes. The log sheet (Figure 12.1) which you complete for the group might also satisfy the agency's file purposes. If you are keeping the groupwork recording separate from individuals' files, you may be able to cross reference briefly (for instance, 'Ann was a member of the Tuesday Group for eight weeks, during which time she gained enough confidence to go shopping independently by the end of the group. See The Tuesday Group folder for details').

Confidentiality can be complex to define in work with individuals or families, and it is even more so when it comes to groupwork. Individual group members' written files should be confidential from each other (unless permissions are given otherwise), and group recording should normally only be available to those involved in the group. Questions of privacy, confidence and disclosure should be an explicit aspect of establishing the ground rules, so the question of recording highlights rather than creates these issues (Chapter 6). Indeed, a discussion of how the group will be recorded can act as a trigger to open up concerns about confidentiality, power and the 'authorities'.

WHY ARE YOU RECORDING?

In considering who you are recording for, you also address the question of why you are recording. There are often many purposes:

- to *describe* what is happening currently in the group, a 'snapshot' of the group in any one session
- to *reflect* on what has happened and to analyze the processes and dynamics at work
- to *measure* movement and change in respect of individual members and the group overall
- to *evaluate* the impact the groupwork is having on the group and its members; what is working well, what less so
- to *account* for the work of the group to others outside the group, such as the agency or perhaps a wider audience.

In some circumstances you might also be considering writing the groupwork experience for a wider audience, through a policy document or publication in a journal such as *Groupwork*.

If the recording of the group fits into a larger scheme, this should be made explicit to group members. For example, records on individuals' participation in a motoring offenders' group contributed towards a final write-up on each person who they and their supervising probation officer received, and this could feed into any subsequent work on probation (Hutchins 1991: 246). In some cases formal data might be collected to compare the progress of one group against others in the same programme.

Methods of recording

It is important that the process of recording fits with your aims for the group. In other words, if the group is intended to be an empowering experience for participants, how can this be reflected in the way the group records itself? Group members who ordinarily perceive your agency as distant and powerful might have an experience through the group which changes that perception, or at least gives them another perspective. The way in which they are involved in collecting and holding information about the group could be a significant factor in changing these perceptions. For example, the 12 participants of a group for violent offenders were each given a personal folder so that they could retain their own notes and handouts from the group (Canton *et al.* 1992: 46).

Recording sounds like a rather stuffy activity, suggesting a collection of dry sentences destined to be lost in a dusty file, retrieved only in the case of a crisis or an inquiry. However, the act of recording in groups can be creative and an integral part of the group itself; activities involving the flipchart, for example, might not be labelled 'recording', but they can often fulfil some of these functions. If it is impractical to store them in their flipchart format, they can be typed up and copied for participants. Questionnaires, evaluation sheets, small group drawings and the like are all capable of forming part of the group's record.

In addition to these written forms of keeping record, there are other media which might be more suited to the dynamism of a group. Video and audio tape provide another eye and ear on what is happening in a group. Novices to videotape often need to overcome a preoccupation with what they look like rather than what they are doing (Chapter 7), but when they progress beyond this stage video offers a unique record of the group. Of course, group members must agree to video and be aware of how it will be used, and when it will be erased. The practitioners who used video in the Groupwork Project found group members were very welcoming, though there were a few groups (such as that for teenage boys who had been sexually abused) where the leaders were self-censoring and did not propose the use of video. Careful consideration needs to be given to obtaining the informed consents of group members, though it is interesting to speculate whether such courtesy is offered in respect of other (more durable) forms of recording, such as file records. The video, of course, records practitioners and service users both, whereas file records are a one-way street.

Methods of recording are closely related to methods of organizing feedback in the group. The summarizing activity which closes each session is part of any system of feedback, but it is likely to be at the level of the whole group rather than the individual. Opening channels for feedback between group members and between workers and members should aim to be as creative as possible, using a variety of the action techniques described in Chapter 7. For example, Peake and Otway (1990: 128) used letters to communicate congratulation and disapproval in equal measure to individual members of a group for girls who had been sexually abused. As long as levels of literacy allow, letters have the advantage of being 'paced', in that both the writer and the reader can take their time in composing and digesting the contents, and a letter can be treasured beyond the life of the group in the way that spoken words cannot.

A pattern to recording: the groupwork log

We have already emphasized immediacy as a significant factor in successful groupwork recording. In addition to this, a systematic approach helps streamline what can become a cumbersome and time-consuming occupation. Developing a pattern to the groupwork record eases the workload and aids the continuing search for themes (Chapter 10). It is also invaluable when it comes to the final collation of the various pieces of recording into an overall summary.

The groupwork log (Figure 12.1) is designed to be immediate and systematic at the same time. It is best completed soon after each session. The 'window' encourages you to consider the members in relation to each other by drawing how they sat or interacted, in contrast to just listing the names of people present. This graphic representation is more likely than linear prose to help you to make connections and recognize patterns of interaction, subgroupings, levels of participation, absences and so on. It is possible to extemporize, for example by representing power in the group in a

Groupwork log   My name: Date:
Name of the group: Session number:
                        Date and time of session:

Who was present and who sat where? *Draw a diagram in the window.*

If somebody was absent, do you know why? *Is there a need to follow up?*
Consider who contributed most/least? *Is there a pattern? Where does the power lie in the group?*

What were the main **aims** of this session?	What **themes** are emerging for the group?
1.	
2.	
3.	

What was the general atmosphere and **feeling** of this session of the group?

What was **my** main contribution to the session?	What did my **co-worker** particularly contribute?

What I **learned** most from this session as a groupworker was…

Future plans include…

Figure 12.1 The groupwork log sheet

diagrammatic way – circling the networks which seem the most powerful, using different colours to depict constructive or destructive relationships in the group, and the like.

Did the group work?

'Did the group work?' is a simple question with extremely complex answers. Because of the complexity of considering this question, it is important to reflect on why it is worth asking.

REMOTIVATING GROUP MEMBERS

The process of finding out whether the group has worked, and what that means, is satisfying in itself, even if the answer is equivocal. In many cases the group will conclude that it has been successful, and the evaluation will help everybody to feel the success as well as to know it. It can provide a springboard to help members leave the group as successfully as they participated in it.

DEVELOPING THE GROUPWORK

Asking the question, 'Did the group work?' demonstrates a commitment to the knowledge base of groupwork and a desire to add to it. Finding out what elements of the group worked well can help to build your own understanding and share this with others, perhaps leading to specific modifications in a group programme. For example, Harmey and Price (1992) increased the number of sessions with bereaved children from six to ten in response to feedback from the children, who wanted more time to deal with feelings and develop strategies to cope with them.

ACCOUNTING TO OTHERS

As we have stressed on many occasions, groups take place in a wider context. They have the support (or not) of a unit, an agency, parents, families or a community. Groupworkers owe an account to those who have been affected by the group's work. Whether it is a formal evaluation as part of a policy paper, or a brief descriptive account for the community newsletter, most groups have a small 'p' political dimension which makes them of interest to others. Part of the group's credibility comes from its ability to articulate what has worked and what has not worked.

So, whether it is for internal or external purposes, asking 'Did the group work?' is key.

Who defines success?

From the first planning meeting, groupworkers should ask themselves who defines success in this group. There are numerous perspectives, all of which are important to incorporate into a profile of whether the group has worked or not. These stakeholders in the group are likely to have a set of concerns with a different focus.

THE GROUP MEMBERS

- A principle focus of the group members' evaluation is likely to be the personal impact of the group on their lives.

Central to the evaluation must be the members' own definition of what success means. Did they meet their own needs and aims and has the experience of the group and its outcome been satisfactory for each person? Do individual members feel they have contributed to other members' aims, and to the purposes of the group as a whole? Helping to translate broad aims into individual or group objectives helps people to have a better feel for whether they have been successful. For example, a broad aim such as 'improving self-esteem' might be expressed by an individual as 'to feel confident enough to go to my daughter's wedding in the summer, and enjoy it', or by the group as 'to organize a forum to channel our views to the housing department of the local council'. Even so, it remains possible to feel closer to the broad aim without wholly achieving the particular objective.

THE GROUPWORKERS

- A principle focus of the groupworkers is likely to be the groupwork and issues of professional development.

In addition to their concern for the impact of the group on its members, the co-workers will need to evaluate their own part in the success, or otherwise, of the group. How well have they worked together and how have they handled differences? What impact did the various action techniques have and were particular combinations more effective than others? In addition to evaluating action techniques, it is important to audit interactional techniques, learning from how sticky moments were managed. How did the co-workers encourage controversy in a cosy group or calm in a chaotic one?

The co-workers have a professional responsibility to focus on the *groupwork*. For example, the leaders of groups for children who have lived with domestic violence initially accepted all children, but 'the groupworkers gradually tightened up their ideas as to who was likely to benefit' as they learned from their own experience (Mullender 1995: 87). In this way, group leaders can develop their knowledge of what works in groups and enhance their skills to put this understanding into practice.

THE AGENCY

- A principle focus of the agency is likely to be weighing costs against benefits.

Behind most groups is an agency which has sanctioned and supported the groupwork. This may be explicit or implicit, and the workers involved may or may not experience the agency's involvement as supportive. Nevertheless, in paying for their time the agency has a legitimate stake in the evaluation of the group; even when the group is run in a voluntary capacity there is usually an agency or organization (such as a church, voluntary body, etc.) with an interest in its progress.

'It is easier to ask forgiveness than permission' and to present the agency with the fact of a success rather than the hope of one. However, a groupwork service can survive only when there is a groupwork strategy; a group here and there, run in the face of a reluctant or neglectful agency, is ultimately going to prove insufficient to support sustained groupwork. For all these reasons it is important to consider the agency's stake in the group and how the group meets at least some of the agency's aims, so that the findings can be fed into the agency's policy-making structures. If the agency is at the stage where groups are considered a way of servicing large numbers of people at once (stack 'em high), then much work is required to educate the agency to the value of groupwork as a quality, as well as a quantity, service.

Corroborating evidence can be very powerful and, indeed, satisfying. 'I see far more conversation generally in the prison now than there was a year ago and I attribute that in good part to the Dialogue Group' said one prison governor who had never actually attended a Dialogue Group, (Garrett 1995: 61). Your colleagues are part of the agency and their response to the group is important. Feedback may be direct or inadvertent, such as the fact that every probation officer (bar one) in Newcastle referred to the intensive groupwork project over time (Mackintosh 1991: 272). The impact of groupwork on other agency staff can be considerable. Gibson (1992) found that staff attitudes towards older people in residential care tended to limit opportunities for residents ('he'll never come because he's always complaining about his illness'), but a series of reminiscence groups held in a number of residential homes and day centres was highly successful in challenging staff's assumptions about what was possible. The experience of these groups led to a more generous assessment of the older people's capabilities.

OTHER 'STAKEHOLDERS'

- The principle focus of other stakeholders is the most difficult to predict.

People spend relatively little time in the group compared with the time they spend with other people who are significant to them. However, the group might have a considerable impact on these other people, and any evaluation of its effectiveness should consider how this might be included.

Clearly, finding out what effect the group has had on these people presents a greater challenge than discovering its impact on the group members, groupworkers or sponsoring agency. It is not immediately evident who these people are, and they do not form a coherent constituency, in the way that the group members do. Moreover, group members might be in conflict with these people and have strong feelings about how or whether their opinions should be canvassed. These practical and ethical difficulties should be weighed carefully when considering the inclusion of others in the evaluation of the group.

In some cases, members of the group are significant others to each other. Pennells' (1995: 250) bereavement group for children accepted some siblings into the same group. She describes the difficulty of assessing beforehand what the balance of advantages and disadvantages is likely to be with any particular set of siblings, and occasionally it has been necessary to separate them.

Although it is difficult to be certain of the focus of significant others, often it will be centred on the impact on them of changes in the behaviour or situation of the group member. Sometimes the significant others might be able to point to change and progress which group members themselves are, for a variety of reasons, reluctant to admit themselves (for example, the parents of boys who had been sexually abused described by Dixon and Phillips 1994: 89). On occasion, significant others might see changes which are uncomfortable, but which nevertheless signal a success for the group member. Some of the parents of young children with a sibling with a disability noticed more angry behaviour half way through the group; this was taken by the groupworkers as a sign that the children 'were beginning to recognize their own needs and letting them be known' (Ferraro and Tucker 1993: 49), though it might not have been welcome to the parents.

We have been advocating a 'rounded' evaluation, in which many perspectives are taken into account. It would be mistaken to assume that all perspectives will carry, or should carry, equal weight. How much power does each stakeholder have to define whether the group is successful (using the metaphorical activity which began this chapter, how close is each stakeholder's 'land mass' to the area of success in the Sea of Groupwork?)

What contributes to success?

There are so many different aspects of the group that it is impossible to evaluate them all. Which parts have had the most significance, either in sustaining the group or in failing it, is by no means self-evident. Every chapter in this book has pointed to factors which have a bearing on the group's success – planning and recruitment, offering groupwork to individuals, agreeing purpose and ground rules, using a range of appropriate action techniques and interactional techniques, managing the boundary between the individual and the group, co-working effectively, not to mention an awareness of power, oppression, intimacy, difference and group themes. In Chapter 5 we noted the significance of the individual offer of groupwork in promoting successful groupwork by practitioners in the Groupwork Project, but how do we weigh all the various factors involved?

If this were not problematic enough, it is not always straightforward to define what 'success' is. For example, is a group for violent offenders being evaluated for group members' understanding about what triggers violence, their learning of strategies to manage violent feelings, or the impact on reconviction rates? (Canton *et al.* 1992: 52). The different stakeholders described earlier in 'Who defines success?' might each have contrary views as to what success is. This is another good reason to start to ask these questions before the group begins, so that the group is judged by criteria which you consider to be fair. To state your own indicators of success and to help group members to consider theirs early in the group is to enable the group to retain power over the definition of its own success.

One relatively straightforward indicator of success is attendance. In those circumstances where group members can vote with their feet, they will. Peake and Otway (1990) considered attendance to be the obvious measure of success for a group for girls who had been sexually abused. The group started with nine members and ended with nine members, and there was an average attendance of 30/35 sessions. Successful attendance is, itself, a sign of other successes, which in this case were attributed to the provision of transport (female taxi drivers brought the girls to and from the group), the choice of groupworkers, group selection, the rules of the group and the curriculum of the group. Attendance, though an obvious indicator in many respects, needs to be set in context; 50 per cent attendance at a group by someone who is a non-attender at school can be seen as a remarkable achievement. To remind us that we can take nothing for granted, the success of the 'degrouping' technique is measured by the complete dissolution of the group (in this case Hong Kong youth gangs), or its transformation into a more formal youth group (Lo 1992).

It is also important to evaluate the methods used in the group. Craig (1988: 56) canvassed the views of adolescent boys concerning the various activities the group had used, and found that certain activities (such as brainstorming) had been better received than others (such as the pen and paper exercises). This kind of feedback is especially important if you are planning a repeat of a group.

In a group for black children in white foster homes, the overall aim was to foster a sense of black identity, so a major indicator of success might be the terms which the individual members of the group used to describe themselves at the end of the group ('black') as opposed to the beginning of the group ('white').

Indicators of progress

'Success' is a 100 per cent word and, in reality, most groups are likely to achieve a measure of success. It is important, therefore, to have an idea of what will indicate progress. Sometimes these indicators only become evident during the group itself:

> Some prisoners began deliberately reading newspapers in order to be able to contribute to the conversation, and I noticed a steady increase in the vocabulary used by many of them. (Garrett 1995: 61, on Dialogue Groups in a prison)

It is unlikely that a questionnaire asking prisoners, 'do you deliberately read newspapers in order to be able to contribute to the conversations?' would elicit many 'yes's, nor that these same prisoners in the Dialogue Groups would be self-aware of their developing vocabulary. It is even less likely that they would have put these two achievements as their personal goals at the outset of the group. Highly subjective and unquantified though they are, these are nevertheless valuable observations and, if substantiated by others, can be more illuminating than a hundred questionnaires.

Once you and the group are clear about what success might look like, you will have a clearer idea about the travel which will indicate progress. Whether it be a stammer that virtually disappears over the course of the group (Dixon and Phillips 1994: 90), or the fact that a group of Asian women who came to early group sessions in their work clothes now dress up and wear jewellery (Muir and Notta 1993: 128), or that bereaved children start to talk to their parents about their feelings and not just to the groupworkers (Harmey and Price 1992: 26), or that male sex offenders talk about their offences less as though they were passive victims of their actions and more as active participants (Cowburn 1990: 169), there are all kinds of signals which can show that the group is working.

Although it is important not to fabricate indicators *post hoc* which happen to fit the circumstances, it is evident from all the examples above that there are very valid indicators which arise out of the experience of the group. If you have the opportunity to run the group again with new members you will be able to look for similar indicators which have presented themselves in previous groups. Sometimes it is possible to compare similar groups, such as Hopmeyer and Werk's (1993) study of different kinds of family bereavement group.

Methods of evaluation

We do not have the space here to explore in detail the way research methodology applies to groups. In most cases the evaluation of the group is informal rather than formal, and groupworkers can draw from the kaleidoscope of action techniques in Chapter 7 to conduct evaluations which are integral to the groupwork as well as informative and creative. Here we highlight just a few of these.

GROUP DISCUSSION

Open-ended discussion ('How is it going?') is likely to produce soft generalizations which are frequently too unspecific to be useful. Focused questions are more likely to provide information which is of better quality. The questions might focus on the impact on the group member:

'How has the group helped or hindered the way you...?'

or on the group itself:

'If we were to run this group again what would you suggest we keep? What would you suggest we change?'

Imaginative ways can be found to make the evaluation an enjoyable experience, such as the staff development group which used panel discussion, in which all members took part in a draw for membership of two competing teams called the Scoffers and the Flatterers. To trigger an evaluative discussion 'these opposing teams present their evaluation of the course and its results and defend these in debate' (Szmagalski 1989: 242).

WRITTEN EVALUATIONS

The kinds of questions you use to frame a discussion can also form a written questionnaire. 'Running' questionnaires which are introduced at the beginning of the group's life help to make review and evaluation an integral part of the group's experience:

> 'Why did you decide to join the group? What is your vision of an 'ideal' group?

especially when revisited at various stages:

> 'Now that we are halfway through the group, would you recommend a friend who was in similar situation to yours to join?'

Think of ways to make use of the group's lifetime; 'all the participants wrote letters to themselves, addressed and sealed an envelope and entrusted it to a course leader to post to them after six weeks' (Canton *et al.* 1992: 50, writing about a group for violent offenders).

Questionnaires are very flexible and, in addition to both open and focused questions, you can include scales:

> 'On a scale from 0–10 how supportive have you found this group?'

and multiple choices:

> 'Which of the following have been the three most important aspects of the group?'

Questionnaires have been used successfully in situations which might at first seem difficult, such as groupwork with bereaved children aged between six and eight, who at the end of 12 weeks were asked whether 'children should come to such groups and why' (Pennells 1995: 249).

The written testimony of group members can be important when enlisting the support of others such as senior managers in the agency, perhaps with regard to a group's survival:

> We want to keep the group going because we get support from each other and understanding, help, advice, friendship and a sharing of problems. We'd rather have two probation officers in the group than one, but if not, one will do, OK Chief. (Statement by women offenders to the chief probation officer, in Jones *et al.* 1991: 229)

KEEPING A LOG

A regular log, such as the example earlier (Figure 12.1), retains basic data about who was present when and what happened, which helps the search for patterns and themes in the group and a reflection on the way the group has developed.

FLIPCHART QUICK-THINK

Quick-thinks are useful when you want to yield many different ideas, sometimes called 'blue-sky', so a flipchart might productively be used towards the beginning of a group to generate indicators which people consider could be used to show the group is working well.

GROUP PRODUCT

Sometimes the group has a very public product as an outcome. In an article about a group for women whose children have been sexually abused, Otway and Peake (1994: 158–9) reproduce a comprehensive list of what mothers would benefit from when it becomes known that their children have been sexually assaulted. Comprising 18 points, this list was developed by women in the group. It is a concrete outcome which speaks for itself in terms of the value of the group.

EMPIRICAL MEASURES

We have already considered attendance as a relatively objective indicator of success. There may be formal instruments or scales available for the kind of work in which you are involved, such as psychometric testing (Towl and Dexter 1994), allowing you to do a pretest and a post-test to measure changes in individuals' attitudes or behaviours. Barnett *et al.* (1990: 200–1) used a cognition scale to measure changes occurring in female sexual abuse offenders in prison at the end of a ten-session group. The results showed tangible changes, though the authors are rightly cautious of the possibility of the women replying in ways they thought they should, in order to impress the prison authorities. Other indicators were also used to confirm the changes.

SHAPE OF THE EVALUATION

Just as you had choices about the shape for the various action techniques (Chapter 7), so there is a choice about the shape of the evaluation. Principally, this is a choice between individual and group-based evaluations (the two are not mutually exclusive), though some techniques such as telephone evaluations necessitate an individual approach (Home and Darveua-Fournier 1990: 241). The time dimension of the evaluation is also significant. Grindley (1994) noted that the euphoric tone of the evaluations completed immediately after sessions was muted, though still positive, six months later. When is it right to follow-up? Ross (1991: 68) suggests that 'evaluation is rarely successful until after the feelings associated with ending the group have been expressed', yet some evaluations benefit from the accuracy of an immediate response, before memories dim.

Analysis of information gathered

Collecting information is often easier than knowing what to do with it. Groupworkers should view the information which arises from the evaluation as part of an incomplete picture; sometimes it is possible to see just how complete or otherwise the picture is, other times it is less evident what is missing. This is a complex activity which requires the co-workers to consider the information available and to discover patterns, rather than impose them.

There are many reasons why you need to be cautious about any conclusions, both in terms of this group and in relation to any generalizations from this group to others. Towl and Dexter (1994: 258) put the dilemma succinctly:

> First, [is] the problem of defining and measuring change. Second, the problem of establishing whether or not any change is a direct product of participation in the group rather than the result of other events.

To these difficulties can be added the issue of achieving an honest evaluation. As O'Connor (1992: 85) notes, there can be 'a tendency for the facilitators to attend selectively to data which seemed to confirm their original hypotheses'. An uncritical view of your own groupwork results in evaluations which attempt to prove what you already believe, such as Fitzsimmons and Levy's (1996) view of an art therapy group for young people, in which it is evident that whatever happened to the group members, it would have supported the authors' psychodynamic explanation of anorexia and bulimia. Where it is evident that there is no awareness of other possible interpretations and their relative merits, the evaluation loses not just credibility but also interest. It is what you learn, not what you prove correct, which helps you to develop as a groupworker. There are many pitfalls in evaluating your own work if you have a very closed belief system: 'I am still processing what the groups meant for me, and why they worked, but I am sure that a psychodynamic background was a contributing factor' (Gobat 1994: 221). Others must be privy to how any factor contributes to the group working well, and this means an ability to state what would have disproved this factor.

There is a balance between on the one hand a rigid adherence to tightly drawn behavioural indicators, making it near-impossible to demonstrate that the outcome is related to the group experience, and on the other hand an unshakeable belief in the rightness of your chosen approach. An inquiry which does not produce some some surprise does little to extend your practice or the sum of groupwork knowledge.

Groupwork and formal research

There is a need for flexibility in outcome research in groupwork in order to be able to respond to the unintended outcomes, the unanticipated changes and the necessary messiness of groups, and to avoid trivializing what is being evaluated. Formal research into groupwork is guided by an investigative paradigm, sometimes classified as either 'experimental' or 'naturalistic'. The complexity and evolving nature of most groups means that the group's purposes and objectives are likely to change during the life of the group, so that a straightforward 'this is what we set out to do' and 'this is how far we got' is, indeed, too simple. Rather than focusing purely on measurable indicators of effectiveness, it is important to develop forms of evaluation which take account of the broader systems with which the group and its members are in contact, and which focus on 'participants, relationships, activities, intentions, resources, structures and processes' (Gordon 1992: 42).

Examples in the literature of empirical groupwork research are unusual. Weisen's (1991) study of five groups for people with stress and anxiety used a control group of people in a mental health day centre setting who were not exposed to any groupwork, and found evidence that groupwork was effective in alleviating anxiety and improving strategies for coping with stress. No conclusions could be drawn in respect of the most effective number and length of sessions, number of members, leadership style or group activities.

Cwikel and Oron (1991) adopted a 'null hypothesis' approach. They hypothesized that a support group (in this case for people suffering from chronic schizophrenia) would not have any apparent effect, and generated alternate hypotheses which might explain any effects, such as an alternate hypothesis that support group members were not as psychiatrically disturbed prior to their participation as those who did not participate. This approach aims to avoid researchers searching for what they want to find.

Walmsley (1990) used a group approach to help set the agenda and verify her findings when researching into the question of what adulthood means for people with learning difficulties. She tapped into an existing group of five elected members of a self-advocacy group at an adult training centre, combining group sessions at beginning and end with individual interviews in between to paint a picture of adulthood based on the group's perspective.

Linking the evaluation of groupwork to the conduct of a research project, Whitaker (1985: 156) explores this in terms of formal assessments and investigations. She views the main reason for taking informal monitoring a step further as the need to demonstrate the value of the group to others. However, if it is necessary to persuade the purseholders to continue to support a groupwork programme, Whitaker rightly suggests that formal research (couched as it inevitably is in conditional terms) is unlikely to sway the sceptic. However, in the quest to understand why the group worked for some and not for others, what aspects of the group were particularly successful and what factors contributed to this, evaluative research has an important role to play.

Groupwork as a method of research: focus groups

This chapter has focused on evaluating groupwork, but it is also the case that groupwork can be deployed as a *method* of evaluation. A number of authors have suggested how focus groups, for example, can harness the power of groups in research to the benefit of the disadvantaged and oppressed, rather than the political parties and commercial outfits who customarily use them (Home 1996; Swift 1996; Walton 1996). In an unusual study, Atkinson (1993) describes how what began as a research project developed into an autonomous group; her role as a researcher to explore whether older people with learning disabilities could use recall and reminiscence to produce oral life histories became that of a scribe to document their individual and collective memories.

Some models of groupwork propose great clarity and specificity in aims and objectives in order to achieve equally clear evaluations (Preston-Shoot 1988). Other models demand less precision and suggest a more evolutionary approach to group purpose (Mullender and Ward 1991). At a general level, there is no right or wrong approach; at the specific level of your group there are better and worse approaches and these depend on the kind of group you are working with, your own style and the circumstances of the people who are members of the group.

Finally, do not underestimate the value and impact of group members' own statements. Wintram *et al.* (1994: 131) include three powerful statements from members of a women's group which speak more eloquently than any researcher's questionnaire about the impact and benefit the group had for them. Statements of this nature are the most empowering and enduring testament to a group.

Below is one of the evaluations from a 'significant other' in respect of the impact of the group on an individual member.

Portfolio extract

 City Metropolitan District Council   **Social Services Department**

Barbara had initially been referred by her GP to the Community Mental Health Team because of a long-term depression which the GP related to the death of her husband some three years before. Barbara is also registered blind and her limited eyesight exacerbates her mental health difficulties and contributes to her feelings of low self-esteem and self-worth.

Prior to joining The Outings Group, apart from her immediate family and a problematic relationship with a man, Barbara was very socially isolated. The relationship was causing Barbara many difficulties. Barbara was increasingly aware that she was being exploited by this man, however she was unable to find the confidence to end the relationship. Barbara had some fixed ideas around 'no-one else will want me'.

The Outings Group enabled Barbara to build upon her social skills and increase her feelings of self-confidence and self-worth.

Throughout the process of the group Barbara adopted better coping mechanisms and eventually began to make some important decisions herself, significantly, she assertively ended the damaging relationship.

Barbara has since continued to transfer the skills she developed in the group into all aspects of her everyday life.

I believe that The Outings Group was a very positive experience for Barbara and enabled her to develop her own knowledge and understanding of mental health issues in general and increased Barbara's self-awareness in respect of her own problems.

LP Senior Social Worker SS (1998)

CHAPTER THIRTEEN

Endings in Groupwork

About 'Unfinished...'

Endings often evoke a raft of mixed feelings – sadness, relief, celebration, anti-climax, achievement, reflection. 'Unfinished' is designed to help you tap into your own thoughts and feelings about endings and what makes an ending satisfying.

Purpose

The chapter looks at endings from the perspective of individual group members (who may leave a group which continues) and the group itself. Endings are related to beginnings, both seen as the 'ends' of the group, and links are made between the process of closure which describes the endings of group sessions and the process of ending the group as a whole. The group's ending is set in the wider context, especially with regard to the kind of contact, if any, group members have outside the group. The impact of the groupworkers' views of endings (painful or gainful?) is emphasized.

Method

- Read the narrative in the unfinished activity.
- Make notes to answer the question 'how might the reader feel and why?' and answer the questions raised at the bottom of the page.
- Compare notes with your co-worker. How similar and different are your responses?

Variations

'Happy endings' is an action technique which helps complete the circle of beginning and end by asking group members in the first session to draw what they see as a 'Happy ending' for themselves, come the end of the group. These drawings are kept and returned to group members to discuss in the last session.

Consider your responses to the ending of different films. Do you like to know beforehand how a film is going to end, or would this spoil it for you? Do you have a preferred type of ending? How do you respond to equivocal endings, such as in Hitchcock's *The Birds?*

Unfinished...

The tale of gripping suspense had occupied almost all of the weekend. It had started in a commonplace setting, a middle-sized town towards the end of a wet autumn. Its very ordinariness was unusual. It is true that there had been something untrustworthy about the landlord, though only hinted at. And yet it was far from clear that he was implicated. In fact, it was likely that both he and his son were a red herring. Actually, it hadn't been clear until the second half who actually was the victim, which was very clever, because you weren't aware of the anomaly until the house was finally unlocked. The mother was a strange mix, and the complexities of the twins had been skil-fully drawn, including their ambivalent relationship with the agency. And what was the significance of the plum? But, aside from the characters, it was the texture of place and occasion which had maintained the tension for such a long period. How strong to have resisted all temptation to skip ahead and sneak a preview of how it would end. You can imagine, then, the feel-ings when the narrative ran out. Mid-sentence, at the bottom of page 329. The last six pages were blank. Blank! Was it a printer's error? A 'postmodernist' ending by deliberate design? Accident or plan, the reader would never know whodunnit or why.

How might the Reader feel and why?

Think of an occasion from your own experience, recent if possible, where you have felt the need to revisit (mentally) a situation after it has finished.

What was it about the experience of the actual situation which made you wish to replay it?

Notes for the groupworker

Endings can be seen from different perspectives. One perspective is that of the individual group 'careers' of the participants – members and group-workers. Are they leaving a group which will continue after they have gone, or does the group end together? Another perspective derives from the groupwork processes at play; the dynamics of the endings of individual sessions and of the final ending of the group itself. Each kind of ending has common aspects, and each has its own particular characteristics, which we explore in this chapter.

Endings for individuals

The initial offer of groupwork should have included the question of whether the group has a fixed time to run, or whether it is intended to be open-ended. In committing themselves to a group, potential members need this knowledge to make an informed decision, or the knowledge that the group itself will decide once it has met. It is not that one kind of group is preferable to another, but different kinds of group lend themselves to different timescales (Chapter 4). Even in groups which describe themselves as 'ongoing' some kind of renewal is usually necessary, because it can be difficult to sustain the initial energy.

It is useful to think of both the beginnings and endings of a group together. The ending should be anticipated from the beginning. This was displayed graphically in a group for boys who had been sexually abused, where there was a group calendar to give the boys an idea of the overall 'time-shape' of the group, and this helped them to prepare for the eventual ending (Dixon and Phillips 1994: 87).

These 'ends' (as opposed to endings) are like bookends supporting the books in between, and we need to be aware that the nature of any particular group will be heavily influenced by the nature of each of these ends. We can use a continuum to conceptualize the various possible ends (Figure 13.1). At one end of the continuum are those groups where the beginning and ending of the group is the same for all its members (point A). This is the archetypal group, the implicit model for the 'classic' group, but it is only one of many variants. Close to this point is the situation where individuals start and finish one of a programme of groups together (point B). Towards the other end of the continuum is the group with no apparent ends, in which individuals come and go but the group plays on (point C) and a particularly final type is the group where individuals leave to move on to another life stage, such as an admission to a hospital or institution, or death itself (point D). In between these points are many different possibilities. Let us look at each of these points in turn.

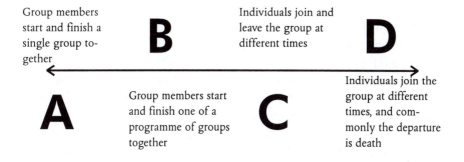

Figure 13.1 Group ends – a continuum

GROUP MEMBERS START AND FINISH A SINGLE GROUP TOGETHER (POINT A)

When the coming together of the individuals *is* the group, and their leaving it *is* the conclusion, we have a group of type A. The elapsed time from start to finish varies (eight to twelve sessions over as many weeks is common but not universal). In these circumstances it is the group which is ending, not just the individual's contact with it and members have been together since the group's inception. We will look in more detail at the particular considerations for endings with closed groups of this nature later.

GROUP MEMBERS START AND FINISH ONE OF A PROGRAMME OF GROUPS TOGETHER (POINT B)

There are some groups which form part of an overall programme, forming part of a 'stepladder' of services for the group members. The programme might consist of the group in question being repeated for different cohorts, such as Norman's (1994) pregnancy group, the first of a two-stage process in which the second stage is a group for both mothers and babies, following the birth of the babies.

Depending on what kind of contact the cohorts have with each other, any single group in the programme could feel much like a type A group to its membership. However, the leaders might make specific reference to the way in which the group's content and structure has been influenced by other cohorts' experiences; or individuals might graduate to other groups in the programme, depending on their progress. A number of the groups in the Groupwork Project were conducted within day centre settings, so that group members were also part of larger, less defined groupings. In these circumstances, where group members have knowledge of each other outside the defined group, beginnings and endings are less sharp.

INDIVIDUALS JOIN AND LEAVE THE GROUP AT DIFFERENT TIMES (POINT C)

Even where the life of the group as a whole is without end, there are endings for individual members. In these circumstances there are different entry and exit points for members regulated by vacancies in the group, and the group itself has a life which is independent of the particular individual people who make up its current membership at any one time. This is best described as a 'replacement' model of open groups (Henry 1988), compared with the drop-in/drop-out model in which membership is very fluid. The replacement approach might equally apply to the group leadership or to an individual couple or family. A group for families at risk met twice a week for three hours, with most families participating for about a year and new families joining as old ones left (Moe 1989: 268).

There are numerous examples of these kinds of groups at other levels in society, such as church congregations and local political groups. These entities are held in trust by the contemporary membership, their purpose greater than the immediate benefits. There is a similarity between these larger groupings and smaller ones such as the Tuesday Lunch Club, where members come and go but the club goes on. Interestingly, our language seems to recognize these differences by finding words like 'club', 'society', 'association' and 'union' as opposed to 'group', which we instinctively feel means something more intimately bound up with the individuals involved. Although there are groupwork processes at work during a lunch club, and the leaders can practise elements of groupwork, the club as a whole is something different to a group.

Special consideration needs to be given to how individuals who are leaving a group at different times are helped to say 'goodbye'. Writing a letter to the group and the group leaders is one way of helping the individual to assess where they are now and formally saying goodbye and perhaps 'thank you' to people who have helped (Davidsen-Nielsen and Leick 1989: 196–8).

INDIVIDUALS JOIN THE GROUP AT DIFFERENT TIMES, AND COMMONLY THE ENDING IS DEATH (POINT D)

It is important to record a special note for those groups where an individual's ending with the group has special significance. This usually arises from the fact that leaving the group marks an important life stage for the individual, such as moving into residential care or some other institutional arrangement.

The most final of endings is death. It can be a shock when a group member dies unexpectedly, but a group might be formed specifically to help dying people to prepare, or new places in the group might be contingent on the opening left by a member who has died. The way in which the taboo subject of death is faced is hugely significant to group members; it is important to honour and remember dead members of the group and to face the fact of death itself, not to perpetuate a collusive silence. Current members, observing the group's treatment of dead members, also observe how their own anticipated death will be handled by the group.

Death is particularly poignant when it means an abbreviated life. A support group for gay men with Aids met every Monday evening for an hour and a half. Over the course of two and a half years, 11 members died. The group leadership also changed, with one leader who had been diagnosed with Aids deciding it was time to leave; his replacement was also diagnosed with Aids a month after assuming co-leadership (Getzel and Mahony 1989: 95).

Endings are influenced not just by the way individuals join and leave the group, but also by the extent to which group members have contact together outside the group. The significance of these two dimensions (illustrated in Figures 13.1 and 13.2) arises from the fact that their focus is less on the group and more on the wider context, which reflects one of our themes in this book, namely the importance of the boundaries between the group and the other aspects of members' lives, and the recognition that – no matter how powerful and influential the experience of groupwork – its members spend much more time outside the group than in it. The extent to which the experience of the group is reinforced or diluted by life outside the group is influenced by the amount of contact between members beyond the group sessions.

Groupworkers must also consider whether it is their own departure from the group rather than that of individual group members which should be planned for. Mullender and Ward's (1991) model of self-directed groupwork certainly alerts us to this important consideration. In addition, the kind of contact which the groupworkers have with each other and with the members outside the group has a significant bearing on how the group's ending is experienced.

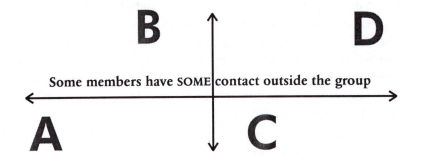

Figure 13.2 Group members' contact with each other

Sessional closure

If the group programme as a whole can be likened to a symphony, then the individual group sessions are its 'movements'. Each session plays its part in the whole and each requires a satisfactory conclusion. What is a satisfactory conclusion and how is it achieved?

FINISHING TOGETHER

We have all experienced groups or meetings where participants have drifted off and where the session becomes more of a fade or a collapse than a conclusion. When a group session ends by depletion it feels unsatisfactory for everybody, those who have left without being a part of a conclusion and those who remained to witness the attrition. A very basic principle, then, is to finish together.

The best way to achieve a concerted closure is to ensure that everybody knows when that is – the agreed time for the end of the session (this includes your co-worker!). People may have buses to catch, children to collect, medical appointments to keep, maybe just a television programme they want to watch. It is important to respect each other's time. Reminding people at the beginning of the session of the time for the end is an opportunity to ask if there is anybody who will need to leave early. The group knows that when this person departs in the middle of a difficult discussion it is not a 'walk-out' but an agreed early exit. This is an important distinction, both for the individual and the rest of the group.

Countdowns to the end of the session alert the group to the passing of time. A reminder that the group is just over half way through can encourage someone who has been sitting on a difficult subject and prevent it being raised just as everybody is ready to leave. Despite their best efforts, most groupworkers will experience some sessions which end in a different time and a different way for different individuals in the group. Ross (1991: 59) describes how one member of a group for 15-year-olds with school-related problems had rushed out of the group in tears without telling anyone why. Even so, she completed the group programme and made good progress at school. Finishing together is an important aim, and groupworkers can facilitate this by their conduct from the very beginning of the session.

EXTENSIONS

> Sometimes at the supposed end of a session, someone would speak of a painful or upsetting incident or memory. (Tribe and Shackman 1989: 164, on a group for refugee women)

Despite the many openings which the groupworkers have created during the course of a session, an individual member introduces an enormous and painful topic just as the session is ending. One of the most difficult decisions is when to extend the ending of a session beyond the agreed time. If the group is going to run beyond its time, it must not happen by default, and the group should make a positive decision to do so; although the groupworker might pose the question, it is the group which needs to answer it. The group agreement (Chapter 6), might already have anticipated this kind of situation and provide a quick response. When the group does not extend its session, the groupworkers might need to spend individual time with the person afterwards, and if this becomes a pattern, the group should be invited to consider whether its last-minute behaviour is more an indication of difficulties with leaving and separation than with the particular issue which is raised.

CLOSURE AND ANTICIPATION

A successful sessional ending is one which looks backward and forward in equal measure. 'Closure' is perhaps the best way to describe the first of these aspects. This means an understanding of the issues which have been raised by the session and their implications for each individual and a shared understanding of progress *as a group*. It is usual for the groupworkers to articulate this understanding, or at least to put it in train. There may be a consensus about what these issues are; if not, closure can only be achieved if the differences have been named and accepted as such. The group need not reach consensus, but it should reach an agreed understanding of the differences.

258 THE ESSENTIAL GROUPWORKER

It is just as significant that there is a sense of closure at the feeling level, too. To feel a sense of conclusion, the group must achieve a sense of *acceptance*. This means that group members might feel differently, but that there is an awareness of these different feelings and, as far as possible, an acceptance of them.

Closure is an opportunity for the group to give itself positive strokes about the progress made, the difficult feelings expressed, the complex issues understood, and the like. Usually several positives from the session can be identified, but where the group really does not feel to be working it is important that the closure allows honest expression of feelings and observations. Though there is a natural desire to end a session on a good note, careful honesty can provide a trigger for reconsidering the group, not necessarily now but as the focus of the next session.

Indeed, anticipating the next and future sessions of the group is an important factor in the summarizing at the close of session. The group can begin to consider how this session has helped lead to the next and what issues arising now should be addressed in the future. This process of setting the agenda might be very explicit (using a flipchart to agree the topics for the next session and reminding people of any specific tasks which they have agreed to do) or more tacit, with quiet agreement about the next phase.

INDIVIDUAL CONTACTS BETWEEN SESSIONS

We discussed earlier the possibility of contact with an individual immediately after a session, especially if there are issues which relate more particularly to that individual. Similarly, groupworkers need to consider whether they will initiate contact with members who have not attended the session but who were expected to do so. Again, these decisions are easier to make if a course of action has already been laid via the group agreement (Chapter 6).

Individuals in the group sometimes want contact with groupworkers between sessions in order to discuss something which is happening in the group. In these situations, it is crucial that the ground rules are carefully discussed. There are some occasions where such contact can be justified (unknown to the groupworker, somebody in the group is at risk from another member); however, in most cases, group issues should be raised *in the group*. It undermines any sense of closure if group members suspect that the closure is only partial and that others will continue the process in their absence between group sessions.

COMPLETING THE CIRCLE: PATTERNS BECOME RITUALS

Successful sessional endings are linked to successful sessional beginnings. Dobbin and Evans (1994: 120) describe the importance in a group for mothers of sexually abused children of 'a collective effort to remember the last session in some detail and to write it in the diary'. Since this act of collective memory can be surprisingly difficult, it helps to provide reinforcement by asking group members at the end of a session to state what they hope to remember at the beginning of the next. Linking into the next session is a powerful way of summarizing this session. So, beginnings and endings are more circular than linear; or, using a wave metaphor to depict the flow of each session, closure should be an opportunity for order to resurface (Manor and Dumbleton 1993).

Rituals help to establish a pattern for each session, and patterns are useful in providing security and stability in the group. The end of each session is a significant transition point for the group, and a ritual ending helps deal with this transition. In a group for five- to seven-year-old siblings of children with special needs, a 'facial dice' was used to close each session. The dice had six facial expressions – happy, sad, surprised, angry, etc. – and group members took turns 'to throw the dice and use the facial expressions to talk about their feelings about what has happened in the group' (Ferraro and Tucker 1993: 47). This ending might seem to be in direct contrast to the unstructured 15 minutes of free play at the end of each session of another group for children (this time with a focus on bereavement, Harmey and Price 1992). Whether structured or unstructured, the common factor is the closing ritual.

The proposed closing ritual can sometimes be too powerful for the members to undertake:

> It had originally been intended to end every session with a ritual exercise asking each woman to make a positive statement about some aspects of themselves or their functioning. This proved impossible: the women could not do it. Unlike their adolescent daughters in previous groups who had managed it very well. But as it became clear, while the girls had someone to take care of them, many of the women had no one. (Dobbin and Evans 1994: 123, on a group for mothers of sexually abused children)

The ending of the group

Käthe Kollwitz was one the foremost artists of her day. In October 1914, her son, Peter, was killed at the age of nineteen, during one of the first major campaigns of World War I. She vowed to create a memorial to her son to commemorate the sacrifice of all the young volunteers. She attempted various designs, put the project aside, and did not return to complete it until 1931. That she was only able to complete it seventeen years after his death should tell us something about how unconvincing is the view that the Great War ended when the textbooks tell us, on 11 November, 1918. For millions of people who had to live with the human costs of the conflict the war lasted much, much longer. (Winter and Baggett 1996; the memorial lies in a German war cemetary near the town of Vladslo in Belgium)

It may not be on the huge scale of the war to *end* all wars, but it is possible to appreciate how endings are seldom neat and how trauma and loss, in particular, reverberate through time. However, we can also make use of this phenomenon to create a positive aftermath. The beneficial impact of groupwork and the positive memories of a group can help sustain those who were members of the group beyond the final session. The group ends but the groupwork lasts. From this perspective, then, endings are best reframed as transitions.

TIME-LIMITED GROUPS

Earlier in this chapter we looked at groups which have no planned ending and discovered that, nevertheless, 'endings' remain significant, because of the many individual endings which the group experiences as its members leave. A group where all of its members leave at the same time cannot avoid focusing on the process of ending and should use this opportunity to involve the group members both in planning and preparing for the end, and in transferring their learning from this experience to other endings in their lives.

There are many parallels between the processes of closure in sessions and ending with the group as a whole. Countdowns are important to pace an individual session, and are similarly valuable to alert group members to how many further sessions the group has available (Ross 1991). The process of completing the circle described in relation to each session is relevant to the whole group cycle, too. Often, activities which were used at the beginning of the group's life might be revisited to end it. A group for children of divorced or separated parents returned to the use of structured exercises and activities in order to consolidate the changes induced by the group. 'The same questionnaire on sibling relationships used at the beginning was used to help members refocus on their sibling relationship as they moved out of the group' (Regan and Young 1990: 29). The sets of six sibling pairs had been helped to move into the 'whole group' and were now encouraged to move back into their 'sibships', each having become a more confident and less uncertain pair of siblings.

Reopening letters written in the first group session and commenting on them in the last is an enlightening way of marking change and progress. It re-connects group members with a time which might well be hazy or forgotten.

UNFINISHED BUSINESS

> It is not unknown for groupworkers to fool themselves into believing that a group will not end because it is so vital to the members: this is … a very serious error. (Ross 1991: 67)

Just as the closure process can be jeopardized by an extension of a session, so indecision about the end of the group itself risks the process of ending. The focus on processes of engaging and group-building should not obscure the equally important process of disengaging and leaving the group. This can be especially difficult when the group has meant different things to different members; for example, some have used it as a launchpad to a more independent lifestyle, whilst others have become heavily dependent on the social company it provides. Groups that do not allow themselves to end may be indicative of groups where there is unfinished business.

Careful group evaluation, as detailed in the previous chapter, should throw light on what each individual has gained from the group and what part they feel it has played in their current situation. By reviewing the group regularly, any wide variations in individuals' expectations of the group should be apparent well before the ending, so that alternatives can be considered for any members who have treated the group as a lifeline. An awareness that individuals might have different finishing lines need not prevent the group from celebrating a communal ending; indeed, it once more reflects the recurrent theme of the acceptance of difference within the group.

There can be forces outside the group which determine its fate, preventing it from being in control of its own ending or its own continuation. Even if the workers and members of the group are united in their attempts to keep a group going, there may be external pressures to close it. Gobat (1994: 217) describes how funding was to be withdrawn from two long-term groups with which she was working, and how this galvanized members into writing a communal letter to the case managers to save the group from termination.

A group should only extend its life after very careful consideration. What is the purpose of the extension? Perhaps a task group requires more time to achieve its goal; it could be that the group is in conflict and needs additional sessions to resolve it. If it is possible to judge how many extra sessions are needed, the group should agree to a specific extension. Sometimes a group which started with one kind of purpose evolves into a group of a different nature; this should be apparent long before the planned end, so that the metamorphosis from time-limited to open-ended group can be monitored and agreed. A planned continuation is different from the group which just cannot bring itself to say goodbye.

FOLLOW-UP

Follow-up work is quite different from extending the group, since follow-up is a process planned from the beginning. A follow-up may entail a group reunion, though it is more commonly on an individual basis. Rather like the offers of groupwork which prepared individuals for the start of the group, follow-ups can help the transition out of the group. Certainly, the individual follow up is likely to deliver an honest account of how long-lasting the effects of the group have been, since the temporary euphoria of a reunion can anaesthetise the actual 'here and now' for each individual. Review meetings might be held at an agreed interval after the end of the group to check on any issues which have arisen, as illustrated by the review with bereaved children six weeks after the group described by Harmey and Price, (1992: 26).

There is at least an equal case to be made for spending time with individuals after the group as there was before it, especially when we consider the relative difficulty of endings compared with beginnings in other aspects of life (compare weddings with divorces, for example).

CEREMONY, RITUAL AND REMEMBRANCE: SAYING GOODBYE

We all have different ways of saying goodbye, and farewells are governed by cultural expectations. The enormous variety in the way in which funerals and wakes are experienced is testament to the range of human responses to endings, from tight inhibition to exorbitant demonstration. An empowered group will be in control of its own destiny and the question of how to mark the group's end should have been discussed and decided long before the end arrives. Groups that have been troubled in the running will likely be troubled in their ending, too. In all circumstances it is important to remember that individuals in the group may have different expectations around endings.

Goodbyes are easier if they have been anticipated. For example, photographs taken in different sessions help to recap the course of the group to remind people how it has developed; displayed at the final session, these photographs are an impressive summary of the group's life and times, and can be shared out for group members to take away. This process is easier when the group has a material product such as Atkinson's (1993) reminiscence group for older people with learning disabilities. 'Our book' was all the more potent because it came to symbolize 'our group' and developed into 'our second book' and 'our third book'. The group's goal became the production of an even bigger and better book of reminiscences. Similarly, the women's group in a drop-in centre produced a resource handbook to help homeless women 'to regain some degree of control over their lives as they actively participated in solving resource-access problems that had plagued them constantly' (Breton 1991: 41). One of the biggest 'group' projects of present times is one of remembrance for the premature endings of many lives, and its product is the Aids quilt, with each life commemorated in a piece of patchwork.

Sometimes the idea of product is actively resisted. For example, in a group for vulnerable children, the co-workers made it clear that the children 'were not there primarily to make finished products (pretty pictures) but to become involved in expressing themselves through the art media and materials' (Clerkin and Knaggs 1991: 52). This same group of children used clay for emotional release rather than the finished product.

We have already noted the significance of patterns in groupwork (Chapter 4), and sometimes these become formalized into ritual. This is at its strongest with ending rituals. Usually some form of celebration is expected. Some groups, especially long-running ones, may have rehearsed 'celebration' at other times during the life of the group. For example, birthdays were a regular occasion for cake and cards and singing in a group for mothers with sexually abused children (Dobbin and Evans 1994: 120). At other times, the end of the group might produce a rare reward, such as the cream cake tea for the prisoners in a women sex offenders group (Barnett et al. 1990: 199). A party to end a group should not, however, inhibit the necessary expression of sad feelings, so that there is an attempt at a false cheeriness.

Termination games are a common ritual, such as the 'End game', in which each person in the group says 'goodbye' to the group and individuals in the group, before leaving the room and waiting outside. Other group members think of anything they would like to say, and the individual outside the room also takes time to reflect further; then the feedback is shared, and the same process occurs with each member in turn (Ross 1991: 63).

OMEGA SESSION

In Chapter 6 we discussed the value of an 'alpha' session before members decide whether to commit to the group. The group has a similar decision about whether to have a special last session outside the mainstream of the group programme, an 'omega' session. For example, the celebration might involve a different venue, a trip out, or even a residential holiday (Rhule 1988: 46). Perhaps it is appropriate to invite others to join the omega session, in the way parents were invited to join a group for bereaved children so they could share their books of artwork, completed during the group; 'the completed book is often used by children later to initiate discussion at home around the death or a particular aspect of their loss' (Harmey and Price 1992: 25).

Feelings about endings: pain or gain?

> A lesson learnt from the experience of running the first support group was that ending was an issue for the staff as much as for the young women. (Norman 1994: 234)

Endings are not just about what you do and think; they are also about what you feel. Tuning in to the possible feelings of group members, and being aware of your own, is no less important now than it was during the course of the group (Chapter 5). How do you anticipate group members will feel about the ending of the group or about their personal departure from a group, and how do you intend to bring these anticipated feelings into the group itself?

The pain of ending seems unbearable to some groupworkers, to the extent that group members in one group were spared the knowledge of ending 'until the end was inevitable': 'they [the group members] preferred to "kill me off" before I "killed" them' (Gobat 1994: 218). The premise seems to have been around an idea of separation anxiety and loss rather than any celebration of success or arrival. Although it is important to be aware of your own feelings, about endings in general and the end of this group in particular, you should also be aware of the impact of your own view of the group's end. If you see it as a time of great pain and misery this is undoubtedly how it will be experienced; if you view it as a time for reflection and celebration this, too, is how it is likely to be experienced. Groups which specifically make active use of a time limit are more likely to celebrate endings as a time to mark success, perceiving the end of a journey as an arrival somewhere else.

Postscript

WHERE WILL IT ALL END?

> Cosmologists are presently pursuing the answer [to the question 'Where will it all end?'] through observations of the value of Omega (the observed density of the universe compared to a critical density). The value of this parameter determines the fate of the universe: if Omega is greater than 1, the universe will collapse into a 'big crunch' (the end!), but if Omega is less than 1, the universe will expand forever (no end!). Omega exactly equal to 1 means the universe will stop expanding at

infinity (no real end). Present observational data puts omega between 0.3 and 1, while theoretical arguments advocate omega equal to 1. (Notes and queries, Guardian, 17 December 1997)

Portfolio extract

We were aware of feelings such as 'where do we go from here?', 'what will I do on a Wednesday afternoon?', 'will we meet up again?' and we felt that these needed addressing. After reading Ross (1991), [we decided to try] the End Game ... The group requested the co-workers to demonstrate this game. I was the one to leave the room and on my return the comments that were made stirred up emotional feelings, and the group voted not to carry on with the game.

...At the end of the last session when we asked for verbal feedback, Mazie said she 'didn't know how to tell us what she was feeling in case we took it the wrong way and were upset'. We encouraged her to say exactly how she felt. Mazie said that she didn't need us any more; she had been involved with mental health services for the past 32 years, but now felt that she had moved on, and would not be back. Both my co-worker and me were delighted with this, as was the rest of the group.

JP (1998)

What better message with which to end this book?

References

Ajdukovic, Marina, Cevizovic, Milena and Kontak, Ksenija (1995) 'Groupwork in Croatia: Experiences with older refugees.' *Groupwork 8*, 1, 152–65.

Allum, Sarah (1990) 'Investigating groupwork: A case study in using a group approach in the initial stages of child sexual abuse investigation.' *Groupwork 3*, 2, 134–43.

Ashe, Mike (1991) 'Meeting prisoners' needs through groupwork.' *Groupwork 4*, 3, 277–83.

Atkinson, Dorothy (1993) 'Life history work with a group of people with learning disabilities.' *Groupwork 6*, 3, 199–210.

Badger, Anne (1988) 'The brothers and sisters group.' *Groupwork 1*, 3, 262–8.

Badham, Bill, Blatchford, Bob, Mcartney, Step and Nicholas, Malcolm (eds) (1989) 'Doing something with our lives when we're inside: Self-directive groupwork in a Youth Custody Centre.' *Groupwork 2*, 1, 27–35.

Ball, Jill and Norman, Annemarie (1996) '"Without the group I'd still be eating half the Co-op": An example of groupwork with women who use food.' *Groupwork 9*, 1, 48–61.

Barnett, Sharon, Corder, Francesca and Jehu, Derek (1990) 'Group treatment for women sex offenders against children.' *Groupwork 3*, 2, 191–203.

Batsleer, Janet (1994) 'Silence in working across difference.' *Groupwork 7*, 3, 197–209.

Behroozi, Cyrus S. (1992) 'Groupwork with involuntary clients: Remotivating strategies.' *Groupwork 5*, 2, 31–41.

Benson, Jarlath (1992) 'The group turned inwards: a consideration of some group phenomena as reflective of the Northern Irish situation.' *Groupwork 5*, 3, 5–18.

Bensted, John, Brown, Allan, Forbes, Carlton and Wall, Rick (1994) 'Men working with men in groups: Masculinity and crime.' *Groupwork 7*, 1, 37–49.

Bernard, Lorraine, Burton, John, Kyne, Phyllis and Simon, June (1988) 'Groups for older people in residential and day-care: The other groupworkers.' *Groupwork 1*, 2, 115–23.

Berne, Eric (1964) *The Games People Play.* London: Penguin.

Bertcher, Harvey J. (1994) *Group Participation: Techniques for Leaders and Members* (2nd edn). London: Sage.

Bethune, Gordon (1998) *From Worst to First: Behind the Scenes of Continental's Remarkable Comeback.* New York: John Wiley and Sons.

Bodinham, Helen and Weinstein, Jeremy (1991) 'Making authority accountable: the experience of a statutory based women's group.' *Groupwork 4*, 1, 22–30.

Booth, Tim (1985) *Home Truths: Old People's Homes and the Outcomes of Care.* Aldershot: Gower.

Bradbury, Malcolm (1975) *The History Man.* London: Secker and Warburg.

Bramson, Robert (1981) *Coping with Difficult People.* Ballantine.

Breton, Margot (1989) 'Learning from groupwork traditions.' *Eleventh Annual Symposium Proceedings of the Association for the Advancement of Social Work with Groups 1*, 3–25, Montreal.

Breton, Margot (1991) 'Toward a model of social groupwork practice with marginalised populations.' *Groupwork 4*, 1, 31–47.

Brown, Allan (1990) 'Groupwork with a difference: The group "mosaic" in residential and day care settings.' *Groupwork 3*, 3, 269–85.

Brown, Allan (1992) *Groupwork* (3rd edn). Aldershot: Arena.

Brown, Allan, Caddick, B., Gardiner, M. and Sleaman, S. (1982) 'Towards a British model of groupwork.' *British Journal of Social Work 12*, 6, 587–603, London.

Brown, Allan and Caddick, Brian (1993) *Groupwork with Offenders.* London: Whiting and Birch.

Brown, Allan and Clough, Roger (eds) (1989) *Groups and Groupings: Life and Work in Day and Residential Centres.* London: Tavistock/Routledge.

Butler, Sandra (1994) 'All I've got in my purse is mothballs! The Social Action Women's Group.' *Groupwork 7*, 2, 163–79.

Butler, Sandra and Wintram, Claire (1991) *Feminist Groupwork.* London: Sage.

Caddick, Brian (1991) 'Using groups in working with offenders: A survey of groupwork in the probation services of England and Wales.' *Groupwork 4*, 3, 197–214.

Canton, Rob, Mack, Carolyn and Smith, Jeff (1992) 'Handling conflict: groupwork with violent offenders.' *Groupwork 5*, 2, 42–53.

CCETSW (1995) *Assuring Quality in the Diploma in Social Work.* London: Central Council for Education and Training in Social Work.

Chau, Kenneth L. (1990) 'Social work with groups in multicultural contexts.' *Groupwork 3*, 1, 8–21.

Chorcora, Maire Ni, Jennings, Eddie and Lordan, Nuala (1994) 'Issues of empowerment: Anti-oppressive groupwork by disabled people in Ireland.' *Groupwork 7*, 1, 63–78.

Clarke, Peter and Aimable, Amanda (1990) 'Groupwork techniques in a residential primary school for emotionally disturbed boys.' *Groupwork 3*, 1, 36–48.

Clerkin, Eugene and Knaggs, Belinda (1991) 'Working creatively with children.' *Groupwork 4*, 1, 48–56.

Corden, John and Preston-Shoot, Michael (1981) *Contracts in Social Work.* Aldershot: Gower.

Cormack, Elisabeth (1993) 'Group therapy with adults with learning difficulties who have committed sexual offences.' *Groupwork 6*, 2, 162–75.

Cowburn, Malcolm (1990) 'Work with male sex offenders in groups.' *Groupwork 3*, 2, 157–71.

Craig, Eileen (1990) 'Structured activities with adolescent boys.' *Groupwork 1*, 1, 48–59.

Craig, Rod (1988) 'Starting the journey: Enhancing the therapeutic elements of groupwork for adolescent female child sexual abuse victims.' *Groupwork 3*, 2, 103–17.

Crown, Kym and Gates, Dan (1997) 'Group work with juvenile sex offenders.' In Albert Alissi and Catherine G. Corto Mergins (eds) *Voices from the Field: Group Work Responds.* New York/London: Haworth.

Cwikel, Julie and Oron, Adina (1991) 'A long-term support group for chronic schizophrenic outpatients: A quantitative and qualitative evaluation.' *Groupwork 4*, 2, 163–77.

Daste, Barry M. (1989) 'Designing cancer groups for maximum effectiveness.' *Groupwork 2*, 1, 58–69.

Davidsen-Nielsen, Marianne and Leick, Nini (1989) 'Open grief groups: the resolution of complicated loss.' *Groupwork 2*, 3, 187–201.

DeVere, Merav and Rhonne, Ossi (1991) 'The use of photographs as a projective and facilitative technique in groups.' *Groupwork 4*, 2, 129–40.

Dixon, Gary and Phillips, Michelle (1994) 'A psychotherapeutic group for boys who have been sexually abused.' *Groupwork 7*, 1, 79–95.

Dobbin, Deb and Evans, Sarah (1994) 'Staying alive in difficult times: The experience of groupwork with mothers of children who have been sexually abused.' *Groupwork 7*, 2, 256–69.

Doel, Mark and Sawdon, Catherine (1995) 'A strategy for groupwork education and training in a social work agency.' *Groupwork 8*, 2, 189–204.

Doel, Mark and Shardlow, Steven (1989) 'The practice portfolio.' Sheffield University.

Doel, Mark and Shardlow, Steven (1995) *Preparing Post-Qualifying Portfolios.* London: CCETSW.

Doel, Mark and Shardlow, Steven (1998) *The New Social Work Practice: Exercises and Activities for Training and Developing Social Workers.* Aldershot: Arena.

Doel, Mark, Shardlow, Steven, Sawdon, Catherine and Sawdon, David (1996) *Teaching Social Work Practice.* Aldershot: Arena.

Douglas, Tom (1976) *Groupwork Practice.* London: Tavistock.

Douglas, Tom (1983) *Groups.* London: Tavistock.

Douglas, Tom (1991) *A Handbook of Common Groupwork Problems.* London: Routledge.

Drakeford, Mark (1994) 'Groupwork for parents of young people in trouble: A proposal.' *Groupwork 7*, 3, 236–47.

Drower, Sandra (1991) 'Groupwork and oral history: Raising the consciousness of young people during social transition.' *Groupwork 4*, 2, 119–128.

Duffy, Bernadette and McCarthy, Brian (1993) 'From group meeting to therapeutic group.' *Groupwork 6*, 2, 152–61.

Edgar, Iain (1992) 'The dream in groupwork practice.' *Groupwork 5*, 2, 54–64.

Erooga, Marcus, Clark, Paul and Bentley, Mai (1990) 'Protection, control, treatment: Groupwork with child sexual abuse perpetrators.' *Groupwork 3*, 2, 172–90.

Fatout, Marian F. (1989) 'Decision-making in therapeutic groups.' *Groupwork 2*, 1, 70–79.

Ferraro, Georgina and Tucker, Julie (1993) 'Groupwork with siblings of children with special needs: A pilot study.' *Groupwork 6*, 1, 43–50.

Finlayson, Sheila (1993) 'Working with a family group of bereaved children.' *Groupwork 6*, 2, 93–106.

Fitzsimmons, Janet and Levy, Rosemary (1996) 'An art therapy group for young people with eating difficulties.' *Groupwork 9*, 3, 283–91.

Francis-Spence, Marcia (1994) 'Groupwork and Black women viewing networks as groups: Black women meeting together for affirmation and empowerment.' *Groupwork 7*, 2, 109–116.

Garland, J.A., Jones, H.E. and Kolodny, R.L. (1976) 'A model for stages in group development in social work groups.' In S. Bernstein (ed) *Explorations in Groupwork*. Boston: Charles River Books.

Garrett, Peter J.T. (1995) 'Group dialogue within prisons.' *Groupwork 8*, 1, 49–66.

Getzel, George S. and Mahoney, Kevin F. (1989) 'Confronting human finitude: Groupwork with people with AIDS.' *Groupwork 2*, 2, 95–107.

Gibson, Faith (1992) 'Reminiscence groupwork with older people.' *Groupwork 5*, 3, 28–40.

Glassman, Urania and Kates, Len (1991) *Group Work: A Humanistic Approach*. London: Sage.

Gobat, Helen (1993) 'Groupwork with parents of learning disabled adolescents.' *Groupwork 6*, 3, 221–31.

Gobat, Helen (1994) 'Ourselves and others.' *Groupwork 7*, 3, 210–222.

Gordon, Kenneth H. (1992) 'Evaluation for the improvement of groupwork practice.' *Groupwork 5*, 1, 34–49.

Grindley, Geraldine (1994) 'Working with religious communities.' *Groupwork 7*, 1, 50–62.

Grossman, Bart and Perry, Robin (1996) 'Re-engaging social work education with the public social services: The California experience and its relevance to Russia.' In Mark Doel and Steven Shardlow (eds) *Social Work in a Changing World: An International Perspective on Practice Learning*. Aldershot: Arena.

Habermann, Ulla (1990) 'Self help groups: A minefield for professionals.' *Groupwork 3*, 3, 221–35.

Habermann, Ulla (1993) 'Why groupwork is not put into practice: Reflections on the social work scene in Denmark.' *Groupwork 6*, 1, 17–29.

Harmey, Nuala and Price, Bernie (1992) 'Groupwork with bereaved children.' *Groupwork 5*, 3, 19–27.

Heap, Ken (1979) *Process and Action in Work with Groups*. Oxford: Pergamon.

Heap, Ken (1985) *The Practice of Social Work with Groups*. London: NISW No. 49.

Heap, Ken (1988) 'The worker and the group process: A dilemma revisited.' *Groupwork 1*, 1, 17–29.

Henchman, David and Walton, Susan (1993) 'Critical incident analysis and its application in groupwork.' *Groupwork 6*, 3, 189–98.

Henry, M. (1988) 'Revisiting open groups.' *Groupwork 1*, 3, 215–28.

Hirayama, Kasumi K., Hirayama, Hisashi and Kuroki, Yasuhiro (1997) 'Group treatment programs for alcoholism in the United States and Japan.' In Albert Alissi and Catherine G. Corto Mergins (eds) *Voices from the Field: Group Work Responds.* New York/London: Haworth.

Hodge, John (1985) *Planning for Co-leadership: A Practice Guide for Groupworkers.* Newcastle: Groupvine.

Holstein, Barbara B. and Addison, Doreen L. (1994) 'Groupwork for mental health providers: Using the Enchanted Self concept.' *Groupwork 7*, 2, 136–44.

Home, Alice (1996) 'Enhancing research usefulness with adapted focus groups.' *Groupwork 9*, 2, 128–38.

Home, Alice and Darveau-Fournier, Lise (1990) 'Facing the challenge of developing group services for high risk families.' *Groupwork 3*, 3, 236–48.

Hopmeyer, Estelle and Werk, Annette (1993) 'A comparative study of four family bereavement groups.' *Groupwork 6*, 2, 107–21.

Hutchins, Kathryn (1991) 'The Telford motoring offenders education project.' *Groupwork 4*, 3, 240–48.

Jones, Marion, Mordecai, Mary, Rutter, Frances and Thomas, Linda (1991) 'The Miskin model of groupwork with women offenders.' *Groupwork 4*, 3, 215–30.

Kerslake, Andrew (1990) 'Groupwork training: A case study.' *Groupwork 3*, 1, 65–76.

Kohli, Kavita (1993) 'Groupwork with deaf people.' *Groupwork 6*, 3, 232–47.

Kurland, Roselle and Salmon, Robert (1993) 'Groupwork versus casework in a group.' *Groupwork 6*, 1, 5–16.

Kurland, Roselle and Salmon, Robert (1997) 'When worker and member expectations collide: The dilemma of establishing group norms in conflictual situations.' In Albert Alissi and Catherine G. Corto Mergins (eds) *Voices from the Field: Group Work Responds.* New York/London: Haworth.

Lacoursiere, R. (1980) *The Life Cycle of Groups: Group Developmental Stage Theory.* New York: Human Sciences Press.

Lang, Norma (1986) 'Social work practice in small group forms.' In N. Lang (ed) *Collectivity in Social Groupwork: Concept and Practice, Social Work with Groups,* special issue, *9,* 4.

Lebacq, Marie and Shah, Zaffira (1989) 'A group for black and white sexually abused children.' *Groupwork 2*, 2, 123–33.

Lee, Francis W.L., Lo, T. Wing and Wong, Dennis S.W. (1996) 'Intervention in the decision-making of youth gangs.' *Groupwork 9*, 3, 292–302.

Levine, B. (1979) *Group Psychotherapy.* Englewood Cliffs, NJ: Prentice Hall.

Lewis, Gun (1992) 'Groupwork in a residential home for older people: building on the positive aspects of group living.' *Groupwork 5*, 1, 50–7.

Lo, T. Wing (1992) 'Groupwork with youth gangs in Hong Kong.' *Groupwork 5*, 1, 68–71.

Lo, T. Wing (1993) 'Neutralisation of group control in youth gangs.' *Groupwork 6*, 1, 51–63.

Lorde, Audrey (ed) (1994) *Sister Outsider: Essays and Speeches.* California: The Freedom Press.

Lordan, Nuala (1996) 'The use of sculpts in social groupwork education.' *Groupwork* 9, 1, 62–79.

Lumley, Jenny and Marchant, Harold (1989) 'Learning about groupwork.' *Groupwork* 2, 2, 134–44.

Mackintosh, Jane (1991) 'The Newcastle Intensive Probation Programme: A centralised approach to groupwork.' *Groupwork 4*, 3, 262–76.

Manor, Oded (1988) 'Preparing the client for social groupwork: An illustrated framework.' *Groupwork 1*, 2, 100–14.

Manor, Oded (1989) 'Organizing accountability for social groupwork: More choices.' *Groupwork 2*, 2, 108–22.

Manor, Oded (1996) 'Storming as transformation: A case study of group relationships.' *Groupwork 9*, 3, 128–38.

Manor, Oded and Dumbleton, Miriam (1993) 'Combining activities and growth games: A systems approach.' *Groupwork 6*, 3, 248–65.

Martin, Nicola and O'Neill, Eddie (1992) 'Groupwork with teenage cancer patients.' *Groupwork 5*, 3, 62–73.

Masson, Helen and Erooga, Marcus (1990) 'The forgotten parent: Groupwork with mothers of sexually abused children.' *Groupwork 3*, 2, 144–56.

Matzat, Jurgen (1989) 'Self-help groups as basic care in psychotherapy and social work.' *Groupwork 2*, 3, 248–56.

Matzat, Jurgen (1993) 'Away with the experts? Self-help groupwork in Germany.' *Groupwork 6*, 1, 30–42.

McCaughan, Nano (1988) 'Swimming upstream: A survey of articles on groupwork in social work journals 1986–87.' *Groupwork 1*, 1, 77–89.

McCluskey, Una and Miller, Liza Bingley (1995) 'Theme-focused family therapy: The inner emotional world of the family.' *The Association for Family Therapy 17*, 411–34.

McGuire, James and Priestley, Philip (1991) *Offending Behaviour.* London: Batsford.

McKay, Mary McKernan, Gonzales, J. Jude, Stone, Susan, Ryland, David and Kohner, Katherine (1997) 'Multi-family therapy groups: A responsive intervention model for inner-city families.' In Albert Alissi and Catherine G. Corto Mergins (eds) *Voices from the Field: Group Work Responds.* New York/London: Haworth.

Mischley, M., Stacey, E.W., Mischley, L. and Dush, D. (1985) 'A parent education project for low-income families.' *Prevention in Human Services 3*, 4, 45–57.

Mistry, Tara (1989) 'Establishing a feminist model of groupwork in the probation service.' *Groupwork 2*, 2, 145–58.

Mistry, Tara and Brown, Allan (eds) (1997) *Race and Groupwork.* London: Tavistock/Whiting and Birch.

Mistry, Tara and Brown, Allan (1991) 'Black/white co-working in groups.' *Groupwork 4*, 2, 101–118.

Moe, Rigmor Grette (1989) 'Groupwork as early intervention in high risk families.' *Groupwork 2*, 3, 263–75.

Muir, Lynne and Notta, Hardev (1993) 'An Asian mothers' group.' *Groupwork 6*, 2, 122–32.

Mullender, Audrey (1988) 'Groupwork as the method of choice with black children in white foster homes.' *Groupwork 1*, 2, 158–72.

Mullender, Audrey (1990) 'Groupwork in residential settings for elderly people.' *Groupwork 3*, 3, 286–301.

Mullender, Audrey (1995) 'Groups for children who have lived with domestic violence: Learning from North America.' *Groupwork 8*, 1, 79–98.

Mullender, Audrey and Ward, David (1989) 'Challenging familiar assumptions: preparing for and initiating a self-directed group.' *Groupwork 2*, 1, 5–26.

Mullender, Audrey and Ward, David (1991) *Self-Directed Groupwork: Users Take Action for Empowerment.* London: Whiting and Birch.

Muston, Ros and Weinstein, Jeremy (1988) 'Race and groupwork: Some experiences in practice and training.' *Groupwork 1*, 1, 30–40.

Norman, Caroline (1994) 'Groupwork with young mothers.' *Groupwork 7*, 3, 223–35.

O'Connor, Imogen (1992) 'Bereaved by suicide: Setting up an "ideal" therapy group in a real world.' *Groupwork 5*, 3, 74–86.

Otway, Olive (1993) 'Art therapy: Creative groupwork for women.' *Groupwork 6*, 3, 220–1.

Otway, Olive and Peake, Anne (1994) 'Using a facilitated self-help group for women whose children have been sexually abused.' *Groupwork 7*, 2, 153–162.

Parkinson, Frank (1993) 'Coping with trauma.' *Groupwork 6*, 2, 140–51.

Paulsen, Mary Lou, Dunker, Kenneth F. and Young, Joan G. (1997) 'Activity group for emotionally disturbed children' In Albert Alissi and Catherine G. Corto Mergins (eds) *Voices from the Field: Group Work Responds.* New York/London: Haworth.

Payne, Malcolm (1991) *Modern Social Work Theory: A Critical Introduction.* London: Macmillan.

Payne, Malcolm (1998) 'Social work theories and reflective practice.' In R. Adams, L. Dominelli and M. Payne (eds) *Social Work: Themes, Issues and Critical Debates.* Houndmills: Macmillan.

Peake, Anne and Otway, Olive (1990) 'Evaluating success in groupwork; Why not measure the obvious?.' *Groupwork 3*, 2, 118–33.

Pennells, Sister Margaret (1995) 'Time and space to grieve: A bereavement group for children.' *Groupwork 8*, 3, 243–54.

Phillips, Julie (1989) 'Targeted activities in group contexts: The analysis of activities to meet consumer need.' *Groupwork 2*, 1, 48–57.

Preston-Shoot, Michael (1987) *Effective Groupwork.* Basingstoke: Macmillan.

Preston-Shoot, Michael (1988) 'A model for evaluating groupwork.' *Groupwork 1*, 2, 147–57.

Preston-Shoot, Michael (1989) 'Using contracts in groupwork.' *Groupwork 2*, 1, 36–47.

Preston-Shoot, Michael (1992) 'On empowerment, partnership and authority in groupwork practice: A training contribution.' *Groupwork 5*, 2, 5–30.

Randall, Lynda and Walker, Wendy (1988) 'Supporting voices: Groupwork with people suffering from schizophrenia.' *Groupwork 1*, 1, 60–6.

Reid, Ken (1988) '"But I don't want to lead a group!" Some common problems of social workers leading groups.' *Groupwork 1*, 2, 124–34.

Regan, Sandra (1997) 'Teleconferencing group counselling: Pre-group public phase.' *Groupwork 10*, 1, 5–20.

Regan, Sandra and Young, Jan (1990) 'Siblings in groups: Children of separated/divorced parents.' *Groupwork 3*, 1, 22–35.

Reynolds, Jill and Shackman, Jane (1994) 'Partnership and training and practice with refugees.' *Groupwork 7*, 1, 23–36.

Rhule, Clare (1988) 'A group for white women with black children.' *Groupwork 1*, 1, 41–7.

Rice, Susan and Goodman, Catherine (1992) 'Support groups for older people: Is homogeneity or heterogeneity the answer?.' *Groupwork 5*, 2, 65–77.

Rimmer, Joyce (1993) 'A Cruse family circle.' *Groupwork 6*, 2, 133–39.

Ritter, B. and Hammons, K. (1992) 'Telephone group work with people with end stage AIDS.' *Social Work with Groups 15*, 4, 59–72.

Robertson, Rona (1990) 'Groupwork with parents of sleepless children.' *Groupwork 3*, 3, 249–59.

Ross, Sue (1991) 'The termination phase in groupwork: Tasks for the groupworker.' *Groupwork 4*, 1, 57–70.

Ross, Sue and Thorpe, Andy (1988) 'Programming skills in social groupwork.' *Groupwork 1*, 2, 135–46.

Rowland, Derrick (1995) 'An outdoor teamwork programme for a group of first year sixth formers.' *Groupwork 8*, 2, 177–88.

Sarri, Rosemary and Galinsky, M. (1967) 'A conceptual framework for group development.' In R. Vintner (ed) *Readings in Group Work Practice*. Michigan: Campus Publishers.

Schonfeld, Heino and Morrissey, Mary C. (1992) 'Social workers and psychologists as facilitators of groupwork with adults with a learning difficulty: A survey of current practice.' *Groupwork 5*, 3, 41–61.

Schutz, W.C. (1973) *Elements of Encounter*. California: Joy Press.

Schwartz, William (1976) 'Between client and system: the mediating function.' In Robert W. Roberts and Helen Northen (eds) *Theories of Social Work with Groups*. New York: Columbia University Press.

Senge, P.M. (1990) *The Fifth Discipline: The Art and Practice of The Learning Organization*. New York: Doubleday.

Senior, Paul (1993) 'Groupwork in the probation service: Care or control in the 1990s.' In A. Brown and B. Caddick (eds) *Groupwork with Offenders*. London: Whiting and Birch.

Shulman, Lawrence (1984) *The Skills of Helping Individuals and Groups*, (2nd edn). Illinois: F.E. Peacock.

Shulman, Lawrence (1988) 'Groupwork practice with hard to reach clients: A modality of choice.' *Groupwork 1*, 1, 5–16.

Silverlock, Leslie and Marion (1995) 'Teachers, learning, ego and groups.' *Groupwork 8*, 2, 217–230.

Smith, G. and Corden, John (1981) 'The introduction of contracts into a family service unit.' *British Journal of Social Work 11*, 3, 289–314.

Suk-Ching, Elaine Au Liu (1995) 'An integrated, feminist socio-economic model: Groupwork with nurses in Hong Kong.' *Groupwork 8*, 3, 285–301.

Swift, Paul (1996) 'Focusing on groups in social policy research.' *Groupwork 9*, 2, 154–68.

Szmagalski, Jerzy (1989) 'Staff development through groupwork in Polish community agencies: "The Centres of Culture".' *Groupwork 2*, 3, 237–47.

Taylor, George (1996) 'Ethical issues in practice: Participatory social research and groups.' *Groupwork 9*, 2, 110–27.

Taylor, John, Miles, Di and Eastgate, John (1988) 'A team development exercise.' *Groupwork 1*, 3, 252–61.

Taylor, Paul (1994) 'The linguistic and cultural barriers to cross-national groupwork.' *Groupwork 7*, 1, 7–22.

Thomas, Kenneth W. and Kilmann, R.H. (1974) *Thomas-Kilmann Conflict Model Instrument.* Sterling Forest, Tuxedo, NY: Xicom.

Towl, Graham (1990) '"Culture" groups in prison.' *Groupwork 3*, 3, 260–8.

Towl, Graham J. and Dexter, Polly (1994) 'Anger management groupwork with prisoners: An empirical evaluation.' *Groupwork 7*, 3, 256–69.

Trang, T. and Urbano, J. (1993) 'A telephone group support program for the visually impaired elderly.' *Clinical Gerontologists 13*, 2, 61–71.

Trevithick, Pamela (1995) '"Cycling over Everest": Groupwork with depressed women.' *Groupwork 8*, 1, 15–33.

Tribe, Rachel and Shackman, Jane (1989) 'A way forward: A group for refugee women.' *Groupwork 2*, 2, 159–66.

Tropp, Emmanuel (1978) 'Whatever happened to groupwork?.' *Social Work with Groups 1*, 1.

Tuckman, B. (1965) 'Developmental sequences in small groups.' *Psychological Bulletin 63*, 384–99.

Turkie, Alan (1995) 'Dialogue and reparation in the large, whole group.' *Groupwork 8*, 2, 152–65.

Vintner, E.E. (1974) 'Program activities: An analysis of their effects on participant behaviour.' In P. Glasser *et al.* (eds) *Individual Change Through Small Groups.* New York: The Free Press.

Walker, C.E., Bonner, B.L. and Kaufman, K.L. (1988) *The Physically and Sexually Abused Child.* New York: Pergamon.

Walmsley, Jan (1990) 'The role of groupwork in research with people with learning difficulties.' *Groupwork 3*, 1, 49–64.

Walton, Pat (1996) 'Focus groups and familiar social work skills: Their contribution to practitioner research.' *Groupwork 9*, 2, 139–53.

Ward, Adrian (1993) 'The large group: The heart of the system in group care.' *Groupwork 6*, 1, 64–77.

Ward, Adrian (1995) 'Establishing community meetings in a children's home.' *Groupwork 8*, 1, 67–78.

Ward, Dave (1998) 'Groupwork.' In R. Adams, L. Dominelli and M. Payne (eds) *Social Work: Themes, Issues and Critical Debates*. Basingstoke: Macmillan.

Ward, Dave (1996) 'Editorial.' *Groupwork 9*, 2, 107–9.

Ward, Dave and Mullender, Audrey (1991) 'Facilitation in self-directed groupwork.' *Groupwork 4*, 2, 141–51.

Weinstein, Jeremy (1994) 'A dramatic view of groupwork.' *Groupwork 7*, 3, 248–55.

Weisen, Rhona Birrell (1991) 'Evaluative study of groupwork for stress and anxiety.' *Groupwork 4*, 2, 152–62.

Whitaker, Dorothy Stock (1985) *Using Groups to Help People*. London: Routledge.

Williams, Antony (1991) *Forbidden Agendas: Strategic Action in Groups*. London: Routledge.

Williams, Patricia J. (1997) *Seeing a Colour-Blind Future: The Paradox of Race*. London: Virago (1997 Reith Lecture).

Winter, Jay and Baggett, Blaine (1996) *1914–18: The Great War and the Shaping of the 20th Century*. London: BBC Books.

Wintram, Claire, Chamberlian, Kerry, Kuhn, Marlene and Smith, Jo (1994) 'A time for women: An account of a group for women on an out of city housing development in Leicester.' *Groupwork 7*, 2, 125–35.

Subject Index

Author Index